BORSCHT BELT BUNGALOWS

Memories of Catskill Summers

IRWIN RICHMAN

TEMPLE UNIVERSITY PRESS

PHILADELPHIA

BORSCHT BELT BUNGALOWS

Memories of
Catskill Summers

Temple University Press, Philadelphia 19122
Copyright © 1998 by Temple University
All rights reserved
Published 1998
Printed in the United States of America

Interior design by Kate Nichols

♾ The paper used in this publication meets the requirements of the American
National Standard for Information Sciences—Permanence of Paper for Printed
Library Materials, ANSI Z39.48–1984

Library of Congress Cataloging-in-Publication Data

Richman, Irwin.
    Borscht belt bungalows : memories of Catskill summers / Irwin
Richman.
        p.   cm.
    Includes bibliographical references and index.
    ISBN 1-56639-585-2
    1. Jews—New York (State)—Catskill Mountains Region—Social life
and customs.   2. Jews—Recreation—New York (State)—Catskill
Mountains Region.   3. Richman, Irwin.   4. Catskill Mountains Region
(N.Y.)—Socal life and customs.   I. Title.
F127.C3R37 1998
974.7′38004924—dc21   97-22662

Contents

Photographs follow pages 34, 100, 142, 174, and 204.

Acknowledgments

I have consciously thought about writing this book for thirty years. My mother and my wife have urged me on. I have observed thousands of people in the resort industry, and I have talked to hundreds of them over many years. I thank them all, but I won't attempt to make a list. My major library resource has been the Heindel Library of Pennsylvania State University at Harrisburg, where the staff has been very helpful. Ruth Runion-Slear, our interlibrary loan wizard, has been especially important in locating material for me in exotic places; for example, she found a novel about the Catskills (translated from Hebrew) in a library in West Virginia. I have also had cooperation from the Sullivan County Historical Society in Hurleyville, New York.

William (Bill) Mahar and John Patterson, the Humanities division heads (now called school directors), past and present, of Penn State/Harrisburg have been supportive; Bill not only cheered me on in faculty development conferences, he also helped me obtain funding to offset some expenses incurred in preparation of the book. Howard Sachs, our associate dean for research, has been a major facilitator. His office provided funds for photographic work, photocopying, and the services of Renee Horley and Jane Hollinger, who have done much of the typing. Howard has a great personal enthusiasm for the project and arranged for me to have the services of several graduate students in American

Studies as research assistants. The best of them has been Matt Singer, now of the Philadelphia Museum of Art. Additionally, Howard used his computer wizardry to prepare the floor plans printed in the book. He is indeed the graduate dean for all purposes. Our former provost, Ruth Leventhal, never saw me in the hall without asking, "How's the book coming?" It helped keep up the momentum. Our present provost, John Bruhn, has always been cooperative when extra support was needed. Author Simon Bronner, our resident book machine, has offered suggestions and, since he can read Yiddish, has even provided me with several sources that I might have overlooked. Michael Barton, another American Studies colleague, is always good for a cogent comment, if not always a pertinent one—but he, unlike the rest of us, grew up in Nebraska. Making amends, he regularly searches the Web for "Catskill" entries on my behalf.

My thanks also goes to Michael Ames, my editor at Temple University Press, his colleagues, and the staff at P. M. Gordon Associates for their help and confidence. All photographs in *Borscht Belt Bungalows* not specifically credited were taken by the author.

I am technologically and mathematically challenged, but I have had the good fortune and good sense to have done something about these shortcomings. Therefore, as an American Studies person, I dedicate this book to the mathematicians in my life: my wife, Dr. M. Susan Richman, whose computer skills and sharp intellect performed miracles on the manuscript, and to our sons, Alexander Eugene and Joshua Solomon, our *nachas*.

BORSCHT BELT BUNGALOWS

Memories of Catskill Summers

Introduction

"*Vie a Heen Zol Ich Gayn*" and "*Mein Yiddishe Momme*" are two songs that Borscht Belt singers could count on to bring down the house.[1] If you wanted to leave your bungalow or hotel audience on their feet, stomping, applauding, shouting for more, end your 1950s or 1960s act with one of these workhorses. "*Mein Yiddishe Momme*" ("My Jewish Mother") evoked the image of the self-sacrificing, presumably immigrant, Jewish mother bathed in the warm glow of Sabbath candles. "*Vie a Heen Zol Ich Gayn*" ("Where Shall I Go") struck an even more elemental chord among Jews as a popularized version of the saga of the wandering Jew. "What place shall I choose, one that is destroyed or one that is going to be destroyed?"[2] After lamenting that "to the left, to the right, all doors are closed to me," the song ends on a note of glory celebrating the new State of Israel. Putting aside this last message, many American Jews used the title "*Vie a Heen Zol Ich Gayn*" as a rhetorical question on more trivial occasions. The answer might be to Miami Beach, to Lakewood, or to the Catskills. If "the Catskills" was chosen, more specific answers were needed: to a hotel, to a *kuchalein*, or to a bungalow colony; and then to the Frank Villa, to the Sunshine Colony, or even to Richman's, my family's place.

The immigrant Jews who came to the United States in several waves in the nineteenth century were greeted by the xenophobia that fed the nativist movements. The American Party, The Anti-Masonic Party, and the Know Nothing Party were anti-foreign and by extension anti-Catholic and anti-Jewish. Many of the new arrivals had been tradesmen in Europe and many became peddlers in America. For a number of old-stock Americans, their first interaction with a Jew was with a man with a pack on his back. Many, though not all, Jews prospered, some as merchants and bankers. As Jews became more numerous and more visible—and richer—animosity grew. One of the earliest public expressions of the desire to restrict Jewish access to recreation came in 1877 when Judge Henry Hilton barred the important German-Jewish banker Joseph Seligman, a friend of Ulysses S. Grant, from registering as a guest at the Grand Union Hotel in Sarasota Springs, New York, which Hilton managed. Seligman was prevented from staying at the hostelry even though he and his family had spent previous summers there. Two years later, Austen Corbin, president of the Manhattan Beach Corporation, announced that he would not allow Jews in his exclusive Coney Island hotel because, "We do not like Jews as a class."[3]

Barriers were clearly going up to separate Jews, no matter how refined they might be, from 'the better elements of society.' Jews were to be excluded from the workplace, if possible, restricted in their access to private universities, and kept out of resorts. Some Jews hid, or tried to hide, their identities in order to go to Christian-only vacation spots. Some changed their names. Steinbergs became "Stonehills" and Schwartzes became "Blacks." More Jews, however, reacted by purchasing or creating their own resorts.

In 1883, the Fleischmann family, Jews of Hungarian origin, bought sixty acres of land near the town of Griffin's Corners, soon to be renamed Fleischmanns, New York. The family leader, Charles F. Fleischmann, was the Cincinnati yeast and distilling magnate. Fleischmann and his relatives and friends soon built homes of unheard of luxury in the Catskills of Ulster County, the northern Catskills. Fleischmann's own home even boasted an artificially heated, spring-fed, outdoor swimming pool. The door was now open. Less affluent Jews bought boarding houses, and soon the nearby towns of Hunter and Tannersville were also Jewish resorts.[4] Their potential clientele was enhanced when a nativist nightmare came true. About 2,378,000 Jews, mostly from Eastern Europe, emigrated to America between 1880 and 1924 (when restrictive legislation halted the flow). Most were driven out of their homelands by grinding poverty and harsh anti-Semitic governmental policies. Nearly all of them settled in big cities, and over half chose New York City. Most of them came from small towns, or *shtetlen* or *shetlach,* fewer came from big cities like Lodz, Vilnius, Warsaw, and Odessa.[5]

For the most part, these Jews were not nature lovers, but they appreciated the fresh air to be found away from the crowded, malodorous cities. Small numbers, however, did relish nature. A selection of Catskill-based naturalist John Burroughs's widely read essays, glorifying nature, were even translated into Yiddish.[6] Some of these Jews were farmers in the old country, and a few wanted to re-create their old-world ways in America. Because of its proximity to New York City and its cheap land, the lower Catskills, especially the Neversink Valley of Sullivan County, were very attractive.

Easily accessible by the Midland Railroad and its successor—the New York, Ontario, and Western Railroad—the region was publicized by the railroads in their annual publication *Summer Homes,* which first appeared in 1878. Railroad influence, here as elsewhere, led to more picturesque local names. Think of the poetic names along the Main Line of the Pennsylvania Railroad as it runs from Philadelphia to Paoli: Bryn Mawr, Swarthmore, Ardmore, and so on. These were bestowed by the railroad. So, too, in New York. Centerville became Woodridge. Sandburg emerged as Mountaindale. Sheldrake's Pond became Loch Sheldrake; its body of water became, redundantly, Loch Sheldrake Lake. Pleasant Lake became Lake Kiamesha.

Thanks to the railroads, New Yorkers flocked to Sullivan County. Gentile farmers soon took in boarders, and boarding houses and hotels grew in importance. Some were semielite, most were not. Most simply catered to working-class Irish and German immigrants. Jews first entered into this Christian world of farms and summertime resorts "as early as 1892 in the person [of] Yana 'John' Gerson recognized . . . as the first Jewish farmer in the area." The Gersons began with an abandoned farm in Glen Wild, near Woodridge, and soon built a successful dairying operation and a boarding house.[7] Others followed.

Jews were not welcomed, but they persisted. Former hotel owner Cissie Blumberg recalls that when her father bought land for a resort in Lake Huntington he had to contend with "a Ku Klux Klan and a thriving German American Bund, . . . as well [as] a Property Owners' Association whose charter included a covenant restricting the sale of property to Jews."[8] The Sha-Wanga (later Shawanga) Lodge, near Wurtsboro, is an early example of a major Christian hotel that was sold to Jews. "It was poetic justice . . . that the Dan family, Jewish purchasers of the Sha-Wanga, had brochures printed that were identical

3

to those their Christian predecessors had, except that they replaced 'No Hebrews Accommodated' with 'Kosher Cuisine Featured.'"[9]

For a variety of reasons—including its closer proximity to New York City, the railroad, and Sullivan County's warm embrace of the road and the automobile (which the predominantly gentile, nature-loving resort communities of Ulster County abhorred)—Sullivan County's resorts flourished. Jews flocked there and Christians yielded to them, with more or less grace. As Sullivan County flourished, it drained Jewish summer trade from the older resort areas of Ulster County north of Ellenville.

From the 1920s through the 1960s, Sullivan County became the preeminent summer resort for American Jews. Its hotels became the models for those in Miami Beach and, indeed, those built later in Las Vegas. There were also less celebrated aspects of the Jewish resort industry that, while they served more people, were less influential than were the hotels. These were the *kuchaleins* and the bungalow colonies that dotted the countryside. The tale of their rise and fall and transformations is the substance of this book, which, in some degree, is also a study of the Jewish American quest for both separation and assimilation. It is my story, my family's story, and the story of at least hundreds of thousands of American Jews who have a bungalow colony in their past.

Many of us live lives very different from those of our childhood. It's been said that Archie Leach reinvented himself as Cary Grant. I and many thousands of Jewish adults who grew up in the period from 1920 to 1960 have, to one degree or another, reinvented ourselves. We are in our thirties, forties, fifties, sixties, and seventies; some are even in our eighties and nineties. With few exceptions, we are not the often chronicled show business types, but we are corporate CEOs, small businessmen and businesswomen, public servants, accountants, doctors, dentists, lawyers, teachers, and professors. Most of us are at least solid middle class. We're all over the United States. You might not find many of us in Nebraska, but California, Florida, and New York are full of us—and there's a large contingent in Nevada. What we share together is a childhood of summers spent in the Catskills of Sullivan County, New York. We didn't go to hotels; we stayed in the lesser known, but far more numerous, resorts of the region. It's not a past people boast about, but it is a past people will reveal with prodding, and they will probably have some semisweet nostalgic memories. Unlike former President George Bush's feelings toward Kennebunkport, Maine, we don't feel tied to our ancestral summer places. In fact, most of us reject them. Few who now summer at East Hampton willingly discuss their earlier summers in Mountaindale or Woodridge. My roommate in undergraduate school, and a future physician, always laughed at the "dungalow colonies."

As I read Stefan Kanfer's *A Summer World* (the best book to date about the Catskills, the 'Jewish Alps'), I looked for information on rooming houses and bungalow colonies—the *kuchalein* (literally "cook for yourself")[10] resorts—which, without any doubt, catered to more people than did the hotel industry, especially the two hotels that get the most attention, Grossinger's and The Concord. Relatively little information is included on the less-renowned resorts. Furthermore, some of it (i.e., on bungalow colony pricing) is wrong.[11] I believe the reason Kanfer's book falters in its treatment of the *kuchaleins* and the bungalow colonies is the same reason it gives too much attention to Jennie Grossinger; it concerns the availability of primary research materials. Bungalow colony owners, like most hotel owners, were not writers; many were illiterate immigrants. They left few, if any, memoirs.

There simply was no bungalow-oriented book equivalent to the Jennie Grossinger inspired—and no doubt subsidized—*Waldorf-in-the-Catskills*.[12] The primary sources for the bungalow story are memories of people who were there and a few novels and tapes—no literary or cinematic gems, nothing celebrated. There is no mention of bungalow colonies in Oscar Israelowitz's *Catskills Guide*,[13] but plenty on the hotels. Most people who spent their summers in the Catskill *kuchaleins* and bungalow colonies never thought of it as a noteworthy experience. Some of us with a Catskill background were perhaps a little ashamed of the ghetto in the hills where we spent our summers. I've written about Pennsylvania German culture, but—except for one article on "The Jewish Drinking Glass" written for *The Journal of Popular Culture*—I have not written about my culture.

In the 1990s, a critical mass of Catskill alumni reached the age of nostalgia. Scholarly conferences now explore our past.[14] Catskill childhoods are being reevaluated and revealed. New York's trendy *Village Voice,* for example, ran an article entitled, "The Lost Daughters of Zion Return to the Catskills: A Journey to the Source of Jewish Identity, Featuring Gefilte Fish, Matzoh Ball Soup, Boiled Chicken, Pot Roast, Corned Beef, Potato Kugel, and Memories."[15] The author, Donna Gaines, had grown up in the Jewish tradition and had gone to a *yeshiva,* but she rejected it all. She not only became a rock groupie, she also consciously and defiantly had herself tattooed—a serious violation of Talmudic law. Now in middle age, after a weekend at The Concord, she has come to a realization: "In the Catskills I'd [be able to] celebrate the eternity of Jewish life."[16] At about the same time, the more normative Jews and gentiles who read the resolutely middle-class-oriented *Lancaster (Penn.) Sunday News* are invited to immerse themselves in Sullivan County's living nostalgia: "At Resorts in Catskills, Everyone Is Family."[17] The message that the Catskills are worthy of another look also resonates with the young. A *Newsweek* article, "Young Fogies," reports on a "Generation X" that is uneasy about the future and nostalgic about the good old days. The article notes that in some New York City circles "nothing says, 'Let's get serious' like a trip to the Catskills."[18] Sullivan County is a reconsidered promised land.

I grew up in, and with, the bungalow colony industry. My grandfather, Abraham Richman, was a well-known personality in the resort community. He knew everybody—and they knew him: from the famous Malke Grossinger down to many an obscure *kuchalein* owner. He was a *macher,* a mover, in the community. One of his favorite causes was Congregation B'nai Israel in Woodbourne, New York, which he helped to found, and which he served as president for many years. I was born in 1937 and, as a little boy, I would go with him on his fund-raising trips on behalf of the *shul* (synagogue). We visited hotels and bungalow colonies throughout Sullivan County. Grandpa was gregarious, a charmer and raconteur. It was the rare resort owner who didn't offer him and his driving buddy (Grandpa never learned to drive a car) at least a *schnapsel* (a drink) or two, a piece of cake, and some fruit; some offered a banquet. These were always occasions of reminiscence and nostalgia, as well as successful fund-raising. On one of these forays, I learned that "Old Lady Grossinger" (Malke) used to carry her money in a garter that held up her stocking. "That's where she went to get the money for a contribution," Grandpa told me. He was proud that he got a contribution from her—right after he extracted one from her husband. "Don't tell Selig," she cautioned Grandpa. It's first-hand experiences such as these, combined with my education, that make me uniquely able to write the story of the *Borscht Belt Bungalows.* Stated simply, as an elderly Jew once observed: "By myself, I'm a book."

The Bungalow Colonies

We don't know who first used the word bungalow for these rentals that evolved from shacks, but he or she had a "country club mind" because the name took. Why bungalow colony? I feel this is a borrowing of allusion thanks to the movies. "Arts colony" and "Hollywood colony" were both well-known terms in the 1920s and 1930s. The term "bungalow colony" is a perfect one for people aiming toward assimilation, yet living in overcrowded apartment-laden neighborhoods. The young Jewish adults tasting delicious assimilationist freedom at adult Kamp Kill Kare in the 1930s centered much of their social life around their bungalows.[19] Just combine the suburban good-life image of "bungalow" with the exclusive image of "colony" and you have a natural for a resort area that had always made extravagant boasts.

The word bungalow, a legacy of the British Empire, is derived from the Bengali word meaning "a low house."[20] The first American use of "bungalow" in this sense is found in an 1879 article in *The American Architect and Building News*, which describes a structure designed by Boston architect William Gibbons Preston and built on Buzzard's Bay, Massachusetts, at the base of Cape Cod.[21] By the late nineteenth century in America, the word bungalow had become synonymous with an upper-class summer home. In subsequent years, popular culture embraced the word. Lines from the long poem "Bungal-ode" by Burges Johnson, appearing in *Good Housekeeping* magazine in February 1906, attests to this.

> *There's a jingle in the jungle,*
> *'Neath the juniper and pine,*
>
> . . .
>
> *And my blood is all a-tingle*
> *As I count each single shingle*
> *On my bosky bungalow.*[22]

Never completely losing its relationship to a bosky (woodsy) retreat, the bungalow came to symbolize comfortable suburban domesticity. The American ideal of the "vine covered cottage" was transformed into a bungalow. Additionally, rural and seaside retreats, however modest, were often called bungalows. The only non-Catskill resort type that consciously used the term bungalow was the "Bungalow Camp," a decidedly WASP institution that was, no doubt, popular among those influenced by Baden Powell and Theodore Roosevelt. One such bungalow camp was operated by Dr. Fillmore Moore at Eliot, Maine. Here "campers were subjected to a regimen of living 'as much as possible in the open air, [eating] the right food in the right way,' [and working] always to some purpose, with an eye for simple beauty, and with plenty of time for play." The so-called bungalows that "they inhabited varied from 9-by-12 feet to 20-by-32 feet in size, and the only solid parts were their framework, flooring, and a batten door, the roof and sides being of stretched canvas."[23]

It is hardly likely that this type of institution was known to the urban masses of European Jews, nor would it have appealed to them. Sullivan County's resorts always defined themselves in terms of hyperbole. When I helped edit my friend Manville Wakefield's *To the Mountains by Rail,* I was struck by the boarding houses—hotels of the 1870s—that described themselves in words suggesting they were on a par with the Waldorf Astoria. Monticello's Exchange Hotel assured guests in 1873 that it could "furnish first-class accommodations, [and] the table will at all times be furnished with the delicacies of the season, and the bar will be supplied with choice wines, liquors, and cigars."[24] Ironically, these resorts never catered to an upper-class clientele.

Later, in the golden age of the hotels, many places added "and country club" to their name, as in "Kutcher's Hotel and Country Club," conjuring up the elegance of an exclusive way of life familiar, if only in the movies, to most guests. In an episode of the television situation comedy *The Brooklyn Bridge,* set in the 1950s, the children of now-deceased parents decide to sell their parents' small bungalow colony in Mountaindale: "The Hollywood Country Club."

> ALICE: Two immigrants from Germany who were never west of Prospect Park West. Where did they come up with the name?
> GEORGE: They loved the movies. It's a good thing they didn't call it "Tara."[25]

George's parents would not have needed to be inhibited; there is a "Tara Acres" bungalow colony between Hurleyville and Monticello.

In post–World War II years, some more pretentious and amenity-enhanced bungalow colonies started to call themselves not "colonies," but "cottages"—thus, "Cutler's Cottages" in South Fallsburg.[26] However, whatever their owners called them, people went to the mountains to rent "bungalows." Interestingly, bungalow is a very Jewish word to people who grew up in the New York City Borscht Belt sphere, and its use and allusions are very different from those of mainstream America, and especially different from California, which has been characterized as "bungalow land." Film and television writer Sybil Adelman

Sage recalls trying to impress a visiting Israeli relative—one who had quickly gained a clear insight into Jewish-American New York culture.

> I circled around the Beverly Hills Hotel, a sprawling Spanish-style stucco structure with acres of unblemished lawn, a star-studded swimming pool and tennis courts, Los Angeles at its flamingo-pink brightest, to show my Israeli cousin Ronit the $3,100-a-night bungalow. Ronit, who had dismissed the city's top tourist attractions—the Farmer's Market, Rodeo Drive and the Venice canals—as clones of things elsewhere, was yawning. "Bungalows I saw in the Catskills," she said, continuing to lean, chin in hand, against the car window, the better to pooh-pooh everything.[27]

There is, indeed, a Monticello bungalow colony called the "Beverly Hills Country Club." Today, you rent a house in the Hamptons, a cottage in the Berkshires, and a bungalow in the Catskills.

Incidentally, there are many "real" bungalows in Sullivan County. These are textbook examples of arts-and-crafts style buildings. In Sullivan County, however, where new is always equated with better, most bungalows have been "improved" with the addition of picture windows, aluminum siding, and other postwar treatments. Our Christian neighbors, the Ampthors, lived in a bungalow, and at least four other year-round houses near us are bungalows. I never knew what these people called their houses, but I bet it was never bungalow. One very assertive bungalow (now denatured) down the road was called "Tony's dollhouse" by locals, after its Italian builder and because of its compact perfection.

Rental bungalows of the colony variety were, and are, architecturally simple. Oral tradition suggests that the first bungalows lacked kitchens and bathrooms. The tenants used outhouses and communal kitchens that were also used by the roomers in the main house. By the 1930s, virtually all bungalows were two- or three-room units, although a very few one-room and four-room bungalows were also built. At least 95 percent of the bungalows had two rooms (kitchen and bedroom) and a bath, or three rooms (kitchen, two bedrooms) and a bath. None had a living room, but many had a porch and, after World War II, frequently these porches were screened.

The exterior architecture was also simple—rectangular or square with gable roofs. They were never set on foundations, but rather on concrete or wooden piers. At many colonies, the piers were hidden by panels giving the illusion that the bungalows had foundations. Often, bungalows were semidetached or double units. This was an extremely common form. In the later 1950s and early 1960s, Hollywood- or Floridian-type bungalows became fashionable. These have the same basic floor plan, but have angled flat roofs and, perhaps, picture windows. Some of these were constructed on concrete slabs instead of piers and were, therefore, lower to the ground. Also, some bungalows were built motel-style, that is, connected to form a row or a court. At Kassack's Bungalows in Woodbourne, the newest bungalows were called "The Floridians." These were court-shaped, had no front porches, and were the most expensive units. Within Kassack's small world of seventy-seven units, "the Floridians" (as the tenants called themselves) were the elite, as were "the Lakefronters" at the fictional Hector's Pond Colony described in the novel *Bungalow Nine*.[28]

Traditionally, bungalows are painted white with green trim. Some bungalows have black or blue trim. Lansman's, a large well-known colony turned co-op, paints the trim red and has adopted red and white as official colors. Their athletic teams wear red and white and their vehicles are red and white. This color coordination, however, is unusual. Knowing the bungalow business as I do, I believe the green and white scheme has to do with economy; white paint is cheapest and, for a long time, green paint was cheaper than other trim colors.

During the years of decline, especially in the 1970s (the "hippie" years), many a desperate bungalow owner tried painting the bungalows with "now" colors: pinks, purples, yellows, and reds, but the effect was akin to a seventy-five-year-old woman putting on Madonna-like makeup. My grandfather would have used the more colorful Yiddish phrase "*Dus kan helfin vie ein toten banchus*" ("this can help as much as cupping a corpse") to describe the futility of this process.[29]

Most bungalows were sheathed in wood clapboard siding, but others were covered in asbestos shingles. Kassack's Floridian units were covered in light green shingles. Sims Resort Colony (note that they dropped "Bungalow"), outside of Monticello, is sheathed in fake stone. I never saw a bungalow sided in wood shingles, the quintessential covering of the arts-and-crafts bungalow. Very few bungalows at ordinary colonies were built after 1960, although many Hasidic and New Orthodox places witnessed building booms in the 1970s and 1980s. When I asked Miriam Damico when the "new" bungalows were built at her well-maintained Moonglow Inn Colony, near Loch Sheldrake, she hesitatingly admitted that they dated from the 1950s.[30]

Most early bungalows were Spartan, but after World War II, there were changes. The first was the "Hollywood Kitchen." By the mid 1950s, there was scarcely a colony that didn't boast of "Hollywood Kitchens" on its sign. A Hollywood kitchen meant that all of the appliances were along one wall, the sink had drain boards, and there were hanging cupboards over the sink, range, and (ideally) over the refrigerator as well. In other words, this was a variant of the modern suburban kitchen. Classy kitchens had tile or pseudo-tile walls and Formica counter tops. Bathrooms also underwent a change. Prior to World War II, bathtubs were virtually unknown in bungalow bathrooms. In postwar bathrooms, tubs and tile walls were introduced, as were large mirrored recessed medicine cabinets and numerous, often fluorescent, lights. All rooms were provided with multiple electrical outlets to power the larger range of appliances of modern life. Traditionally, bungalows lacked heat. When cold snaps hit in August, most people would turn on the oven and open its door. After World War II, many tenants brought along electric heaters. By the mid 1960s, wall-to-wall carpet was common in the bedrooms of larger colonies, and, by the 1970s, some colonies were offering air-conditioning units in their bungalows as well. Air-conditioning and television cable had a phenomenal effect on the community life of the colonies since tenants no longer felt the impulse to leave their units whenever possible.

Landlords were also expected to provide lawn furniture of sorts. Before the war and for a few years following, the predominant chair was an Adirondack type. These were heavy, ungainly to move, and had to be painted each year. Tables and benches were also made of wood. Tenants would often zealously guard the furniture placed near their bungalows and occasionally fought over the question of whose chair belonged where. After the war, metal-framed chairs with wooden slats became popular, and, by the 1950s, bent-metal chairs (popular once again, as *funky*) came into use, as did lightweight-metal umbrella tables. These were followed in short order by aluminum chairs with nylon webbing. Owners felt that heaven had come when these chairs became widely available. They were everyone's dream; they were cheap, strong, light, and could be stacked easily.

Tenants brought their own furniture as well. Joey Adams recalls that everyone brought a hammock.[31] That may have been the case in the 1920s; however, although I do remember hammocks into the 1980s, they were always relatively unusual. The ownership of canvas and wooden folding chairs was more common, and army cots were very popular for sunbathing. This furniture was,

11

in turn, replaced with folding webbed-aluminum chairs and "chaise lounges." One advantage of renting at the same colony season after season, was that the tenants could leave their own stuff in one place over the winter, rather than schlep it all back to New York each year.

"What is a bungalow colony and who goes there?" asks Michael Straus in the *New York Times* in 1956. "A bungalow colony," he answers, "is usually, an oval cluster of cottages bordering a green sward at the opposite ends of which, more often than not, are a day camp for children and a social hall for mothers and the transient fathers."[32] This description is perhaps overly elegant and too restrictive, as subsequent chapters will illustrate. A more recent definition, slightly tongue-in-cheek, holds that "bungalow colony" is "the Catskills word for clusters of white cottages with a handball court and a pool that is always advertised as Olympic-sized even when it is no bigger than a hot tub."[33]

Literature of the Bungalow Colonies

Life in bungalow colonies was usually pacific, petty, and uneventful. It scarcely provided the background of tension and emotion that many authors would find attractive for their novels, and writers of memoirs, apparently, chose to overlook this aspect of their own pasts. One of the very few memoirists to recall a *kuchalein* in any detail is comedian-columnist Joey Adams, born in 1911, whose acerbic remembrances are especially valuable for their early date. He lived the Catskill summers from the 1920s, and *The Borscht Belt* (written with Henry Tobias) recalls a world of rapacious *kuchalein* owners and exploited tenants who, in turn, spent their time figuring how to sneak into the shows provided by hotels for their guests. He remembers the arduous train trips and "hacker trips" to the "Sour Cream Sierras."[34] Despite the early reminiscences, the bulk of his book is devoted to the hotels with which he is clearly smitten—and especially the bigger ones, whose owners are usually depicted as being as warm-hearted and amiable as the small hotel and *kuchalein* owners were churlish and penny-pinching.

In 1987, Henry Tobias wrote his own recollections, *Music in My Heart and Borscht in My Blood,* which is even more star-struck than Adams's. It offers no bungalow stories but does provide insights into the peripheries, such as tales of state troopers and local police who specialized in speed traps designed to harass travelers on their way to the Catskills. He also includes several interesting anecdotes about Charlie Rapp, who played an important role in Catskill entertainment.[35]

The only novel I have located about bungalow colonies is Norman Ober's *Bungalow Nine*,[36] a tale set in a colony in Spring Valley of Rockland County, a bit closer to New York City than Sullivan County. Today this area is a New York City suburb, one from which many fathers could commute to their work daily, although in the 1960s most fathers were weekend visitors. Hector's Pond Colony has all the elements of the classic bungalow colony, including a greedy owner, Hector Mannheim, who rents to a semifashionable young couple, Jason and Ann Cutler. Jason works in public relations for a movie company, and he knows stars. His wife, a former school teacher, now devotes herself to their young daughter, Toddy. Together, Jason and Ann are intrigued and appalled by the social life they encounter at the colony. The lack of privacy and the social divisions between the ordinary renters and the "Lakefronters," whose more expensive units face Hector's pond, surprise them. News of occasional affairs surprises them even more. With them, we visit the casino for tenant meetings where summer rules are made, meet the day-camp staff, and go to Saturday night parties. Ultimately, and based on an actual disaster, we are faced with the single most cataclysmic event in bungalow, or more broadly, Borscht Belt history.

On 19 August 1955, Hurricane Diane hit the Northeast and widespread flooding engulfed many resort areas.[37] Hector's Pond is cut off by flood waters and some bungalows are washed away. Jason and Ann are ultimately impressed by the way the tenants, a mix of middle-class Jews, most in business, pull together to help one another. Jason, who prior to this had, with Ann, decided he never wanted to visit a colony again, even considers giving a deposit on a unit for next year. However, as his adrenaline level returns to normal, he decides that despite the well-run day camp and the colony's potential for emergency camaraderie, bungalow life is not for the Cutlers.

The storm also provides a dramatic focus for Sidney Offit's *He Had It Made*, a *roman á clef* about the Aladdin Hotel in Woodbourne, New York—a hotel that was part of my childhood. Offit married the daughter of the Komito family, which still owns the hotel. The fictional Sesame Hotel is run by Sam and Becky Mandheimer. Their daughter, Marsha, is alienated from the business, but has just divorced her husband and returns with her son to her parents' place. She becomes involved in a summer romance with an ambitious waiter, Al Brodie, who can't understand why Marsha doesn't love the Sesame, which represents to him security and wealth. Marsha's rage reflects the ambivalent feelings of many resort owners' kids, mine included:

13

You think this is Paradise. . . . Well, to me it's a rotten, dirty, filthy place. It cheated me out of everything. You know how many times my cheeks were pinched, how many thousands of times I heard what a lucky girl I was, how they were doing it all for me? You know what my parents were doing for me? Nothing. When I got the measles, my father's biggest worry was that the guests would find out and all the children would go home and it'd ruin the season. How many times did she sit with me in the children's dining room? Wonderful meals! Three squares a day! All I ever heard day and night for twenty years was the hotel, the hotel— should we build a new casino and how much will it cost. She says yes, he says no. And how about the head counselor, he's got a following but he's such a slob. And the laundry man is robbing us blind and the butcher is cheating us on weight and on and on. Good old Mama and Papa, those poor over-worked Mandheimers, killing themselves, dead on their feet and doing it all for me? Well, I think it's ugly and I hate it all.[38]

The novel also details a few interactions between the local gentiles and their reactions to the Jews of summer. This theme is very important in Reuben Wallenrod's *Dusk in the Catskills,* which recounts the story of Russian-born Leo Halper who, with his wife Lillian, runs a small hotel in fictional Brookville, New York, in Sullivan County. The dynamics of their place share many of the same elements with the story of the Sesame, but this work also shows us the winter, or private life of the resort owners, which makes it a useful source. Many of the Halper's problems and life patterns are the same as those shared by bungalow colony owners.[39]

Harvey Jacobs's *Summer on a Mountain of Spices* is about life at Berman and Ferinsky's Willow Spring Hotel, a small family place, near Monticello. I can see many aspects of my resort childhood reflected in the story of the Bermans's nephew, Harry Craft. The book also gives rich glimpses of the often polyglot Sullivan County country roads and the liveliness of Monticello, Sullivan County's county seat. For example, Harry experiences the very real Old Liberty Road:

Old Liberty Road . . . a path of turns and hills, ruts and bumps, led to the Willow Spring, along with a heavy population of other hotels, kocha-layns [*sic*] where the women cooked for their families in communal kitchens while the husbands and kids waited in bungalows without toilets, and the high-hedged homes of early settlers who saw the neighbor-hood change. . . . The final mile to the Willow Spring went past Ham-merman's Shady Rest, a nest of bungalows, the Elmsmere Arms Hotel, the class of the neighborhood, a colonial cottage with a red well and white latticework that belonged to a retired sheriff, a small forest waiting development, another bungalow colony, poorest of the poor, Wishnin-skiwitz Park, then, on the left, Mrs. Kar's battered house and chicken coops . . . her Feshtoonkana slum. . . . The hotel driveway was past a sign surrounded by colored Christmas bulbs. WELCOME TO THE WILLOW SPRING HOTEL. BERMAN AND FERINSKY OWNERS AND OPERATORS.[40]

Another vividly descriptive novel is *Thunder over the Bronx* by Arthur Kober, which provides insights into the lives of those who went to the resorts and has some wonderful vignettes abut the adult camps of the Borscht Belt, where young unmarrieds went to mix. Kamp Kill Kare is nominally in Connecticut, but from the description it could be in Woodbourne or any other place in Sullivan County. At Kamp Kill Kare, "bungalow" was used in the Beverly-Hills-Hotel sense of the word, but on a less classy level. When Bella from the Bronx arrived, she received a "rowdy welcome from Harry Horowitz, who was at the desk and who assigned her to the same bungalow she had been in last year." After she let "one of the waiters take her suitcase to her bunk," she quickly opened it and removed "a pair of canary colored trunks, a pair of pale blue socks, her yellow sandals, a fuzzy blue sweater, a pair of long yellow earrings and a length of baby-blue hair ribbon."[41]

Later she went to a pajama party at Benjic's bungalow, the accommodations of a new-found friend. "There was an odd collection of people assembled in Ben-jie's bungalow. The men, resplendent in gaudy bathrobes, wore scarves which were intricately knotted in the latest Hollywood fashion. Although most of the girls were in pajamas, there were one or two in negligees of a sickly pink hue."[42]

Lastly, there is Martin Boris's novel *Woodridge 1946* in which the author, himself the son of a bungalow colony owner, characterizes the region very nicely. Speaking through his character Phil, Boris puts the cart before the horse when he describes the hotels that by the 1940s "had grown to a business rival-ing the best that Miami Beach had to offer."[43]

Then there was those farmers who wished to be more than debtors to the land yet less than hotel owners. These middle-roaders developed their own way of life, becoming summer landlords instead of grandiose innkeepers. They built multiple-dwelling rooming houses and individual bungalows all with kitchenettes to permit light housekeeping. Each major hotel had its satellites of these kinds of units, and there was as little rivalry between bungalow colony and hotel as there was between the Earth and Moon.[44]

The mountains had an uniquely diverse clientele:

Between the Fourth of July and Labor Day the mountain ghetto swelled a hundredfold. Jewish life and character then was more rich and varied than at any other time since the days of King Solomon. The new high priests were the hotel owners. Low priests were the rooming-house landlords whose forte was pacifying half a hundred Brooklyn and Bronx matrons for ten weeks. Enriching the mix was the variety of summer help that staffed the hotels: busboys, waiters, bellhops—college boys—each one of them gawkier, hungrier and hornier than the next.[45]

The action in *Woodridge 1946* takes place in a typical but fictional resort luncheonette, "Ourplace," run by Phil and his wife Arlene, in the real town of Woodridge, New York. Phil was worried about the future. Could the Borscht Belt last another five years?

Once the airlines got wise and brought the fares down, people would discover a whole new world out there. GIs returning home, like knights from the Crusades, would tell tales of the wondrous places they'd been to. And the offspring of the present vacationers were a new breed: children of post-Depression America, they were the first generation not worried abut saving money. Restless, hard to please, quick to bore and certain never to return to what had satisfied the three generations before them. It was just a matter of time.[46]

The descriptions of the luncheonette ring true to the memories of my life in the Catskills. Phil and his wife Arlene share a troubled marriage and work hard over the long hours of the summer season. Luncheonettes in resort towns are often open until two or three every morning. The summer of 1946 was good, but Phil, amazingly prescient with all the benefits of an author writing in the late 1970s, is afraid that all of his work is probably wasted as far as the future is concerned. "All he wanted was five more good years to salt away a bundle then sell out for whatever he could get and semiretire to a liquor store. Hopefully, a fresh start with her, if she were willing to let bygones be bygones."[47]

All of these books present a remarkably unified image of a resort area that held great allure for a first generation who were overjoyed to be in the country. Reuben Wallenrod muses as the Holocaust looms:

> Who are you and what are you Leo Halper, who was born somewhere in a little village in Russia, came to America as a youth, worked in New York sweat shops and walked now amidst these beautiful Catskill Mountains. Who are you, Leo Halper, who strolled about these grounds so beautiful with trees and flowers and a lake and playfields and a casino, while hundreds of thousands of people had no place to lay their heads? You had her wide peaceful spaces and blue skies and green trees, while over there old men, women and children were pressed into filthy boxcars with black fear hovering over them and cruel eyes peering from every corner.[48]

These characters were typical of the people who were the builders and the early tenants. They often brought their children into the business, although some, or many, like Marsha, rebelled. The tenants still rented. Then came the third generation and the fourth, and the ties were broken as society opened up for New York's Jews and as family and social conditions changed. It is a world of fond memories that is shared in the documentary *The Rise and Fall of the Borscht Belt,* which, although hotel-oriented, includes interviews with bungalow people.[49] It is a world now gone.

A. Richman,
Woodbourne, New York

Grandpa was born in Russian-ruled Lithuania, near Wilna, in the 1880s. He was about ninety-six when he died in 1978. We were never certain of his age because his accounts varied, and some of his friends claimed that he lied about when he was born. Grandpa was a liberated, worldly young man who ran away from home at thirteen, after his mother died and his seventy-year-old father married an eighteen-year-old bride. "We fought," he recalled as an old man. "She had a hard life." Grandpa stayed away for five years. "When I came home, my father didn't recognize me. I was clean-shaven, except for my mustache, and I wore a blouse. I looked like a real *goy*, a Cossack!"[1]

Abraham Richman arrived in America in 1905, and the next year he sent for his wife. Before Bayle left Europe, she and her family posed for photographs by "Rembrandt à Vilne." I, of course, know that Lithuania's capitol is Vilnius, but it was always "Wilna" in my family. My grandfather was a founder, and for several years the president, of the Wilner Benevolent Association, a self-help and burial society founded in 1906.[2] Grandpa, who settled in Brooklyn (he only spent a few days on the Lower East Side), remembered going to the mountains for the first time to stay "a few weeks" two years after he arrived in America. Usually he went to a small hotel while Grandma stayed home. A plasterer by training in the old country, or *der heim,* he soon became a building contractor. (Grandma ran a grocery store in the Williamsburg section of Brooklyn.) He liked "the mountains," as he always called Sullivan County. The "*luft* was *gesmach*" ("the air was delicious/healthful"), Grandpa would say in his brand of "Yinglish."[3] In the late 1920s, Grandpa retired, and a few years later Grandma followed. Now they started to go to the country for the summer. They went to a *kuchalein,* a rooming house, in Woodbourne, on a farm run by one of the Jewish farming pioneers of the area, the Rosenshein family. (Some of the fifth generation Rosensheins still live in the area but they no longer farm.)

When my parents were married in 1931, they honeymooned at a hotel in Woodbourne, The Sky House, run by Grandpa's crony, Archie Schwartz. The following summer, they joined my grandparents at Rosenshein's. My older brother, Seymour, born in 1932, was a rooming-house kid. After two years at Rosenshein's, my parents and grandparents moved closer to Woodbourne, to the Reddish's *kuchalein* (about three fourths of a mile out of town). Unlike the Rosensheins, the Reddishes were city folk who came to the mountains for the summer.

My mother has told me stories about the trials of *kuchalein* life during that period, the same trials as those comedian Joey Adams recalls afflicting his mother. The *kuchalein* simply had community kitchens and everyone had to share sinks and eating space. You didn't have your own icebox—just a share of one. Joey Adams's memories are humorous and deadly accurate:

The joy of the whole world for a *kuchalane* wife is her first morning in the community kitchen. As our GI's fought for every inch of land on Guadalcanal, so did each woman fight to establish a beachhead at one of the two sinks. Armed with Brillo pads and scouring powder, each lived by the motto: "Take the sink and hold it!" Even the two ovens and the breadbox became battle grounds. Everybody fought for the best spot in the icebox too. The status symbol was the two cubic inches assigned to you, and the top shelf on the front was equivalent to a triple A rating in Dun and Bradstreet.

Every jar of goodies had a label. The little lump of farmer cheese, already turning yellow, was tagged "H. Potkin." The pickled lox in the wax paper said "J. Traum." One always heard such anguished cries as, "Somebody's been at my stewed prunes"—"Who spilled and left the shelf so dirty?"—"All right, so it was a little yellow, but did I give you permission to throw out my farmer cheese?"

In the dining room, each family was assigned a large table seating up to ten. Seniority counted for nothing. Whether you were an old customer or just an old lady, you were strictly on your own. The big accomplishment was to land the best table near the only window—which looked out on absolutely nothing.[4]

Rooming houses were the pits, and many people at that time realized it. I never experienced one as a resident, and by the time I became conscious of my surroundings—the mid to late 1940s—community kitchens were definitely declassé. I remember being in a few during this period, but most did not survive the 1950s, although a small number definitely limped on into the 1980s. I remember my surprise in seeing one at a well-kept South Fallsburg colony, little used, but there.

In 1936, Grandpa said, "enough" (actually "*dayanu*") to rooming houses and decided to build a summer house for his family. Originally it was to be a single-family house, but then he, or more probably Grandma, figured "why not make a few bucks by renting a few rooms." So Grandpa became a "farmer." All owners of bungalow colonies in his era were referred to as "farmers." The appellation, of course, had its origins in the backgrounds of the first *kuchalein* owners, who were active in agriculture. When tenants talked about their "farmers," they meant landlords. The story of the evolution of the *kuchalein* is put forth in a 1928 article in *The American Hebrew*. Writer Isaac Landman, who was keenly interested in the Jewish Agricultural Movement of the early twentieth century, went to investigate the charge that "The Catskill Mountains, particularly Ulster, Sullivan, and Orange Counties,"[5] were really just a resort area where Jews played at farming.

As regards the masses, their vacationing in the Catskills is usually spoken of with a sly, cynical glance at . . . those Jews in that section whom we label as farmers. Common report has it that these Jews are only pseudo-farmers maintaining their places not for the purpose of making a living out of the soil, but to keep boarders in the summer time. Their agricultural claims, it is said, constitute a blind for crowding as many of the metropolitan Jews from the crowded districts into their farmhouses as these will accommodate, farming being the side-show and excuse for running profitable boarding houses.[6]

His tour of the region showed him Jewish farming really was viable: "[I saw] barns of which any Kansas or Indiana farmer might well be proud. I saw herds of cattle, T.B. tested, sleek, and big producers. I saw cow barns in which there were fewer flies than in some New York tenement homes." He also learned that taking in summer visitors "enables them to stay in the country and pay off their mortgages. I saw workers of every description from the big city, happy that their families, within their means, can have a long vacation in the Catskills."[7] And he was also very impressed by the resort business and how it helped the farmer from the top rank of luxury hotels on down:

At the other extreme are the farm-boarding and farm-rooming houses. The Jews who are farming in this locality and who "take boarders" or "rent rooms" during summer months have solved the problem of making their niggardly farms pay, and, what is perhaps equally important, the question of vacations for the families of the city working classes. These farmers have translated the "Tourists Accommodated" sign, hung in great numbers before farmhouses throughout the country, into a long season-vacation for those who have no automobiles and who never tour, unless it be in city buses. From the exclusive club, with its select, swell patronage we descend to the anciently built, poorly furnished, badly lighted, and in some cases, hygienically almost impossible farmhouse, which will board for the entire season from June through September anywhere from eight to thirty-seven families, coming from the tenements of Brooklyn and the Bronx, from East New York and Jersey City.[8]

He became convinced that only summer guests could save most farmers.

In the first place, practically everyone of these men came out of New York ghettos with no farm experience; only with a wish, a will to be independent of the sweatshop and free in the open. In the second place, they purchased their farms with very little cash investment, but loaded down with heavy mortgages. In the third place, the farms they acquired are worn out, deserted by the native cultivators, practically abandoned because the soil no longer was capable of giving a return for the toil and labor expended upon it.

The crop itself then, notwithstanding the educational assistance as well as the financial aid the farmers receive from the Jewish Agricultural

21

Society, can never yield sufficiently to support a farmer and his family. What is the farmer to do? What these Jews in the Catskills are doing is solving a real rural economic problem to which genuine attention ought to be given by our farm economists.[9]

The Jewish Farmers have come upon a brilliant marketing ploy.

What they are doing is bringing the market for their crops to their own doors.

Just read that line again.

Instead of *seeking* the market in urban places and selling at whatever price the crop may bring, they bring the market to their own doors and obtain a metropolitan Broadway or Hester Street price for the crop.

For instance, at the time I was in the Catskills the Dairymen's League offered a little less than five cents a quart for milk. These boarder-farmers, however, sold milk to their boarders at fifteen cents per quart. Eggs were bringing thirty-three cents in New York; these farmers sold their eggs to their boarders at sixty-five cents a dozen, and saved the cost of packing and shipping. The vegetables these farmers raise ripen at a season when the market is literally glutted. These farmers sell their vegetables direct to the boarders at the price that these people are accustomed to pay in East New York and in the Bronx.

Moreover, the Jewish farmers who take in boarders or who rent their rooms to tenants that do their own housekeeping, have improved the market not alone for themselves individually but for their entire neighborhoods. Many of these boarding-housekeepers and small landlords do not raise sufficient of their own to sell to their people They buy from their neighbors, at a price higher than these neighbors can obtain in the open market away from home. And these latter, too, save the cost of packing and shipping.[10]

Not only is this good for agriculture, but it helps all Jews.

There is another phase, however, which is as important as the farmers' problem. It is this: The room renters are the families of the men who work at the machines in town. They rent a room in which a mother and two or three children live, for a price ranging from $50 to $150 for the season. The season is as long as the renters wish to make it—"the longer the better," said one of these landlords, "because the longer they stay, the more of my crop can I sell directly to the purchaser."

Their children are always in the open. They obtain for them fresh milk, in many cases from T.B. tested cows; eggs which they themselves can go out and gather in the chicken-coops; vegetables which are pulled right up from the ground; *"Se is doch m'chayeh,"* ["It's a pleasure to be here"] as the mother of three youngsters who were having the time of their lives said to me.

In addition, the husband, knocking off at noon on Saturday, comes up for the weekend by train, by bus, by traction, by automobile, when six or seven of them club in to pay for the journey. They spend a day and a half in the open.

"This is paradise," said a man in a hammock who was a machine operator, gesturing at the magnificent mountain panorama that stretched out before us.

And when we get right down to it, to quote an ancient Rabbi, "Who is happy? He who is satisfied with his lot!"

These masses of the New York metropolitan district are just as satisfied with their lot in the boarding and rooming houses in the Catskills as are the people in the "country club," where there is golf every day and dancing every evening, and where they dress up for dinner.

There are several types of these boarding and rooming houses. At the bottom is the farmer who rents every room in his place and provides kitchen facilities for everyone of his tenants. I saw places where there were as few as three families and one where there was thirty-seven families. Next comes the enterprising farmer, who in the winter season, builds shacks for his prospective tenants. This man will house seven or eight tenants in his farmhouse and as many in the shacks as he can provide for. [Read 'bungalows' for 'shacks.'] Then comes the boarding houses, which range from accommodations for three families who are looked after and boarded entirely by the farmers, to small sized hotels, specially built, accommodating as many as a hundred and fifty people and more. At the top, of course, stands the summer resort, which caters to "class." And I met one man who abandoned the boarding end of his agricultural business two years ago because, specializing in egg raising and selling his products in his vicinity at city prices, he can now make his farm pay.[11]

Charles Brett, a New York stockbroker, first visited the Catskills in 1919 when he was seven. Going to the mountains with his grandmother, his aunt, and two cousins, they stayed at a place in Mountaindale called *Eliyuchem*. He remembers the owner meeting them at the train station with a wagon drawn by two horses. It took an hour to travel about eleven miles along the rural dirt road to get to their place. "We called it a farm—it had chickens and cows—but there really wasn't any farming." The family split the forty dollar summer rent. Soon conditions would be less primitive.[12]

Many farmers felt that building rental properties, especially bungalows, would provide for their future—when farming became too hard. Farmers also had another reason for liking bungalows—they were easy and inexpensive to build. In a time without building codes, most farmers could easily build bungalows themselves. Cheapness meant that debt could be kept to a minimum. "They could be framed of the same local pine and hemlock that was used for practically everything from framing chicken coops to girdering and flooring" large commercial structures.[13] Ann Macin recalled this progression. She moved to Greenfield Park from the Lower East Side with her parents in 1916 when she was six. In 1933, her father gave her five acres of land on which she built ten bungalows, buying the lumber on credit. She kept adding bungalows on through the 1950s until she had twenty-three.[14]

Grandpa never practiced agriculture, but he was a "farmer" and a landlord. As columnist Dave Barry has observed, "If you were to make a list of the most unpopular professions, you'd have to include landlord, which generally ranks, in public-opinion polls, down with attorneys, journalists and salmonella."[15]

Bungalow colony lore is full of nasty observations about owners' cupidity and nastiness. My grandparents had their quirks, but they were basically very nice people in their dealings with tenants. In later years, when I traveled to many colonies, I came to the basic, if unsurprising, conclusion that usually the more financially strapped a landlord was, the more devious he or she was. At the more successful places, the owners were often described as "real nice guys."

I was born in January 1937, and, with neither cause nor effect, by June 1937 Richman's was ready for the first season. Grandpa had bought three-plus acres of woodland on Route 42, one-half mile from Woodbourne, the previous year. Why Woodbourne? Well a *landsman* (countryman) had introduced the town to him on his first trip to the mountains—and he liked it. In later years, Grandpa would show me other tracts of land he had considered before buying his for six hundred dollars. One of these made me drool. It had almost two hundred acres plus a house—three miles from town on a secondary road. Its price was a thousand dollars. Part of this tract was to be developed in later years as a bungalow colony—Jacoby's. Whenever I went there, I yearned to own that view of the mountains. Why did Grandpa turn this piece of property down? Because it was too far out. It was really considered prestigious to be only one-half mile from town—you could walk there! Plus, it was about an eighth of a mile from Reddish's, where the family had spent several summers. My mother recalls that the reason the family went to Reddish's, leaving Rosenshein's, was that they had flush toilets. "Outhouses were terrible and dirty and they smelled," Mother recalled.

Our road was, and remains, mostly Christian and residential. When you turned onto Route 42 from Woodbourne, the scene—with the white-steepled Dutch Reformed Church, the neat houses, and the great maple trees—was almost New England. Only one bungalow colony was between town and our place, and the next bungalow colony was a quarter of a mile up the road. A working farm was across the street from us.

Grandpa had part of the land graded and filled, and he dug the cellar hole. One small spring kept the cellar hole damp; instead of relocating, as a builder should have, he built on his original spot. My mother still has trouble with that spot, with a wet and occasionally flooded basement. Originally the plan was to rent out three rooms. Distinguishing us from the usual *kuchalein* was that each room would have its own kitchen downstairs, and every bedroom had a washbasin. Hot water was provided by the coal- and wood-burning cookstove that was kept going all summer in the main kitchen. When extra hot water was needed, you could light a gas heater in the downstairs bathroom. Laundry was done in a tub, with cold water only, behind the pump house that also served as our storage shed. Often women carried pots of boiling water from their kitchens to the laundry tub.

My parents and grandparents often told me, independently, that in 1937 the house was considered a showplace; people came and wondered at its size—and its privacy. The house had beautifully plastered walls throughout, although the added kitchens were plywood paneled. Grandpa imported special craftsmen from New York to do the trim and the floors. When an average carpenter earned five dollars a day, these specialists commanded ten dollars. And all of this was within walking distance to town!

Rent for the season (July Fourth to Labor Day) was ninety dollars, and Grandma (who ran the business) collected three dollars per week from each tenant for "gas and electric." Gas was supplied from propane tanks. In a day when

25

a tank of propane cost five dollars and electricity was very cheap and electrical appliances few (irons and an occasional broiler), "gas and electric" was a lucrative profit center. In later years when economic conditions changed, old-time "farmers" would wax rhapsodic about the "gas and electric days." Some tenants arrived a little early and stayed a week after Labor Day—at Richman's this was always allowed, but the lore of the mountains is rich with tales of "farmers" who would turn off electricity and water to their tenants by Labor Day. The season was simply over. Unlike the farmers Mr. Landman described, these "farmers" had no fresh produce to sell.

Grandma, always the business brain in Woodbourne, looked around for ways to maximize income, and in 1939 my grandparents added a new kitchen downstairs and a small bedroom over the porch. Grandma and Grandpa used the living room as their bedroom and the summer kitchen was also used as a kitchen.

Since the summer kitchen was so public, the tenants who used it—and we only had one set, people who, except for one year, were with us for the whole forty years we operated the place—ate in the dining room at the far end of our big dining room table. Mrs. Dubofsky always set a tablecloth on her end of the table, over ours, and they usually ate at the same time we did. Five Richmans and two to four Dubofskys ate at the table. Grandma almost never sat at the table, she served and would often eat before or after the others. Recent studies, from a feminist perspective, have been made of this ethnic phenomenon, which we accepted as normal.[16]

Not only did the major outside door open into the summer kitchen, but so did doors to the four individual tenant kitchens, the downstairs bathroom door, as well as the door to our kitchen, which was also the major passageway. The front door, which opened into the dining room, was rarely used. Privacy during the day was rare, during the nighttime it was nonexistent. Jews were accustomed to crowded conditions in Europe, and too often crowded conditions in New York as well, so that the swell did not appear unusual to us. This crowding phase of the immigrant and postimmigrant experience is explored very well in Neil and Ruth Cowans' *Our Parents' Lives*.[17]

From 1939 through the 1950s, the house was packed. There were six Richmans. Each tenant room averaged four people as well—twenty tenants—parents and children—and on special weekends, like the Fourth of July, tenants often had guests. Twenty-six people in that house and guests. As was typical of the period, things were calmer during the week, when the fathers were working in the city. By the 1940s, most fathers no longer worked on Saturdays and, accordingly, they arrived on Friday evening and stayed until Sunday evening when they made the trek back to New York City.

In the 1920s and early 1930s, most fathers commuted to the country on the "Bull Trains," as the late Friday afternoon trains from New York were called. The trip was arduous. You first had to get to the Hudson Pier at 42nd Street where you got the Weehawken Ferry to New Jersey, from there you could board the New York, Ontario, and Western Railroad to the Catskills.[18] Later, buses, hacks, and private cars would substitute.

My father, Alexander Richman, was one of these commuters. Father was born and grew up in Brooklyn and graduated from the then elite and prestigious Boy's High School. A brilliant student, he won a full-tuition scholarship to Columbia University at a time when few Jews even earned admission. Then, also on scholarship, he earned a M.S. degree in chemistry. Father wanted to be a physician, but getting into medical school in the 1920s was difficult for Jews, and family legend—I never could get a straight answer out of anybody on this— was that he could have gotten into medical school if he went "out of town," but my grandparents would have nothing to do with that. They were the last word in possessive parents and he was the last word in dutiful sons. So he studied pharmacy and became a retail pharmacist. He clerked for two years, then Grandpa bought him an established drugstore in the Brownsville section of Brooklyn at the corner of Eastern Parkway and Hopkinson Avenue.[19] Basically, my father hated it, but being the dutiful son, he hung on, succeeded, and eventually even prospered. Father drove up from "the city" on Friday evening in one of his succession of Chryslers. Like most of the men, he worked until five or six o'clock on Friday and then started his trek, which, at its very best, took three and a half hours. Prior to the construction of 'the Route 17 Quickway' in the 1950s and the New York State (now the Thomas E. Dewey) Thruway, there were frequently monumental traffic jams in towns along the way: Suffern, Middletown, Bloomingburg, and Sloatsburg. Cars often overheated going over the Wurtsboro hills. "Kids would stand at the base of the Wurtsboro mountains, where there's a little creek," recalled *New York Times* sportswriter Mike Strauss. They would not only provide water for radiators, but "for a nickel or a dime, they'd throw water on burning brakes as the cars came down the hill."[20]

Local police set up speed traps and watched carefully for any other traffic law infractions. Perhaps the single most common male reminiscence is of the policemen along the way whom most travelers felt were there to harass them.

And, indeed, as Joey Adams recalled, "The sheriffs and villagers en route [to the Catskills] were none too thrilled with the New York wise guys cluttering up their main drag." They gave out tickets freely for offenses like "driving dangerously near the white line" or "disturbing the peace" (if you blew your horn) in addition to the more usual speeding tickets. "After a short stretch of open road, they'd suddenly hit you with a four-mile-per-hour speed limit."[21] My father's horror tales, and those of his friends, certainly corroborate Adams's observations. At that time they didn't simply give you a ticket. They "would haul you off to the local jailhouse" where "you would plead your case." The local magistrate would often make you post a twenty-five dollar bond that he knew would likely be forfeited when he set a hearing "nineteen days" later. Adams remembers "a handsomely uniformed sheriff with white socks."[22] Mike Strauss, however, remembers "policemen with badges on their overalls"[23] Both existed.

A five-hour trip on Friday night was usual. Seven- or eight-hour trips were not uncommon. The men arrived between ten and midnight. No car ever arrived with only one passenger. My father always brought up a load of tenants, drugstore customers, and friends. During the years of World War II, when gasoline was rationed, father and those of his friends who had access to gasoline would form an elite car pool. When things were really bad, father was forced to take the bus—a very unpleasant experience since wartime buses were overcrowded. By the time buses made their pickups in Woodbourne, it was standing room only for the four and a half to five hours to New York City, without air-conditioning, of course. On these trips, Father often carried along "the little chair"—a miniature, iron-hooped, ice-cream-parlor chair that came with his drugstore. Thus, he was able to sit in the "standing-room only" bus.

In the 1950s, Father was able to adjust his weekends more to his liking. At first he would leave New York City at noon and arrive at about three o'clock. He also started returning to New York City on Monday morning—leaving at six—arriving in time to open the store at nine. Year by year, until he retired in 1959, he was able to whittle away at his summer workweek until he would arrive in Woodbourne Wednesday afternoon and return to the city Monday morning. Needless to say, he seldom had riders along on his newer schedule. However, he never took a vacation as such, and this pattern was typical of many small businessmen of the period.

The arrival of the fathers, of course, meant the arrival of cars. Two-car families among New York's Jewish middle classes was virtually unheard of before the 1960s, and car ownership was far from universal. During the week you walked, which was why being near town was so important.

Before World War II, Richman's modified version of the *kuchalein* was a financial success and, in 1939, a decision was made to add bungalows, which was accomplished in 1940. When the first two duplexes were added to the property, Richman's became a bungalow colony. Since most bungalow colonies started as farm houses or rooming houses, they almost always had a variety of accommodations: rooms, apartments, and bungalows. Cutler's Cottages in South Fallsburg proudly considers itself to have been the first "all bungalow" colony in the Catskills.[24]

The Richman's Bungalows were the height of privacy, if not elegance. Each had its own entry through a porch that had a built in bench. You entered into the kitchen, which had a gas range, a sink, an icebox (refrigerators came after World War II), a standing metal storage cabinet, and a gas heater attached to a hot water tank that provided hot water for bathing and dishwashing. Bungalow tenants had to pay for their own gas supply. Most expected a single tank to last for the entire summer—for cooking, hot water, and heat! The ultimate agony, from the tenants' perspective, was to run out of gas a week or, worse yet, a few days before the end of the season and having to buy another tank knowing that the "farmer" would get the rest. Freer spenders routinely allowed for two tanks. On occasion, the big spender even bought three tanks. The kitchen was a principal sleeping room for kids or used as the guestroom; so in addition to a table and four chairs, the kitchen also had a "high-riser cot" (a metal cot with a trundle). The bathroom had a mirror-fronted wooden medicine cabinet over the wash basin, a toilet, and a stall shower.

The bedroom held two three-quarter-size metal beds. These had solid-panel headboards and footboards grained to look like wood, not the brass or pipe-style beds some places used. These metals beds were apparently popular from the late 1920s through the early 1950s, when the demand for more elegant furnishings brought wooden beds into the bungalows. The beds create a drum-like noise if you hit either the head- or footboard. Kids exploited this quality to the fullest. A dresser and two chairs were also in each bedroom. Grandpa had bought (cheap) some Art Deco ladies dressing tables with huge mirrors and limited drawers. There were no night tables or chests of drawers—which were added after World War II when tenants became more demanding. Nor were there electrical outlets; if you had an appliance, you ran a wire from an adaptor screwed into the overhead light socket. All of the single-bulb fixtures like those

29

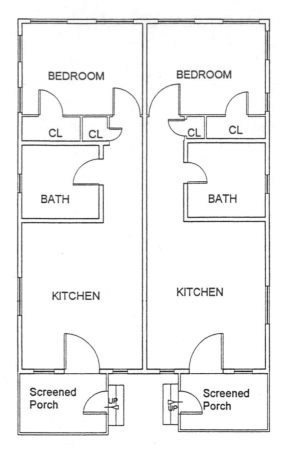

TYPICAL DOUBLE ONE BEDROOM BUNGALOW

in the main house were switched by pull cords. The walls were unfinished plywood but the woodwork was stained and varnished pine. The floors were covered with oilcloth—wall-to-wall in the kitchen and bathroom. Oilcloth rugs were used in the bedrooms. These rugs were especially popular because you could rotate them when they got worn and hide the worn-out spots under a bed. The rugs were usually floral and were patterned after cloth carpets of the period. One clue that we were out of the mainstream came in later years when my grandfather could no longer find rugs. An avid flea marketer, I am amused to see these rugs now offered as collector's items.

The double bungalows cost $1,200 each to build in 1940 and each unit rented for $125 ($250 per double) per season, plus $2 each week for electricity. With taxes on the property around $100 per year and services minimal, the return was very satisfactory. The bungalow rates were raised in 1943 to $250 and again in 1945 to $400 (always plus electric), which would remain their top price. Rooms in the main house also went up during World War II, first to

$125, and then to $300 (plus gas and electric). By 1945, the gross rental income was $3,100 (plus gas and electric). The total cost of house, grounds, and bungalows, including furnishings, had been approximately $6,500. With expenses running about $500 a season (taxes, insurance, utilities, repairs), the return on principal was outstanding—and we had our "free" summers in the mountains.

When the bungalows were built in 1940, another improvement was made at Richman's. We installed a telephone—yes, for three summers we had existed without a telephone; the nearest one probably was in Woodbourne, one-half mile away. Our new telephone, equipped with a coin box, was installed in the summer kitchen. Not having a telephone was fairly usual at the time. We didn't have a telephone in our apartment until 1948. Every street corner in Brooklyn seemed to have a grocery, a drugstore, or a candy store where you could make a call—and they all had errand boys to call their customers to the telephone. In the years before television and private phones were common, neighborhood stores were busy and open until at least 11:00 P.M.

When the war ended, rental demand on the mountains was overwhelming. You could rent anything! Not only did more people have more money and more cars than before the war, but veterans returned home to an incredible housing shortage. Many had to double up with their in-laws. The summer could provide an escape. The "farmers" rallied for the buck. Even chicken coops (not ours) became bungalows. Once I even visited a bungalow at Meyer Furman's colony in Woodbourne, built using one of the outside walls as the colony's handball court—"bang, bang, bang" all day long. Even the rooms with community kitchens were renting easily. In later years, people, such as Miriam Damico who had some of these units at her Moonglow Inn Colony, made money by renting the rooms out by the week or even by the weekend to people who didn't want to commit themselves to a summer rental.

Building materials were scarce, and shoddy construction ruled the day. In 1948, Grandpa, Grandma, and Father—Mother was never consulted—decided to build more bungalows at the rate of one double bungalow a year. In 1949, the first new cottage was built; it was larger than the earlier cottages and it had amenities. It consisted of three rooms: a kitchen that opened through a large arch into a second room envisioned as a dining/sleeping area, a bedroom, and a bath. My brother, Seymour, then a student at Brooklyn Technical High School, drew up the plans to grandparents' specifications. Like the other bungalows, the new ones were built on cement piers. While the bedroom was pan-

31

eled in plywood, the dining room was finished in the newly popular knotty-pine, and the kitchen and bath were tile board that emulated pink ceramic tile. The ceilings were acoustical tile. The ceiling light fixtures were fluorescent circular bulbs (exciting light in the late 1940s). There were wall switches and outlets. Linoleum was used on the floor, and rugs were laid in the bedroom. A fluorescent fixture even shone over the medicine cabinet. The furniture was colonial style for the bedrooms, bought from S. Weiner's in South Fallsburg, which specialized in bungalow colony furniture—and who lasted in business, with modification, until 1989. Of course the dinette sets were up to date—chromium with Formica tops.

The double bungalow cost $4,800 to build and each half rented for $500 (plus electric); $1,000 a year on a $4,800 investment—a very good return. Grandpa acted as our general contractor, and he, himself, made the piers. The new bungalow had screened porches, and we screened the porches on the older units as well. Since the site was woodland, I had been encouraged for the time being to play with my hatchet; I spent many a day chopping down small trees. The major work on the bungalow was done by a local carpenter, John Morton, "the *schicker*" ("the drunk") as Grandpa called him. But he was usually sober, and he was helped by his son. Mister Winter did the plumbing, and Harry Dill, our local hardware store proprietor, did the electrical work. Altogether, the bungalow begun in June was finished by the end of August. Because of postwar shortages, Grandpa couldn't get good wooden siding, so he used white asbestos shingles. The next summer, the same crew built a second bungalow to the same plan, although it was decided to make the scale larger. The bedroom was now almost ballroom size. The cost was $5000, but the rent was the same. This was also our rental unit swan song. Before the new bungalow was completed, family tragedy would change our space allocations.

In the fall of 1949, we had, as usual, all gone up to Woodbourne to be with Grandma and Grandpa for Rosh Hashona. Seymour was his usual self, except for the day before we were due to leave. When he got up that morning, he was very pale. The next day was Sunday, and he continued to be pale. On Monday he was taken to the doctor, and by Tuesday a diagnosis was established—leukemia—a virtual death sentence in 1949. Despite heroic efforts, including taking Seymour to Boston to be treated by Dr. Sidney Farber, who was on the cutting edge of leukemia therapy, Seymour died in April. I was now an only child.

The family was devastated, and as we approached summer, it was decided

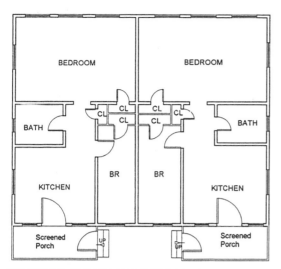

TYPICAL DOUBLE TWO BEDROOM BUNGALOW
Floor Plan I

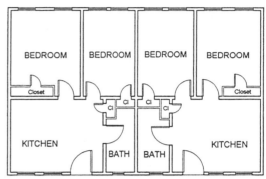

TYPICAL DOUBLE TWO BEDROOM BUNGALOW
Floor Plan II Adapted for Motel Style Unit

(maybe my mother exerted some influence) that we should have a bungalow to ourselves. That year Mother went into the city every week with Father and came back up for the weekends. In past years, once a summer, usually in August, Mother would go into the city for one week—to clean house, we were always told. The trip was an event because we would often be brought a game or a toy on her return, but this weekly trip was a new regimen. During the weekends I slept on the high-riser in the kitchen, but during the week I had a real bed, and I could even have a friend over to spend the night! I, of course, had my meals at Grandma's in the Big House, as the original building was called. In going around other colonies, I found out that "Big House" or "Main House" was common at colonies with rooming house or apartment centers. If the owner lived on the grounds in a private house, it was "the Office." Bungalows were "on the line" or "down the line."

In the meantime, Grandma was able to find friends who would share a kitchen—so she rented out our old room to them. The next winter, Father broke a leg and developed severe diabetes, so Mother's commuting pattern continued the following summer. When I was fifteen, in 1952, Mother resumed staying up for the week—and Father, who had always eaten all of his mid-week meals in restaurants, started to take Mother's prepared meals home to eat during the week. He had also now begun to substantially shorten his week in New York City, first to Thursday, then to Wednesday.

33

Grandma Richman was always a stoic, and, as mentioned earlier, she had seldom eaten with us. But late that summer, we noticed that she would make excuses not to be around at mealtimes—and she was losing weight. By summer's end, I discovered her vomiting after eating. She, of course, denied anything was wrong. By the time she and Grandpa came back to New York City after the season, she couldn't deny her illness anymore, and the doctors recommended exploratory surgery—it was fully metastasized, inoperable stomach cancer. Operation and then ownership of A. Richman's would pass on to the next generation.

Chromolithographic scenic postcard, circa 1950. This typical resort card was one of a large group of scenic cards whose images are often unrelated to the site. They sell the illusion of what Sullivan County should be. The same image was often sold with different legends. This one is from "Woodbourne, N.Y."

The cover of a 1950s promotional piece distributed by the Sullivan County Board of Supervisors. It touted all the reasons to vacation in the mountains. Not only are there great scenery and entertainment, there are "no mosquitos!" Those were imaginary bites everyone got when the sun went down. As an extra inducement, Sullivan County's bungalows and other resorts are "far outside potential atomic bomb blast areas." True enough.

Miriam Damico is the proud owner of the Moonglow Inn in Loch Sheldake, N.Y. Her well-tended colony offers (reading from her business card) "Completely Furnished Cottages" and "Duplex Apts" (1993). Catering to "snowbirds" who winter in Florida, Miriam even provides her guests with bedding and dishes.

The motel-style "New Units" at Miriam Damico's in 1993 were actually built over thirty years ago. The corner units, with cross ventilation, were rented at a premium. The lawn furniture is pressed resin.

Bertha Richman poses on the lawn glider at Reddish's *kuchalein* in Woodbourne in 1936. The Richmans started summering here in 1934 because Reddish's had flush toilets. (Photo: Unknown)

Three guys mugging for the camera. Not even Bertha Richman remembers who they were—they may have been her husband's pals. The photograph was taken at Rosenshein's *kuchalein* in Woodbourne, circa 1932. These single-sex group shots were very common in the 1930s. The three wear street clothing, when suspenders were common. The barefoot man holding his shirt and tie had probably just arrived from New York City. (Photo: Unknown)

(right) Seymour Richman on a lawn glider at Reddish's *kuchalein* in 1934. Note the rough grass. (Photo: Alexander Richman)

(left) The "Big House" was new in 1937 when Bertha and Alexander posed on the porch. Alexander came up on weekends, and Bertha stayed up for the summer. Grandma Richman ran the *kuchalein,* did all the cooking, and ruled the roost. Bertha took care of the kids and did all the rest of the housewifely chores; cleaning, laundry, and so on. She also got along with her mother-in-law. (Photo: Unknown)

The Big House and a bungalow, 1942. The driveway was unpaved and the grounds rough. (Photo: Alexander Richman)

One of A. Richman's "old bungalows" when it was less than five years old. The 1945 picture shows the high cement piers Abraham (Grandpa) Richman used. The Richman bungalows were placed farther apart than most. Note the benches Grandpa made and the bathing suits on the clothesline. (Photo: Seymour Richman)

Hank (Joshua Henry) Rosenfeld, the Herbens' grandson, poses with a shuttlecock glued on his badminton racket. The year is 1952. The sidewalk leads to an old bungalow whose porch is just visible, back right. The two new bungalows are behind him. The old basket swing set is on the lawn. The concrete base with the wooden inset was there to keep people from parking on the lawn.

Woodbourne, N.Y., 1993. Taken from the middle of the new bridge crossing the Neversink River, Route 42 has a New England aspect that only occasionally changes as you go up the road. The Dutch Reformed Church is testimony that even at the height of the resort industry, the vast majority of Sullivan County's year-round residents were and remain Christian. The region's often-parallel societies, Jewish and Christian, usually merge, if at all, at the nearby local volunteer fire company.

A relic of the past, circa 1950. This bungalow, one wall of which served as handball court, survives as a remnant of a large colony that has lost its other buildings. A modern home has been built on the site of the main house. Now used for storage, this strange building in Woodbourne reflects the time when anything could be rented. The basketball hoop reflects the interests of today's owners.

3

Farmer's Life

While many resorts emerged from farms, this was not always the case. Hotel and bungalow colony owners came from differing backgrounds. Some used the mountains as an escape; several saw the industry as a way to move up in the world; others had more personal reasons. Most were immigrants or children of immigrants.

As spring approached, European-born Leo and Lillian Halper of fictional Brookville, who for many years had been year-round Sullivan County residents, made an annual trip into New York City. "They had to hire waiters, bus boys, a band and other help."[1] Not caring for New York City's parking problems, they took the bus, watching the scenery and talking to the bus driver, a country neighbor. Their trip combined business with family obligation. They reminisced about visiting relatives on the Lower East Side: "Leo's sister Bella lived on Norfolk Street. She was a big fat woman who had owned, in former years, a pushcart on nearby Orchard Street." Now she had moved to Borough Park in Brooklyn.[2] The Halpers saw their world changing; they saw the world of the ever more Americanized Jews changing. When they visited old friends, the Toozens, who had lived on the Lower East Side, they slept on the floor. In postwar America, their friends moved to a new house on Mosholu Parkway in the Bronx and "were proud of their spacious house, the modern kitchen, large closets and a garage for the car."[3] These people and others always showed up at Brookville in the summer.

At the very real Richman's, we had a constant stream of friends and relatives who "stopped in" for a few days or weeks. They were welcome before or after the season, but were barely tolerated during our busy time when they had to sleep on a couch, if they were lucky. A long-time summer drop-in was Grandpa's Turkish bath buddy Abram. A giant of a man, with a prodigious capacity for liquor and one eye that wandered as he talked, Abram was a *parshak,* or masseur, at the Turkish baths that my grandfather and his cronies frequented in Brooklyn. Perennially fighting with his wife, in summers Abram would often take refuge at Richman's—in later years sleeping in a bed in the loft over the garage. One of his summer activities was making new *bezims* (brushes), which he used in scrubbing down his clients. These were made by gathering vast amounts of heavily leaved, straight, white oak twigs. About a hundred of these were tightly bound together with string and hung upside down to dry. When mostly dry, but still pliable, the *bezims* were ready to be used. They were soaked in soapy water to soften and then used to scrub you down. I was once given the treatment and found more pain than pleasure. Curiously, in a 1991 issue of *Le Figaro,* a French newspaper, I was reading an article about Tzarist Russia, and there was a photograph of a *parshak* using a *bezim* on a St. Petersburgh aristocrat.[4]

Typical of the nonagricultural farmer of the resort business was rotund, genial Meyer Furman, one of the three Furman brothers who had bungalow colonies in Woodbourne. A teenager, Brian Lazarus, profiled him in *Meyer Furman's Camp Neversink Weekly Camper:*

> Meyer was born in Dorakoe, Romania, on Oct. 28, 1895. Soon after, he moved to Braella, Romania. At the age of six he went to school for six months. He left to work in a grocery store. He soon left his job, and until the age of eleven he worked as a tinsmith assistant.
>
> He came to America in 1907. His first job here was in the fruit business. Later he went into plumbing, but soon after he returned to the fruit business. He met Stella and six months later, on Aug. 1, 1917, they were married. A few months later he went into the Army. When he was discharged in 1919 he weighed 98 pounds.
>
> After this he bought an Army and Navy store. In 1936 he first came to Woodbourne. He liked it so much that three years later he bought

some land and a house here. In 1946 he put up eight bungalows. Meyer now has over 200 acres of land. He is the proud father of four children and he has three grandchildren. Last week Meyer and Stella celebrated their thirty-seventh wedding anniversary.[5]

Despite variations, "farmers" came in two basic varieties. Those who lived in the country all year, and those who lived in New York City and went up for the season. Year-rounders, like our neighbors the Franks of Frank Villa, were members of the minority. Most "farmers" were "New York people" and, indeed, many were building up their summer businesses for retirement years, and many paid for their resorts and met their mortgage payments with money from the city, which, of course, meant New York City. In many of these families, the mother was the "farmer," and she would run the business with the father continuing to work in the city until the colony was big enough to support the family and dad could quit. This was also the pattern at many small and mid-sized hotels as well, even those founded by real farmers. Ben Posner, of the Brickman family, remembers his father (who had married "the farmer's daughter") working in the city to help support the Posner family farm, which eventually became Brickman's Hotel. Other men worked at seasonal jobs, such as coal and oil delivery, where they could get away during the months of June (set-up), July and August (the season) and September (close-up). Weekends from early spring were necessary for renting and early chores. Fall weekends were for leaf raking and general grounds maintenance. If you built, ideally you wanted the work done in the fall so that it could be finished in time for "the season." But the summer was never off the mind of the colony-owning family.

Our family was a variant on the schema. Grandma and Grandpa ran the colony and their comings and goings were as regular as the tide. When they were in New York City, they lived with us. They had lived with my parents from the time my parents were wed, when Mother was fifteen and Father was twenty-four. It had been a semiarranged marriage, as Mother's father was sick and wanted to see his daughter taken care of—he died about one year later, at the age of forty-two.

Grandma and Grandpa would always go to "the country" right after Passover, and they would come back the weekend after Thanksgiving. My mother, father, brother, and I would go to the country for Memorial Day weekend, for the summer (from the last day of school, which in New York City, was the last Friday in June, until the day before school started, the second Monday of September), and again for Rosh Hashona. After Seymour's death, we started spending all weekends in the country when the grandparents were there. Father and Mother, with loaded car, would meet me on Friday afternoon and we would be off; we would stay until Sunday at five o'clock, when we would start back. This pattern remained until I went to college. I was even drummed out of the Boy Scouts because of our weekend pattern. I could never take part in hikes, and I was classified a "parlor scout."

When the grandparents arrived in Woodbourne, in late March or April, the weather was cold, and even in May and June there would be cold days and nights. Because the house did not have central heat, Grandma and Grandpa would live in our room before and after the summer. This bedroom, which opened onto the kitchen and the bath, would be their living area as it was heated by the coal-fired cookstove that was kept going from when they arrived in the spring until they left in November.

My grandfather never learned to drive, so my father would drive his parents up to the country each year. While up there, their life revolved around their "place," or "*plotz*" as they referred to it. Most of our neighbors were gentiles, and my grandparents had little to do with *"der anti-Semiten,"* although they were slightly friendly with two neighbors: the Ampthors, an elderly couple, and Edith McKenna, who lived with her "brother" (we were told) Mr. Smith, who was the Woodbourne postmaster. Grandma and Grandpa walked to Woodbourne and up the road to visit with the Franks and the Abe Furmans. As a rule, bungalow colony owners were not very sociable with their brethren—after all, they were the competition. Though my grandparents belonged to the local resort owners association, they never had faith in it. Always feeling, and probably rightly so, that it was run for the benefit of the local hotel and bungalow *machers* (movers). Grandpa looked down on most folks in the business because he "didn't have to eat from the bungalows." His major income was derived from the mortgage business. My grandparents were especially friendly with several merchants in town, particularly the Herbens, who ran a grocery. When the Herbens retired and went to live in New York City, they returned in the summer as our tenants for a number of years.

In spring there were chores of cleaning the grounds of winter's twigs and branches. May and June, after the weather warmed, was the time for planting and maintenance. Neither of my grandparents were much interested in gardening, but we did have a small vegetable garden at the side of the house. Grandpa always hired a goy to dig up the garden and plant some "pickles" (cucumbers), tomatoes, and "scallions" (spring onions). One goy planted a few raspberry bushes and they were appreciated for many years. When the goyim weren't easy to find in the early 1950s, I took over the gardening. In the late 1950s, we needed to add a new drain field, so the garden became lawn and, despite a brief revival in 1970, the area has remained lawn ever since.

Grandma's flowers were typical of those grown from "pieces" given by neighbors. There were lilacs (lavender), roses (a red climber, a pale fragrant climber, and a pink moss), a few snowball bushes, hollyhocks, and "tiger" or day lilies.[6] There was a patch of variegated goutweed, peonies (or "pineys" as the locals called them), some creeping phlox, and Grandma's major gardening effort: her "dallies" or dahlias. They were small pink and red ones that grew on tall plants. She stored the tubers with the Ampthors over the winter. Grandpa especially liked the pineys, and I remember him giving many people starts. The only ornamental plants the grandparents ever paid for were the two peegee hydrangeas that Grandpa planted on the front lawn in the late 1940s.[7] There was a goy selling them. I don't know what the affinity is between Catskill resorts and peegee hydrangeas—perhaps it's that they are carefree and bloom during the late summer—but I've seen them practically everywhere at hotels and bungalow colonies. Since the large showy flower heads keep well as dried flowers, many tenants wanted bouquets to take home at the season's end. Today as you drive along the back roads of the Catskills, whenever you see a peegee hydrangea in a scrubby field, you can be sure that you're at the site of an old resort. It's typical of Grandpa's conservatism that he didn't get his "snow ball tree" until this late date—and then only after much family pleading, especially from me. It was at this time, too, that Grandpa made a pair of wooden cranes as lawn ornaments. He thought they looked nice, and he got the pattern from a goy up the road. In 1988, an antiques dealer offered my mother forty-five dollars for the weathered pair—but we still have them.

In the late 1940s, Grandpa also decided to grow a few fruit trees and he planted a concord grapevine. This was probably stimulated by a goy who planted a small strawberry bed in the vegetable garden near the raspberries. Grandpa and Father—I was along too—went to Sears in Brooklyn to pick out the trees; they chose five apples, a pear, and a plum. In their heyday they added a uniqueness to the place, and tenants watched the ripening fruit with a proprietary interest. At most other places where I've seen fruit trees, the trees were old and left over from farm days—especially if they were some distance from the bungalows, where fallen fruit would not have to be raked. These remote trees were often favored climbing spots for summer kids and the source of weapons for apple fights; most of the fruit was small, green and wormy.

One yearly chore was painting the porches and the cement floors of the showers. Grandpa did this routinely, later my mother did the chore. Every six to seven years the entire colony would be painted. Grandpa had a buddy from New York City named Mr. Cantor who would come up to paint at the end of April on through May and June (sometimes in successive years). He was, of course, paid, and he received room and board. He had been trained as a tailor, but he never liked it; he did enjoy occasional sewing though, and evenings he did mending, sewing curtains, and the like for Grandma.

Up until the time when lead was banned in paint in the late 1950s, Mr. Cantor would mix his own paint from the white lead my grandfather provided. The endurance quality of paint has never been duplicated since lead was banned. When Mr. Cantor could no longer paint, in the late 1960s, Grandpa could not get used to the fact that he couldn't find an individual craftsman and that he needed to deal with a painting contractor. When the place needed painting after Mr. Cantor died, Grandpa found an old Italian man who seemed to be of the old school. He worked for a week then filed for unemployment compensation. Grandpa didn't know what to make of that; it had never occurred to him to pay for unemployment compensation insurance.

At many colonies the painting was done by the owners, or at larger places by the handyman or handymen. Aside from occasional day help we never had a handyman, but I knew many owners who did. All were white,[8] goyim, and often alcoholic. Many owners practiced a fine art of balancing the flow of money and liquor to the level where they kept the handymen dependent, at work, and not too drunk. Their duties included painting, ground maintenance, and small repairs. At large, fairly deluxe resorts, handymen would often pick up the tenants' trash and garbage as well. As bungalow colony owners paid salaries direct from their pockets, most had the cheapest help they could find, and primarily it was seasonal. I witnessed this everyday drama while working summers at day camps run by bungalow colonies. Often owners hired help only for the season, but the Kassacks—Leo and Sophie who had a big colony in Woodbourne—had "Dick," a picaresque character, who worked for them year-round. They housed him, fed him (never at the table), and doled out liquor, beer, and money for years. In addition to Dick, the Kassacks hired another handyman or two during the summer.

A complex handyman character is portrayed in the film *Sweet Lorraine,* in which a local falls in love with the owner's granddaughter. When she is surprised that he knows so much about the family hotel, he tells her that all the locals know about the resorts because many of them use the facilities late at night or in the off-season![9] Often large colonies and co-ops now hire year-round caretakers who live on the property during the off-season to guard against vandalism and theft, as well as handling maintenance problems.

The most important spring activity was the annual ritual called renting. Up until 1952, renting was no problem. If you had space during the war or right after, you rented it out. If you had vacant units, you had a line of prospective renters. After 1952, the market became softer. The industry was overbuilt, and, with the easing of the housing shortage and the beginning of suburbia, the lure of the Catskills began to wane. This period was one in which larger colonies, those that offered more and more amenities, thrived and were profitable. Many could afford incurring large debts for improvement.

Offering "new and better" was a Catskill tradition. "At every bungalow colony there were 'guarantees,'" remembers Joey Adams. "For instance, the proprietor's wife guaranteed improvements every year, but they usually turned out to be a new bulb to replace the old burned-out one."[10] In the 1950s and 1960s, these "guarantees" included new pools, new casinos, tennis courts, and other amenities that small places could not afford. And promises had to be kept. Many small colonies, those which didn't or couldn't develop a specialized clientele, went out of business. We lasted.

Bungalow tenants can be subdivided into two major groups: individual renters and groups or cliques. These latter ones were friends or relatives who rented a block of units together. In both of these categories there were long-time tenants and variety seekers. The long-timers liked the same place year after year. The novelty seekers would change places every season. The long-term clique was the bungalow colony owner's dream. Some owners had them year after year, earning the reputation of "never having a vacancy." There was a dark side, however. Some of these "lucky owners" suffered financial disaster when a clique, after many years, would break up or decide to go elsewhere. The owners now had to find new tenants for a colony that many prospective tenants did not even consider—because "they were always full."

The "real" dream tenants were those who gave you a deposit before they left at summer's end. At Richman's, we expected a fifty dollar or hundred dollar deposit. If you didn't have rentals tied up over the winter, or if expected tenants canceled, come spring you put out the "bungalows and apartments for rent" signs. You might put an ad in the paper, and you called everyone you could think of to let them know about your vacancy. When you had vacancies you became a prisoner to your colony. Someone always had to be on site in case a tenant should come. Shoppers usually came on the weekends in late April or early May. If you didn't rent by Memorial Day, you would lower the rent and "run a sale"—twenty-five to fifty dollars off. If you didn't rent by July Fourth, you had a "fire sale"—and took half price or anything you could get. On this point, Kanfer errs when he says that everyone ended up paying about the same rent.[11] I remember many unpleasant weekends waiting to hear the sound of a car driving into our driveway when we had a unit, or worse, units to rent.

Tenants were expected to pay in full upon arrival. There was anguish if they waited a day or two or suggested a payment schedule—what would happen if they backed out? When payment was made by check—the check would be deposited as quickly as possible. The Season was serious business. You either made the money in the eight weeks (July Fourth to Labor Day) or you lost it.

Larger places often had payment schedules that called for periodic payments over the winter. Payments were due 15 January, 15 March, and 15 May, with the balance due (about a third) upon arrival. Miriam Damico remembers carrying people at her "Moonglow" with installment payments over the summer, but this was less usual. Large colonies would also hold "reunions" at a restaurant in the city during the winter. This proved a good ploy for collecting deposits and delayed payments. Miriam Damico now throws her reunions in Florida, where most of her tenants winter.[12]

As the season of 1950 approached, we were in a quandary. Grandma was dying of cancer. How and what would we rent? The decision was made to rent the bungalows but not the house because Grandma insisted on going up to the country after Passover. Weak and ill, with an incision that had never healed, Grandma died in early May on a couch that Grandpa moved into the kitchen, near the stove. There was still time to rent for the season. Grandma would have approved.

That summer saw a number of changes. We moved from our bungalow into the main house. My parents took over their old room, but I insisted on privacy and was given the small room over the porch. Other factors also had an impact on Richman's. My father, then in his forties, was, at his father's urging, thinking of retiring, and my mother wanted a modern kitchen. Tenants were balking at individual hot water heaters and gas tanks in their units, in line with the post–World War II demand for bringing amenities up to a standard that many people were now enjoying at home.

As mentioned earlier, laundry was initially done in cold water in a tub behind the pump house; indeed, my mother recalls the first year at Richman's, before an artesian well was drilled, when she and the other women took their laundry down to the river (about a quarter-mile walk). There they pounded the clothes (including my diapers) on rocks in a scene out of Eastern Europe. But the postwar popularity of Laundromats and home clothes washers spread to the colonies, and in 1950 Grandpa cut a door in the side of the pump house and put in a Bendix clothes washer—the model with a window in the front so that you could watch the clothes go around. This machine came into use just as television became popular, and it was a common comedian's butt—people deciding whether to watch the Bendix or the TV! Ha, Ha! The water was still cold, but it didn't touch your hands. It cost twenty-five cents per load to use the machine. For the first few years, a few frugal housewives continued to use the tub and washboard out back, but eventually the machine won everyone over. In the late 1970s, we replaced the old washer and raised the charge per load to thirty-five cents. The larger colonies had multiple washers; some even installed dryers. Our people always hung their clothes to dry on clotheslines, among the trees near the pump house. As elsewhere in society, Monday was the traditional laundry day and always the busiest day. Unlike the mode at the larger colonies, our washing machine was not coin operated. People were honor-bound to pay. Whenever they heard the machine going, my grandmother or my mother would go to see who was using the machine—or if I were unlucky enough to be around, I would be sent to scout. The money collected was kept in a tin can. In the days before we supplied hot water, the washing machine was a moneymaker. Some of our tenants sent their laundry out to be done by Laura Hill who lived up the road, and commercial laundry trucks were common sights at larger colonies in the postwar years.

Water was always a problem in the country, and Richman's, like most colonies, depended on artesian wells; we had three, and they would be inspected once or twice each summer by inspectors from the New York Department of Health. Our first well, the one in the pump house, was drilled in 1937 and topped by a pump that created a racket. The pump house itself is about ten-by-twelve feet, and it doubles as a tool shed and a place to store lawn furniture. The open gable has racks for storage. The first well was 107 feet deep, drilled by a team of locals, the Concklins, who lived in Livingston Manor. They would do our other wells as well. That same year, Grandpa had a shallower well drilled halfway between the house and where the earlier bungalows would be built. This one was topped with a hand pump and gave delicious cold water. One of my brother's and my regular chores was to fill a pitcher of water before meals. During my grandmother's time, when the stove was kept going, someone regularly walked to the well to get a *chinik* (kettle) full of water, which was always kept on the stove. Grandma used this water to wash dishes as well as to make tea—always served in a glass. On laundry day, *chiniks* of boiling water would be carried out to the washtubs. As kids we all liked to play with the pump. How fast can the handle go up and down? How fast a stream can you get? Adults discouraged this contest. I still have a scar on my finger as a souvenir of one of these contests, when I got my hand caught in the wrong place.

After the "new bungalows" (as they were always called) were built, our well couldn't keep up with the demand. Following a summer of drought, a new well was drilled about a hundred feet back from the new bungalows. It was over 240 feet deep. The new pump was housed in a new pump house that was strictly utilitarian and scarcely larger than an outhouse. It just contained room for the pump and someone to service it. Water pumped from here went to the tank in the old pump house, from which it was distributed. When the town of Fallsburg, of which Woodbourne is a hamlet, put in "city water" in the late 1950s, all private wells were condemned for drinking purposes and we were forced to remove the pump from the outside well. I still regret that and remember the cool water—often served with rust flakes from the pump. Years later, many of the old-time tenants also would wax rhapsodic about the old pump.

The new town water system, coming just a few years after the expensive drilling of the new well, was upsetting. Father and Grandfather devised a dual water-usage scheme. Town water (which was and is metered) would be used for the sinks and showers. Our well water would go for toilets. This system was used until the mid 1960s when it dawned on me that the maintenance of the pumps, which were ever more costly to keep in working order, was more expensive than the water bill would be. Most bungalow colony owners welcomed "city water" in the short or long term. During my childhood, there were regular horror stories about colonies that ran out of water in August; their wells or springs just gave out from demand during a dry spell. I remember the August jitters that came before we drilled our new well, they were second only to the springtime "will we rent?" worries.

Closely connected to the water problem was sewage. Here the concern was not bacterial contamination of water (chlorine could take care of that if you got caught), but the dreaded smell. One of our black family jokes today concerns a well-known resort whose semitreated effluvia fouls a nearby lake. As we drive by on New York Route 52 in summer, the pungent odor permeates the air; "The Air of Summer!" we call out in chorus. At most places, ours included, gray-water disposal was simple and direct—shower (we had no tubs) and sink water simply drained under the buildings through holes in the floors. There were no foundations under any of our bungalows or our tenant kitchens. Toilets were handled by septic tanks. Overflow at places with heavy demand and poor drainage went into the cesspool (that's where the smells came from). There were no drain fields. Every year right after our last tenant left, the "honey dipper" or septic tank cleaner would come and empty our two tanks—one near the new bungalows and one serving the old bungalows and the house. Over the years we were fortunate in that we never had a smell problem. In the late 1950s, New York State became much stricter about sewage disposal, and we were forced to capture gray water and put in two drain fields—which established two new areas of grass to mow, enlarged the parking lot, and eliminated the last vestiges of our vegetable garden.

A word or two about parking lots—ours was always grass, and I never saw a bungalow colony with a paved parking lot. Some had gravel and grass. Most were grass and ruts. I remember visiting my great-aunt Rose and great-uncle Willie at a colony in South Fallsburg in the 1970s, where the parking area looked like nice grass. Returning from our visit, we discovered that the car had sunk into the marshy soil and we had to call a tow truck to get it out.

The last major changes to our house came in the 1950s when tenant demands and Mother's demands came together. If Father wanted to retire and move up to the country (they planned to go to Florida in winter), renovations had to be made. A central hot water system was put in and gas lines were run to the individual bungalows from large tanks behind the main house. The house was enlarged, remodeled, and heat was installed. The regimen of changing over from "summer hot water" to "winter hot water" (i.e., from the circulating system to one only serving the central core of the main house) was complex and would cause many problems over the years. Plumbing and hot water problems were, and still are, endemic to bungalow colonies where many installations are "Rube Goldberg contraptions"—usually motivated by a desire to save money and the often low-quality work of local craftsmen. After all, the Catskills is a seasonal area with seasonal income. In season, as during spring set-up, waiting for the plumber or the heating people to service the hot water system was a standard occupational problem. Getting a worker was especially difficult in the summer, when craftsmen typically worked eighteen-hour days.

With the installation of heat, my mother gleefully had the stovepipe dismantled. As a matter of fact, right after Grandma's death the stove was put to pasture. A gas heater was put in the kitchen to replace the heat needed before and after the season, and the bathroom gas heater heated water. The stove, however, remained in place until the 1970s when my wife and I added a family room onto our house in Pennsylvania. We moved the stove down there and used it during the years of soaring oil prices. We loved the radiant warmth. We also came to appreciate why Mother disliked the stove so—it was dirty. Ash, wood debris, coal dust, and coal ash were all unpleasant realities.

The changes made to the main house were extensive. A new living room was added to the old parlor (the grandparents' bedroom), which was to become a dining room. Our old bedroom would become a modern kitchen and a private bathroom complete with our own tub. It was all chic. Mother remembers that there had been a tub in our downstairs communal—family and tenant— bathroom when the house was built, but Grandpa took it out. "It used too much hot water," she recalls. "There was never much hot water, anyhow." Our family bedrooms upstairs had the sinks taken out; this allowed for the enlargement of my parent's closet, which had sliding doors installed. One of the downstairs kitchens was converted into a storage room complete with a large cedar-lined closet.

The new kitchen was built by Kaplan Cabinetmakers in South Fallsburg. All of the cabinets were of then-fashionable birch wood with pink Formica, chrome-trimmed countertops. The kitchen featured a built-in oven and burner components and other modern pleasures. Curiously, after Mother got the new kitchen, she seldom used it, except for baking or for its large refrigerator—she found it too compact. To this day, she uses the two kitchens side-by-side.

Father always got my goat when he'd lecture me or announce to others, "I only put in heat for you and your mother. My father and I could do fine with the coal stove." This was especially irritating as someone else did the work. My father was the only family member totally immune from any work around the colony. I never saw him so much as pick up a twig from the ground. He always vowed he would start taking care of the grounds after he retired—but, of course, he didn't.

Grandpa slept in the new living room during the summer and in an upstairs bedroom before and after the season. The living room remained unfurnished until 1959 when Father finally retired. Father's drugstore was in what was politely described as a changing neighborhood, and, in the late 1950s, drug-inspired burglaries and holdups became a problem. During the Christmas holiday season in 1958, Father was held up at gunpoint three times. Although, by this time, he was taking pride in his now successful business, he felt he had to get out. In the spring of 1959, he liquidated his business. My parents, much to my mother's regret, gave up their Brooklyn apartment and moved to the country. Our city furniture now filled the new rooms. It was a strange sensation for me to look past fine furniture, through the window, and see trees! I was accustomed to urban landscapes; summertime meant bungalow furniture and city hand-me-downs.

Once retired, my father decided that he needed a garage to go with our newly paved driveway. While we had a huge horseshoe drive from the very beginnings of Richman's—because it eased getting in and out—the drive was simply smoothed earth onto which, each spring, several loads of small pebbles or crushed stone were laid. Mother always hated this because it was dusty and dirt was tracked into the house. She wanted the drive to be blacktopped. Finally this was done, but it was done in true fashion that showed Grandpa's hand. To save money, only the area near the house was paved. The rest of the driveway continued to get the annual application of gravel for as long as we ran the colony. Another annual rite of spring was to find a goy who had gravel or crushed stone—or who had topsoil. Since most of the lawns had been marshy woodland, they had been filled and subsidence was a problem requiring annual attention.

Over the years, my father's attitude toward cars and car maintenance changed. Before World War II, Father traded in his Chrysler every two years and he always kept his car in a neighborhood garage "with service," which meant that when he brought the car in it was dusted off by an attendant and washed several times a week. These cars, like most cars of the period, were black, and they were always gloriously shining from repeated waxing, washing, and buffing by garage workers. His last black car was a 1941 model, and I remember it very vividly from years of driving up to the country. Wartime restrictions made it impossible to trade in cars, and so the car lasted a long time.

During the car's glory days, my father and mother would "go to New York" (from Brooklyn) to see a movie at one of the great movie palaces—the Paramount, the Roxy, or Radio City Music Hall—and occasionally they took my brother and me. It was wartime and gasoline was strictly rationed, but my father sometimes could get an extra tankful through one of his friends—or occasionally on the black market. His favorite spot to park was at Rockefeller Center—right on the street where the famous Christmas tree glitters each holiday season. In those days, the streets of Manhattan were almost empty of cars on weekends.

After the war, there was a rapid escalation in the cost of garages "with service" and my father gave up that luxury, parking the car in a nearby lot where he could have it washed on a fee-per-visit basis. Neither that car, nor its successor, retained its pristine appearance. The rising cost of garages with service was not Father's only postwar annoyance. Another was the perceived independence of postdepression car dealers who wouldn't deal with him as he liked. He said, in effect, "The hell with them. I'll keep the car till it falls apart," and he did. The old Chrysler lasted until 1952 when it was replaced by a new, gray Chrysler Windsor. I had campaigned hard for a nonblack car, hoping for maroon, but gray was a step in the right direction.

Plans for a garage were talked about for years and finally the decision was made to build; the lumber and other materials were ordered in the autumn of 1959, but the carpenter, John Morton, proved unexpectedly busy. He promised to be available the next spring. When early winter came, the folks discovered just how uncomfortable the uninsulated house could be in really cold weather. They had planned to go to Florida for the winter in any case, so they went earlier. For many years my father and grandpa had gone to Florida for February and March, the traditional Floridian season. Yes, they left their wives and kids home. We kids did get a basket of kumquats and a carved coconut when they came back. These jaunts stopped when Seymour died. Now the plan was to resume the pattern—but with Mother going along.

One day in March they went out to eat. When they left the restaurant, my father, who had an incredible memory, forgot where he parked his car. He soon became even more confused, and he was taken to the doctors; the diagnosis was a brain tumor. Flown back to New York, he died several days after surgery at Mt. Sinai Hospital. He was fifty-two. Years before, as an estate-planning move, my grandparents had given the bungalow colony to my father, now ownership passed with the rest of Father's estate to Mother, who was a very traditional woman of her time. She didn't drive, nor had she ever seen the inside of a checkbook—but she learned. Back in Woodbourne that spring, Mother and Grandpa decided to go ahead with building the garage "that he had wanted"—after all the wood was there and John was available. The frame garage was attached to the old pump house and it was a sizeable structure built to house two cars. It was extra deep and wide and had a high gable roof with a garret reached by a flight of stairs. Grandpa put a bed up in the attic that he lent to friends, especially Abram the *parshak*. The garage was the last building project at Richman's. Over the years the garage would serve a surprising number of functions: a synagogue, a place to store lawn furniture, a casino, and of course, a place to keep the car over the winter. The garage with its two overhead doors and blacktop floor cost $1,500 to build. In later years, I painted it red.

As Grandpa had said in his unique syntax, "I don't have to eat from the bungalows." The bungalow business was never the family's principal source of income. Grandpa was in the mortgage business. As father accumulated capital from his pharmacy, he would invest, too. Actually, right after World War II, father wanted to invest in the stock market but was talked out of it by Grandpa, whose memories of 1929 were especially vivid.

The first home in which we lived after I was born was an apartment on Whipple Street in Brooklyn. In later years, I learned that we resided there because the Cohens who owned the building couldn't pay their mortgage interest—and since Grandpa owned their mortgage he figured he'd get some of his interest back via "free rent." That apartment was in a two-family house, which is now a convent, and, as a Jew, I still like to joke that I grew up in a convent. When World War II broke out and gasoline rationing was instituted, my father was forced to ride the streetcar to work several times a week, and this would not do at all. Father was fastidious: a very good dresser who never liked to be caught up in a crowd. Consequently, we moved to 1565 Eastern Parkway to be within walking distance of his store, at the corner of Eastern Parkway and Hopkinson Avenue. We lived there until after Seymour's death. Mother, especially, couldn't face life in that apartment with the memories of her dead son.

As a result, Father made one of the few independent decisions of his life— one in which his parents were not consulted. He and my mother chose their next apartment themselves. It was in an upscale neighborhood at nearly three times the rent of the old apartment. Father didn't have the nerve to tell his parents about the move until they were due back from the country. They had a fit—especially Grandma, who knew every technique of control *via* guilt. "If you had to move," she said repeatedly, "and pay such a rent, why did you get such a big apartment? Papa and me, we could get a furnished room somewhere in the winter." Despite Grandma's misgivings, the cost was worth it. This apartment had elegant paneling and parquet floors, a tiled bathroom with a shower stall and a sunken tub, and service stairs. Mother hated to leave it in later years, and she is still nostalgic about it. When we moved to East 34th Street and Kings Highway, we really entered into mainstream middle-class Jewish society. Mother had a regular mah-jongg group and a regular cleaning woman, Estelle; most laundry was sent out; and we regularly ate at Chinese restaurants.

By the time I became conscious of such things, Grandpa and Father had shifted their sphere of mortgage operation from the New York scene, including the ice cream factory that they briefly owned, to the "Mountains," as Sullivan county was always known in our house. I have never understood why the family never bought a house in New York: renters in the city, landlords in the country.

The family mortgage business provided me with an unusual insight into the bungalow business. Mortgage supplicants with whom the family dealt were usually people who owned a property and wanted to expand the facilities, install a swimming pool, or make some similar improvement. Husband and wife would usually show up during the summer, sometimes calling first, usually not, to meet with Grandpa. If Father was there he'd sit in; Grandma never did. She, however, was scrupulously briefed and informed. She would never let outsiders see her business machinations; Grandpa was always to star. The meetings invariably took place in the dining room—and very often with me in a corner. At the sensitive times when money was being discussed, the door between the dining room and kitchen was closed and tenants had to knock if they wanted to pass through on the way upstairs. We only dealt in first mortgages and by the time I was eight, I knew what a chattel mortgage was (i.e., one on all personal property). The family always insisted on a chattel mortgage before agreeing on a property mortgage. Grandpa and Father were scrupulously honest in their dealings. They never took money under the table for granting loans, a practice often resorted to by desperate "farmers" whose credit ratings were not very good. Credit ratings were purely arbitrary and determined by the lender. Our interest rate was the maximum defined by law, 6 percent (at a time when banks paid savers 2 percent interest on deposits). Interest and principal payments were always made in a lump sum at the end of the summer. We didn't have monthly payments. Why did customers come to us, instead of going to banks? Remember that in the 1930s through the 1950s banks were not the friendliest places for people of modest means and they often didn't want to deal with small business people as borrowers. Additionally, the stench of anti-Semitism permeated most of the local banks. Since many of our clients were European born, perhaps they also felt more comfortable with personal moneylenders than with banks. And, of course, our rates were competitive.

By the mid 1960s, after my father's death, the business was phased out. Banks had entered the field more rigorously, and by that time increasing numbers of small places were failing and going out of business. Those places that remained good credit risks required six- or seven-figure financing, and this was an area where Grandpa never felt comfortable, especially without Grandma or Father for advice. His usual loan rate was in the $10,000 to $35,000 range. Loans were for ten, fifteen, or twenty years. I would often be handed a certified check prior to its being given to a client. "Feel what $25,000 is like, *mein kind*" (my child), Grandpa would say. A 1956 article in the *New York Times* reported that "the bungalow and rooming house people say they have spent $500,000 on refinements since the close of last season."[13] Clearly in this league, Grandpa was a major player.

Most *kuchalein* and bungalow colony owners slowly built up their businesses. After World War II, a new element of bungalow colony owner emerged. He was less farmer-like. He was a small businessman who, as a wartime profiteer, had amassed a lot of money and was now looking for a place to put it. "Hitler's millionaires," Grandpa sneered at these vulgarians. A few larger colonies changed hands for sizeable sums. Lawyer Sonia Pressman Fuentes remembers her parents selling their all-bungalow Pine Tree Bungalow Colony in Monticello for $225,000 in the postwar years.[14]

Despite the postwar prosperity, debt was a way of life for most resort owners; hotel men and bungalow colony owners alike. In the documentary *The Rise and Fall of the Borscht Belt,* hotel owner Ben Posner recalls that "everyone was in debt."[15] As Sullivan County historian Bill Smith notes, "The resorts in the Catskills always had trouble borrowing money to put in improvements or just to stay afloat."[16] Henry Tobias explains: "Because of their short season, summer resort owners were regarded as poor credit risks."[17] Tobias also notes that "shrewd businessmen . . . invented new ways to dodge creditors."[18] I recall many stories about bungalow colony owners ducking into doorways when they glimpsed creditors in town or hiding out on their own colony when bill collectors came to call. "A merchant knew that if he didn't get paid . . . by 15 August when the season reached its peak, or by Labor Day, at the latest, the chances were that he would have to wait until the following season to collect his bill."[19] If ever! It was not uncommon for resort owners, hotel men, and bungalow owners alike to build up as big a debt as possible over several years and then threaten to go bankrupt. This would force their creditors to take a discount on their bills.[20]

The Richmans were always conservative. After applicants met with Grandpa in the dining room, a time was set for a visit to see the property. These inspections were always scheduled for when my father would be up so he could provide transportation and consultation. I never missed an opportunity to visit the outside world, and I went along on site visits whenever I could. I tramped through innumerable colonies and small hotels. I saw the old community-kitchen *kuchaleins,* which gave the industry such a bad name, and the latest in modern bungalows, and everything in between. If a preliminary visit looked promising, another trip would usually be undertaken after Labor Day when we could inspect every unit. It was on the preliminary visits that I saw, in operation, the little stores that "farmers" at remote colonies operated to supply their tenants with food—often at high markups. Some farmers would be angry if husbands brought up food from the city. Tenants there would have to sneak food in suitcases and such because those landlords watched like hawks as they unloaded their cars or arrived by taxi from the town after a long bus trip. The stores typically sold groceries, dairy products, and produce. They almost never dealt in meat because most places were at least ostensibly kosher and kosher meats require special handling. Town butchers usually made deliveries to these places giving a commission, of course, to "the farmer."

In the discussion about whether or not to grant a mortgage, the discourse generally centered on two features—the number of "units" and how the place was maintained. Of course, clients were asked what their annual rentals and expenses were, but less credence was given to these factors because my family knew how easily these figures could be fudged. Bookkeeping in the bungalow business was very casual and, until the early 1960s, it was rare for even fairly large places to employ the services of an accountant. The "books" that did exist were closely held. Location also played a role; although they appreciated the farmer's store as a profit center, Grandpa and Father wanted the site to be a reasonable distance to town and on a main road as well. They avoided places Grandpa described as being "*en dred off en barg*"—idiomatically, 'in the middle of nowhere.' By the time I could drive, in the 1950s, I passed Richman-mortgaged colonies in most directions. Since they were all on or near main roads, they were easy to keep track of. I would occasionally point them out to friends.

Once a mortgage and its terms were agreed upon, we called our lawyer Monroe Davis, Esq., of Woodridge, who did all of our legal work in the post–World War II years. (I don't know who his predecessor was.) The papers were drawn up (the client paid for this) and a certified check was handed over. Customers were usually married couples, and once they signed up, they entered the family conversation not as people but as resorts. Grandpa would report seeing Mr. Joyland in the village that day. "Joyland" was the name of the colony, not the people who owned it.[21] Only those folks whose name was on the colony would get called by name, and it was their only identifier. Our colony was always simply "A. Richman's Bungalows," and most places were known by the owner's name. Unlike hotels, colonies were less likely to have cute or exotic names. The biggest colonies in the Catskills were Cutler's Cottages in South Fallsburg and Mason's in Monticello. Each had at least one-hundred-plus units (I never counted). Nor were they our clients. But tucked away among Kassack's, Godlin's, Meyer Furman's, Abe Furman's, and Ben Furman's, there was a Frank Villa and a smattering of "Kare Frees" and "Sunshine Colonies," again none of whom were our clients. Occasionally, colonies had Yiddish names like *Grine Felder* (Green Fields).[22]

The people to whom we had lent money were usually very hard workers, and, for the most part, they were city dwellers who came up for the season they were building their futures. Unfortunately, for many, the years of struggle led to very little. Numerous colonies would be abandoned in later years. The luckier ones sold out to Hasidim or the Modern Orthodox Jews, who are now the major bungalow renters in the region. Some of our clients also had children who worked and helped build the colonies. Some kids, not only those of our clients, were forced to work and still resent it today. Novelist Martin Boris bitterly recalls that his bungalow-owner father "worked him hard, very hard."[23] Occasionally colony owners tried slightly illegal ways to increase their income. One day I picked up the local paper to read that one of our mortgagees had been arrested for running an illegal poker game. That fall when we saw him we asked him about it. Mister "Krinsky" laughed and said, "Yeah, I've been doing it for five years and I just got caught."[24] He kept on running his game for at least fifteen more years until he and his wife sold out to Hasidim. The "Krinskys," he was lean and spry and she a mountain of a woman, were jovial. When they came to pay their mortgage payment, they usually brought a basket of apples from a particularly fruitful tree on their place. One would-be client, to whom we didn't lend money, was a woman who supported her colony by working as a prostitute in New York City during the week. We heard rumors, and she later told my mother they were true. She didn't get a mortgage because her place was, in Grandpa's words, "a real shit house." She eventually made out pretty well on her property when it burned down and she collected the insurance money. In times of stress in Sullivan County there were always a lot of fires: usually after Labor Day, especially in dead of winter. We wryly called them "bungalow renewal" or "hotel remodeling" fires. Because so many were and still are, no doubt, arson, Sullivan County has high fire insurance rates.[25]

As August approached, talk of mortgages became more and more frequent. How was Goldberg's season? Is Mrs. Shady Nook feeling better? Is Solowitz still working in the city?[26] September was coming when the clients would have to make their mortgage payments. And after Labor Day they came, like the creatures in Noah's Ark, by twos. A surprising number came in person. A few simply mailed their checks in. Grandpa did not like these clients. He wanted the full business report that came with each visit. Those who came got tea and cake and would talk about their season, how well or poorly they did. Many would bring a small gift like the Krinsky's apples. Occasionally there were requests for extensions in principal repayment, which were often granted. But you had to pay the interest: no ifs, ands, or buts. When a mortgage was paid off, the customer was provided with a "Satisfaction Piece."

While very few loans were made after my father's death, some mortgages continued active until the mid 1970s. Grandpa and Mother were very worried in the late 1960s when one of their clients who owned a small hotel in Woodbourne, called the "Maple Lawn," was unable to pay even the interest and Grandpa would have to foreclose—something he hadn't done since the depression when he was much younger. Fortunately a developer bought the hotel and turned it into apartments (with Grandpa and Mother holding the first mortgage). Eventually this money was realized.

When my father retired, "someday" came true. After walking around the colony two or three times and never picking up a stick, he decided that the job of grounds keeper was not for him. He simply didn't like to bend down or get his hands dirty. Grandpa, who didn't mind getting dirty occasionally, hated to mow grass—always a continuing chore. At Richman's, Grandma Richman always mowed the lawn, about an acre and a half with a push reel mower, nonpower assisted. Seymour was, of course, too noble for the chore. When I was thirteen, lawn mowing was pushed on to me, and I put in two summers of hard labor until, at fifteen (1952), I rebelled. "No power mower, no grass cutting." I won, and Father saw that our neighbor, Art, who had an auto repair business, had just bought a monster of a garden tractor from Sears. He figured that this was the way to go since Art could service our monster as well as his own. We made a trip to the nearest Sears store in Kingston, New York, and bought the rig. With it came a sickle bar for high grass and a mechanical reel for maintenance cutting. The rig was gasoline operated and looked like an oversized garden tiller. You walked behind it and tried to control its self-propelled wheels. It had a will of its own. We also bought the optional cart, which could be attached to the tractor, but only when the mowers were off. This was intended to be used in lieu of a wheelbarrow for hauling, but it proved to be more trouble than it was worth. Since I couldn't yet drive, I did enjoy tooting around in my power-driven wagon, and I would often give rides to the kids on the place. We retired the monster in the early 1960s and got a new rotary-blade push mower, and, a few years later, our first riding mower. At larger colonies the grass was often cut using gang mowers hauled by a farm tractor, with grass around the individual bungalows being cut by hand with a push reel mower. By the late 1950s, the larger places started using equipment similar to familiar suburban paraphernalia. For me, grass cutting was a long-time commitment. I cut the grass weekly throughout high school on those weekends in the country.

In September 1953, I went off to college, and a new grass cutting pattern emerged. It was decided (for me) that, since Grandma had died the year before, it would be best that I go to Woodbourne after college in early June and keep Grandpa company. The pattern continued through my undergraduate years. When school was over I was picked up by my father and driven to Woodbourne where the grass was yet uncut. I would then deal with knee-high grass that had to be cut and raked. Life in Woodbourne before the season was boring. For recreation, I could take a walk. Radio reception wasn't very good in the mountains—the only station we could get was WVOS, "The Voice of Sullivan County," which, at that time, was very heavy on farm reports. We didn't have TV until my parents contemplated moving to the country some years later. Some evenings Grandpa and I would walk down to the village where my mother's friends, the Dominions, lived. They had television that, in the days before cable, provided a very snowy show in fringe areas such as Woodbourne. On the weekend, my father generally "wanted to relax," and he was loathe to let me drive his car, so I stayed put. I always liked our colony best in the springtime; the mountain air was clean, it was quiet, and there were no tenants around. Forced into sociability, I often longed for solitude that didn't exist during the season.

When I was sixteen and just graduated from high school, my summers took a radical change. I was quietly sitting on the front porch one day in June, painting a nude picture (from a photo, not from life—these were the 1950s and this was Sullivan County), when a blue Studebaker pulled into our driveway. My mother went out to talk to the caller who, as she later related, asked her whether she had any kids she'd like to send to camp. She replied "No, but I have a kid I'd like to send to work." Soon I was employed in a day camp, and I started to move in the world of the big bungalow colonies—those with swimming pools, casinos, professional entertainment, and day camps.

When I was a little kid, "camp" was a very scary word around the house. It was like the "boogey man." You'd be sent to camp if you were bad. I never knew kids who went to camp, except an occasional Boy Scout camp, because until we moved to East 34th Street, we had always lived well below our economic means, and working-class kids didn't go to private camps for the summer. When I went to my high school, James Madison, I made new friends, and a number of them had gone—and still went—to camp, and their tales were fun. One of my regrets is that I never called my folk's bluff and asked to be sent to camp.

The bungalow colony day camp was relatively new in 1953. I had heard about this innovation, which had been borrowed from hotels a few years before. Day camps simply allowed mothers to have "a real vacation" in the summer. From nine to five, five days a week, they got rid of their kids, except for lunchtime when the kids would walk home for lunch. Remember, at this time in New York City, most smaller kids still walked home from school for lunch. At some of the larger colonies, the option of camp lunches was offered so that mothers could have uninterrupted days. I worked in two colonies, both in Woodbourne: Meyer Furman's and Kassack's, first as a counselor, then as arts-and-crafts counselor, and finally as camp director for three years.

In the mid 1950s, as larger colonies offered more and more facilities, our clientele changed and so did our price structure. In 1953, "a spokesperson" reported in the *New York Times* that, "The majority of the bungalow colonies . . . and rooming houses . . . is standing loyalty [*sic*] by last year's tariffs." "Loyalty" had little to do with it; renting had just become more difficult, but more desirable colonies were raising their rents. "In some cases where many improvements have been introduced rates will go up." The unnamed spokesperson also claimed, "Bungalows are renting for anywhere between $300 and $850 for the season, and an average rooming house is going to $175 to $250."[27] The bungalow price range is inaccurate at both extremes. Since we did not offer a pool and other amenities, we had to lower our prices in order to rent. In 1956, we adopted a new rent scale. Rooms were $225, small bungalows were $275, and new bungalows were $450, with no extras. Since expenses were also going up, the colony, like many others, was no longer as profitable as it had been. At a larger colony with all facilities, a one-bedroom bungalow, like our old ones, was renting for $600 to $800 and a two-bedroom one, like our larger ones, rented for $1,000 to $1,200, plus extras. The extras were not gas and electric, but rather day camp fees of $65 to $125 per child and entertainment fees that ranged from $35 to $150 per adult couple. In subsequent years, we raised our rates modestly. In the mid 1960s, the rooms went up to $300 and the small bungalows to $375. Continually escalating operating expenses, escalating taxes, and soaring energy prices following the oil embargo made the colony only marginally profitable. Before my father's death in 1960, he used to say that the colony would always provide a roof and enough to eat. By the mid 1970s, even though we owned the colony free and clear, this was not true. In the 1990s, it is not unusual for the rental in large colonies to be $4,000 to $5,000 for the season, plus extras that would also have gone up with inflation.

How did our tenants change? I recall the buzz that went through the colony when, in the mid 1950s, we rented to the Karotkins—a couple in their late sixties. While some of our tenants had been with us a long time and were near this age, the Kays, as everyone called them, were the first tenants at Richman's without young children. Behind their backs they were called the "old people." Within the next few years, most of our crowd was old people. By the mid 1960s, we didn't have any resident children. Most of our tenants actually tended to have come from the old-world Polish village of Antapol—and I frequently considered writing a history called "Antapol: A Catskill Restructure," which would have sounded very scholarly. I was chilled when I saw "Antapol" etched into an interior window of the United States Holocaust Memorial Museum commemorating communities whose Jewish population was destroyed. From the early 1960s, our crowd solidified, and we rarely had a vacancy until the end of the 1970s when death and desertion broke up the old crew. Louie Resnick died on the lawn while playing cards. His widow and her friends moved on. And although we found new tenants easily, they were not the kind my mother liked. The colony was not as profitable as it had been, it was no longer *hamish* (home-like) with a familiar crowd. These were no longer the people who had invited Mother and Grandpa to their children's weddings and their grandchildren's bar and bat mitzvahs.

In 1980, it was discovered that my mother had bladder cancer and, although she recovered quickly after treatment, she didn't want to continue to run the colony; she decided to go out of the business. Several old customers who had been with us for thirty to forty years were shocked. Mother didn't want to sell, she wanted out of the business. She simply didn't rent, and for two years the bungalows stood vacant. When we were visiting a nearby hotel with an expanding colony, I mentioned to one of the partners that we had bungalows to sell; an agreement was reached. In 1982, the bungalows were put on flatbeds and moved through the fields and across the river to their new location. The main house, the pump house, the garage, and the chicken coop remain, looking for all the world like a big private house on a big lot. Since our sales contract stipulated that no debris be left, not even the piers on which the bungalows stood exist today. Once on the grounds, however, you can see sidewalks that lead nowhere gradually being covered by vegetation. My mother now spends her summers at the house in Woodbourne. Our small colony had a much more dignified end than most; rotting remains of colonies mar many Sullivan County roadsides.

How did real farmers and bungalow colony farmers get along? Pretty well as a rule, but of course there were tensions when tenants trespassed onto farm land, often in pursuit of wild berries. My grandparents knew a number of local farmers, both Jewish and gentile, and often purchased produce from them. When the grandparents returned to "the city" after Thanksgiving, they always brought gallons of cider with them, recycled in glass jugs, which they bought from a local. During World War II when eggs were rationed, they could always buy eggs from the local farmers. They even acquired a special egg container that allowed them to mail us eggs in the city, where they were scarce. Various Jewish farmers also would have cattle kosher killed, and my grandparents knew them well enough so that they could acquire beef without ration coupons. As dairying and general farming declined, large-scale chicken farming became important to the county in the 1950s. And it was here that tensions arose. Pioneer large-scale chicken farming stank, literally. And tenants didn't like it. A consortium of resort owners eventually forced the closure of the largest egg operation in the mountains, the Mt. Pride facility near Woodbourne.[28]

Advertising and Renting

Joey Adams recalls that his folks answered a newspaper ad to find their *kuchalein,* and he describes the circumstances with customary wit, which barely masks his disdain for the period: "In the *Daily Forward,* Papa had read of a small boardinghouse which advertised 'Rooms and bungalows and apartments to rent for the summer. Do your own cooking; Rates very reasonable; Beautiful view; Private lake nearby; Heller's Bungalow Colony—Monticello, N.Y.'"[29] In a few days, "although it was only the first week of April, Mr. Heller called personally to set the deal. The way he described his *kuchalane,* it sounded like Monte Carlo instead of Monticello. Mister Heller even offered to cart us to see this paradise 'anytime in April or May before the season starts so you can choose the best place.'" Papa Adams learned that there was no such thing as a free lunch: "How could Papa refuse? Here was a chance for a free ride to the mountains on Sunday and 'You could even take the kids along; there's no obligation on your part.' Of course, if you didn't hire the rooms there was a small charge for the ride, but this you didn't find out until later. Even if you did take the rooms, Heller still tried to chisel gas and food expenses for the Big Trip." Who was Heller and what was his place like? "Heller was a local merchant in Monticello who ran the shoe store. For the price of two pair of sneakers he had bought a hunk of property with a farmhouse. He had added some rough cabins, hung out his roadside shingle and was in business. The colony consisted of twelve rooms in the main house and three bungalows, with one big community kitchen."[30]

His parents' mistake was answering an ad rather than relying on word of mouth. If you pursue the Yiddish press or the English press of the period, you see relatively few advertisements for bungalows or *kuchaleins,* usually only a dozen or so. In this business, it wasn't really necessary to advertise unless your colony was very remote and off the beaten path, or if you were an exploitative character who had tenants for a single season, like Mr. Heller in Adams's tale. Most owners were not like that, but it is significant that the business has always been a marginal one for most "farmers." They were trying to make a living from tenants who wanted the most for their money—and both sides often pushed as hard as they could.

We read the ads in New York papers, but rarely did we see an ad placed by anyone we knew. Furthermore, the business was not lucrative enough to support more than the most minimal advertising. When we saw an ad for someone we knew, we understood that they were in trouble. One year in the 1950s, we started seeing posters all over our Brooklyn neighborhood for "Romantic Hotel Barlou" in South Fallsburg. Where was this place, we wondered? On our first trip up to the country that year, we indeed, passed Hotel Barlou. It was a renamed dump. We joked about "Romantic Hotel Barlou" where "mouse meets cockroach." It taught us a lesson about resort advertising that most people seemed to understand: Fiction was more common than fact. Such advertising continues today. In the classified section of *Der Yid: Voice of American Orthodox Jewry,* a newspaper that incorporates both English and Yiddish, there is a Yiddish heading that translates as "Katskillim." Some of the ads are in English, others are in Yiddish. One ad advertises "two Olympic [size] pools." Another offers an "air cond *Shul*" as well.[31]

Most renting was done by word of mouth or by prospective tenants scouting out the place, personally. It was not unusual for a prospective tenant to take a bus up from the city to the town of his choice and to walk up a road, stopping at places till he found one he liked and could afford. When done without a car, this search was usually a male chore. When renting was slow, bungalow colony owners often met incoming buses, asking the disembarking passengers, "You want a bungalow?" We were never that desperate.

Joey Adams's mother learned her lesson at Hellers, and the next summer she heard about an Ellenville *kuchalein* called Boxer's Dairy Farm, run by the wife of a real farmer. "When Mrs. Boxer learned through a neighbor that Mama was interested, she came to solicit our business in April." Boxer was a great saleswoman. "When we saw her we could almost smell the country. She seemed to symbolize the vacation we were so eagerly looking forward to."[32]

If a family owned their own car, or could borrow one, both husband and wife would come. My father, like Heller in Joey Adams's remembrances, would sometimes bring prospective tenants up with him. Having a business in the city helped find clients. Once, in the late 1950s when renting was rotten, Father even invited a prospective tenant and family up for a weekend in June. They came, but were really only interested in a free weekend. That weekend was, for me, an especially miserable experience—every time the prospective tenants left the place "to take a ride around," I was sent with them to make sure they didn't rent elsewhere. Fortunately, we never offered a free weekend again.

At Richman's, apart from Grandma making Seymour and me any age that suited the moment, promises made were generally kept, but I very well remember hearing tales similar to those Adams recalls. Many of these pertained to transportation. At a place like Heller's, the owner promised to take people to town or to the lake, but on many occasions reneged, or at least didn't provide the transportation as often as the guests would have liked. Outright lies were often told in promising prospective tenants that nonexistent facilities, such as pools and casinos, would be "ready for the season."

One interesting variant had to do with parents telling their children about facilities that didn't exist. One year we had two families with teenage girls who were very unhappy, as teens often can be. I was a teen at the time, too, and the girls told me that they had agreed to come to a bungalow for the summer because they had been assured by their parents that we offered a pool and a casino! The parents had rented at Richman's to save money, but had told their daughters what they wanted to hear.

Very few customers were ever comfortable with the status quo. They always wanted to hear that next year would be better. At Richman's, there was never anything more contentious each year than the mattress question—especially as the clientele aged. Mother was always getting requests for different mattresses. Each spring we had the annual ritual that I would laughingly call "The Ballet Folklorico de Woodbourne," which entailed switching mattresses from bungalow to bungalow—only Mother could always keep score of who had, and who should get, which mattress. What prowess! I hated the annual scene, especially since Grandpa and I were the usual carriers. Once you got all the mattresses to their new summer destination, you had to put the mattress cover on. Never a pad—"People won't use a pad." The technique entailed rolling up the cover, then two people unrolled it over the mattress. In the 1970s, bed boards became a hot item and we charged extra if you wanted a sheet of plywood under your mattress; installing these was another unpleasant chore. The largest part of the summer's preparation was cleaning the bungalows. Many new tenants asked if the bungalow would be clean upon their arrival. My mother had the cleanliness standards of her generation finely honed, as did most of our tenants. Anyone who did not keep the standards up was described as keeping "a filthy house" and was a "pig."

At Kassack's, where the prices and services were at a much higher level than at our place, I remember a lot more shifting around than mere mattresses and bed boards. Some people would decide, for example, that they couldn't live with a red dinette set, and so kitchen furniture would be shuffled from place to place until all who could be satisfied were. People who rented bungalows were like their hotel-bound brethren in that they wanted the new and different. Very often they forgot that you get what you pay for—and often they just wanted more. Sometimes you could charge extra for the changes, as we did with bed boards. We also did this, along with virtually every colony owner I knew of, with the up-grading of the refrigerator size. Our original 1948 refrigerators were a mere four cubic feet. An upgrade was just twenty-five to fifty dollars per season, which wasn't a very good financial deal for the owner, but it was always necessary "to keep up."

4

"Unzereh Menschen"
(Our People)

There are few, if any, of the traditional bungalow colonies remaining in Sullivan County—the colonies of my youth, the resorts that catered to mostly nonobservant or semiobservant Jewish families with children. Mom and the kids spent the summer; father came up on weekends and stayed up for his week or two summer vacation. Today there are colonies in which the major portion of this lifestyle is practiced, but the religious complexion has changed. It is ultraorthodox and Hasidic Jews who have taken over the colonies, because these families still adhere to a traditional lifestyle like that of most New York City Jews from the 1930s to 1960s.

One of the most frequently reported observations about who went to bungalow colonies and who went to hotels is false. In the 1980s videocassette *The Rise and Fall of the Borscht Belt*, one informant tells you that the upper class and middle class went to hotels and the working class went to bungalow colonies.[1] Now that was probably true in the age of the rooming house, but after the bungalow developed it was often a matter of preference whether one went to a hotel or to a bungalow colony. "My Sam and I don't like formal hotel-type life," a middle-aged woman told Joey Adams's family. "Every year we just prefer a simple bungalow at Madame Geretsky's Villa. Who wants to get dressed three times a day. I get enough of that all winter."[2] While a summer at a hotel for a family was usually more expensive than a summer at a colony, many people on a restricted income would prefer spending a week or two at a hotel to a summer at a bungalow colony. Some saw bungalows as declassé and "automatically looked down on those who were still up to their ears in chicken fat."[3] Writer Bern Sharfman recalls his bungalow days in the 1930s, when his parents dreamed of moving up to the hotels. When father Nathan's business—ladies panties and slips—thrived, he and his family abandoned the bungalows.[4] Conversely, there were many people who could afford to spend their summers at a hotel who didn't care for the hotel regimentation, the need to change clothing at least three times a day, or the hotel diet, and who simply preferred life at a bungalow colony. Furthermore, while some colonies remained rather primitive, others offered semiluxurious accommodations.

Nor were individuals exclusively bungalow or hotel people. My maternal grandmother, long a widow, preferred to vacation at a hotel and did so regularly for many years. She stayed in small hotels, all long gone, for two weeks each summer and sometimes for the Rosh Hashona holidays as well. It was via Grandma's visits that I first experienced life inside the hotels, eating meals in their dining rooms and exploring their facilities as a guest, as opposed to tagging along when Grandpa went fundraising. After Grandma remarried, in her late sixties, she and her husband started staying at a bungalow colony for the summer. You guessed it; they rented at Richman's, and we could keep the revenue, as well as their company, in the family.

We had a number of tenants over the years who would go to hotels for Passover (traditionally the most expensive period) and then come to the bungalows for the summer. We even had one tenant who "took the waters" at Saratoga Springs each July before coming to our colony for the balance of the season. Except for small groups at each end of the spectrum, most Catskill vacationers went to hotels or colonies unfettered by class distinction. Part of this myth of hotels versus bungalow colonies derives from The Concord and Grossinger's fixation of writers about the Catskills. However, while The Concord and Grossinger's had the cream of the market (they were the most expensive hotels in the mountains), the run-of-the-mill hotel was a good deal less glamorous. Many of these hotels were just a step or two up from boarding houses—and many of them had a working-class clientele. The Oliver Hill, The Delmont, the Murray Hill, and the Hotel Furst were very ordinary hotels. Moss Hart was never the social director there as he was at The Flagler (the mountains' first luxury hotel). Nor did Eddie Cantor "discover" Eddie Fisher there,

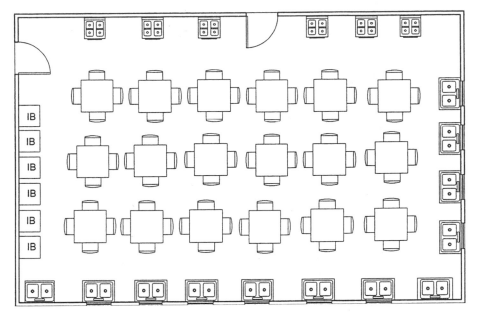

A DELUXE COMMUNITY KITCHEN FOR EIGHTEEN
Each family has its own sink and table. Two families share an icebox and a gas range.

as he allegedly did at Grossinger's. Nor was Buster Crabbe the swimming pro there as he was at The Concord. All these other forgotten hotels were owned by non-Olympian people and catered to a run-of-the-mill crowd. Like bungalow colonies, hotels came in many forms.

Entertainer Elliot Finkel remembers childhood summers at the New Edgewood Hotel in Loch Sheldrake. "It was a fleabag with no bathrooms except for a shack out in the back like an outhouse . . . and the food was lousy."[5] Even at the top hotels, most families crowded into one room. Hotel advertisements regularly stated, "Special rates for children sharing parents' room." Hotel rooms were even more cramped than bungalows because you needed so many more clothes and the closets were often quite small. (Large closets only came in deluxe rooms built after the 1950s.) No self-respecting woman would go to dine in a hotel dining room without packing herself into a girdle or a corset, or be seen wearing the same dress twice.

Complicating the story even more was the fact that many hotel owners also owned bungalow colonies. The Tamarack Lodge in Greenfield Park owned the nearby Sunshine Colony. Guests at these hotel-owned colonies could often use hotel facilities and see shows in the casino. Sometimes, a special entertainment fee was charged for this. The Esther Manor, a hotel in Monticello, bought up the little bungalow colonies "on all sides of us, so we would know who our neighbors would be. And the bungalow renters were entitled to use all of the Esther Manor facilities, watch all the entertainment. And for a little extra they could eat in our dining room."[6] Publicist Phil Leshin remembers that in the summer of 1942 he stayed in a bungalow colony partly owned by Meyer Orkin, owner of the Avon Lodge Hotel, which was about two miles away. He remembers going over occasionally to have lunch at the Avon.[7] This said, there were always dumpy colonies with poor facilities—"shit houses" we called them—that illustrated the stereotype. One of these was "The Fox House," which operated about a quarter mile down the road from us, occupying the remnants of an old hotel built in the 1870s. While it had a few shacks, it essentially was a community kitchen *kuchalein* until it went out of business in the late 1950s. The folks from The Fox House shared our swimming area, and they were decidedly of a different economic class.

Bungalow colony owners were very proprietorial of their "following," which comprised *"unzereh menschen,"* or "our people." The Richman clientele was an interesting mix. We even had a celebrity guest, I'm told. Songwriter Sammy Cahn, Academy Award-winning lyricist of dozens of hit songs, including "Three Coins in the Fountain," was a frequent visitor. His parents were our tenants. This would have been shortly after his first hit. He and Saul Chaplin adapted the Yiddish theater song *"Bei Mir Bist du Schön"* into what became a sensation performed by the Andrews Sisters in 1937. A few years later, he went off to Hollywood where he would spend the rest of his career.[8] My mother remembers him as a "funny looking guy with thick glasses and whose parents owned a restaurant on Graham Avenue." Celebrities weren't our usual folks and we always had a few working-class people, but we also had business people, an occasional writer, lawyers, and bona fide millionaires. One of our "alumni" is president of a Fortune 500 company. The millionaire folks tended to be my grandfather's *lansleiten* (friends from the old country) and long-time buddies—a soft drink manufacturer and a lumber magnate whose business name is well known in the eastern part of New York State. Late-model Cadillacs, LaSalles, Packards, and DeSotos were not strangers in our parking lot. And while we may have been top-heavy with Grandpa's rich friends (it was friends on an equal status, not landlord/tenant), I saw the same pattern in other colonies where I worked and where I knew people. This would especially be true at Lansman's, "the Grossinger's of bungalow colonies." They, like Grossinger's have been effective with their publicity, yet I saw the same groups

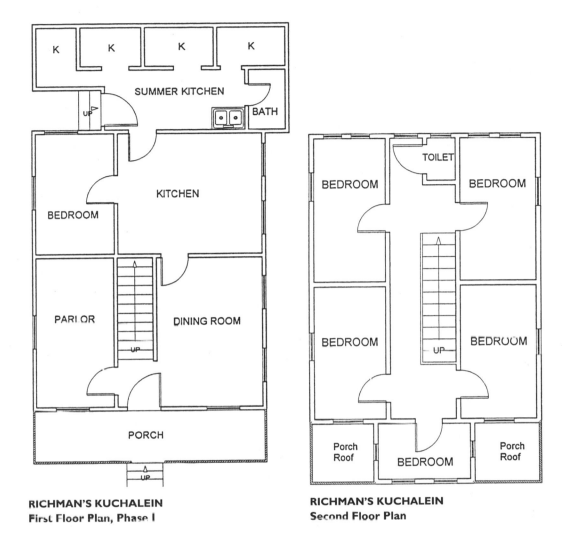

RICHMAN'S KUCHALEIN
First Floor Plan, Phase I

RICHMAN'S KUCHALEIN
Second Floor Plan

at Kassack's and at Furman's. Here, also, there were a few working people, but mostly the tenants were business people, teachers, doctors, lawyers, accountants, and the like.

Two anecdotes vividly illustrate this point:

"Der alte Miron" ("old man Miron"), as Grandpa always called him because he was two or three years older than the rest of Grandpa's cronies, was sitting on the lawn one August day in the early 1950s wearing a new sweater. Another tenant, a lady, gushed, "Mr. Miron, that's a beautiful sweater." In his characteristic gruff way he replied, "It should be. It cost me $32,000." "$32,000," gasped the lady. "Yeah, I bought my daughter-in-law a $32,000 house. The

67

least she could do was knit me a sweater." A $32,000 house on Long Island in the 1950s is today's $350,000 house.

When I was working at Kassack's, we put on a different, pirated musical comedy each summer. Once we decided to do *Guys and Dolls,* which included the song "Take Back Your Mink." The performers were all age eleven through thirteen. The girls in the chorus were asked to provide their own mink stole for the number. This was not discriminatory. No one blinked an eye, but they all showed up for dress rehearsal with at least one garment from mama's closet. Some brought two or three for us to choose from. The 1950s were dressy, and a middle-class bungalow lady felt nude without a mink in the closet—and a mink-trimmed cashmere sweater was a necessity for less formal occasions. Our Mr. Miron's wife took the mink fixation to an extreme. She even wore a mink jacket to carry out the garbage. "It's my old one." When Mrs. Miron went food shopping, however, she plucked her own chicken to save the twenty-five cent plucking fee paid to the chicken flicker.

What was daily life in the colonies like? The answer is to some degree divided into the facilities that the differing colonies had. It also varied with time span, but there were always two distinct times on the colony calendar: "The Weekend" and "During the Week." During the week was the staging and recuperation period for the weekend. During the week, the colonies were matriarchies; on the weekend, they were paternally centered.

A colony, whether large or small, was a world unto itself. Even when other colonies were close by, there was seldom socializing back and forth except for dating teenagers and intercolony softball leagues, which became popular during the postwar years. For the mothers, the week had its responsibilities: Cooking, cleaning, and laundry continued as in the city, but, of course, quarters were smaller than in the city and meals were simpler. We had tenants who had cleaning women or even full-time maids, a phenomenon described in *Bungalow Nine.*[9] Most women tried to get the chores out of the way in the morning and then, apart from lunch and getting supper on the table, they could "enjoy the country." Monday was invariably laundry day, although this rule started to break down in the 1960s and 1970s. Thursdays or Fridays were the food shopping days. For many women, Fridays were especially busy; Friday was a serious food preparation day and also the day to go to the beauty parlor for a perfect hairdo for the weekend.

Food supplies came from three or four sources. Because food costs were invariably more expensive in the country than in the city, many husbands would bring food up with them on the weekend—of course this was often tricky in the days before plastic bags and Scotch ice. Naturally, men who arrived by car could bring more than those who traveled by bus. My father would do the bulk of our weekly shopping in the city and arrive with the trunk full of fruit, vegetables, groceries, and meat in an ice chest. Many kosher butchers in Brooklyn and the Bronx, where most of the Catskill clientele came from, would deliver meat to their customers in the mountains. After all, in many city neighborhoods, food business fell off precipitously in the summertime.

Like many colonies, we had daily delivery of milk and dairy products. In Woodbourne, there was a decided difference in milkmen. The goyim had a year-round milkman who delivered Crowley's dairy products; the Jews had summer milkmen, the Kanowitz brothers, who sold Dairylea and Breakstone products. The bigger colonies near the towns (and near competition) got their deliveries early in the morning (in a resort area, retail deliveries began at 8:30 A.M.; smaller places, further out, like Richman's, had afternoon deliveries. Hymie Kanowitz arrived like clockwork at 5:15 P.M. at Richman's, where his visits were an important marker of each day. Additionally, there were other food vendors who came on a less regular schedule, including an occasional vegetable vendor. Several times a summer, peddlers would come around selling women's and children's clothing. These were festive occasions, and usually profitable to the vendor. While many "farmers" demanded a kickback for allowing peddlers onto their places, we never did.

What wasn't delivered could be bought in the village. Since most tenants lacked cars during the week, if they shopped in the village they carried the food home. Women with babies would put food in the carriages. Mothers with older kids took them along as carriers. In Sullivan County there were, and are, two large towns; Monticello (the county seat) and Liberty. There were many small towns as well—of which Woodbourne was typical.

Since Richman's was only about a half mile from town, many of the women or their kids made daily bread and newspaper runs, *The Mirror* and the *Daily News* were the most popular daily papers. Many people bought the *New York Times* on Sundays. Some tenants read the *Jewish Press,* and copies of *The Forward* and *The Day* were also common at Richman's. There was (and is) a kosher bakery in Woodbourne, although now it is a summer-only business.

While women did their housewifely chores in the mornings, kids played, dreamed, and roamed. As little kids, we had a sandbox and homemade swings that hung from a beam Grandpa affixed between two trees. Our swing supply was enhanced circa 1945 when Grandpa bought a wooden swing support that held four basket-shaped swings, each about three feet long with wooden sides and hammock webbing in between. Grandpa said they had been used after World War I to exercise critically wounded soldiers. As the baskets wore out—kids being more active than the multiple amputees, the swingers they were designed for—they were replaced with homemade seats and a ladder. I saw these same swing sets at many small colonies. In 1950, at my urging, although I was already too big for it, we got our first store-bought playground equipment. I went with Father to Macy's in Manhattan to pick it up. It was an early backyard metal "jungle gym," painted red, green, and yellow. It had three swings, a ladder, and a teeter-totter. The staking device, meant to give it stability, never really worked, and the support always bounced when you swung on it. However, it survived through many children into the early 1980s. Its skeleton and its predecessor's still stand on the grounds at Woodbourne waiting for us to reinstall the swings, which were taken off each fall to be stored until next spring. At larger colonies, before the war, homemade equipment prevailed, afterward, commercial playground equipment was installed. By the day camp era, the play equipment at the colonies was similar to that found in big city playgrounds. These included batteries of swings suspended on pylons imbedded in concrete, sliding ponds, see-saws, and monkey bars. Some places, including Kassack's, had a kid-powered merry-go-round. We at Richman's also had a homemade see-saw that Grandpa built—it was balanced on a tree stump. Since this see-saw didn't have any governor, we loved to see who could bounce who off the other end. We also played box ball and hit the penny on the sidewalks. As we grew older, baseball, Ping-Pong, and badminton were fun games. Larger colonies often had a handball court, which we lacked. They might also have a basketball hoop or two, which we similarly lacked. Most larger places would have a full-fledged softball field—instead of our makeshift bases on the lawn.

Grandma Richman had an unfortunate habit that always affected my brother and me. It was her version of "guarantees." When prospective tenants came to rent, they often asked, "Will there be ten-year-old boys for our ten-year-old son to play with?" Grandma would always assure the prospective tenants that she had a ten-year-old grandson, even if we were six or fifteen at the time.

5

The River and the Woods

ight after lunch the whole colony, except Grandpa (who always napped after lunch) and Grandma (who manned the post), would come together for the trip down to the river to swim. This was a substantial operation. While most colonies offered access to a river or a lake, usually cottages were set back from the water because of the perceived bugginess around water in the evenings. Although we had screens on windows and doors, screened porches were rare before World War II. Soon after Grandpa bought the ground for the colony, he bought a thin strip of land going down to the river, about one tenth of a mile up the road. It was ten feet wide and one hundred or so feet deep. At that point along the river, the drop from the bank to the river was precipitous, so grandpa built a set of wooden steps going down to the water. At this spot the river was also very shallow. Lack of an area to sit and shallow water obviated the charm of the rhododendron-filled banks. It was here that mother came to do the laundry when I was a baby. Grandpa had paid forty-five dollars for this strip of land, which lay between two year-round houses in which goyim lived. From age eight or so, as soon as we were old enough to have solo access to the road, we would sometimes go down to the river here—no doubt upsetting the homeowners on both sides. We would gingerly descend the then rickety and today vanished stairs, go to the water's edge, and throw rocks into the river. Every year from the early 1950s on, one of the homeowners would ask Grandpa to sell him the strip. Finally, over my objections, Grandpa relented and got $350 for the lot, and I lost my pride of ownership in the funny sliver.

A year after Richman's opened, Grandpa bought a right-of-way from a neighboring farmer, George Vantran, which gave us access to a wonderful swimming spot on the river. The walk was long and a bit adventurous. In later years, George wasn't crazy about all of us tramping through his fields, but in 1938 the $150 for the right-of-way was a lot of money.

After lunch (not too soon, mind you; you couldn't go into the water for an hour after you ate lunch lest you get stomach cramps and die), the expedition to the river would form. Anxious kids in bathing suits carried towels and wore sneakers. Mothers in bathing suits carried extra towels; wooden life preservers (series of balsa wood floats held together by straps); inflated, well-patched inner tubes (you never used a new one, only a tube that could no longer serve on a car); bags of cookies, candy, and fruit (you shouldn't starve); and dry clothing (if you wore wet clothes or got chilled, you might get polio, which was every parent's nightmare).[1]

The ragtag band, often including the fathers on weekends, would walk along the road toward Woodbourne for about one tenth of a mile, and then the fun began. First you had to step over the low barbed wire that topped a rock at the corner of the farmer's pasture. Every year, George would put up new wire; every July we would take a wire cutter there and cut it down. Then you were in the active cow pasture—often with cows in it—always with "cow flop," as we called it. Of course, you wanted to avoid stepping in a fresh patty, but I remember the soft, stinky experience very well.

At the end of the pasture, the next barbed wire fence terminated at a tree that stood about two feet from the wire-topped stone wall separating this pasture from the next field. You threw your inner tube over the fence, and, walking sideways with barbed wire fore and aft, you carefully passed into the old-fashioned hay field bordered by rhododendrons, evergreens, and deciduous shrubs, which sloped down toward the river. This field was covered with a mixture of grasses and, long before anyone dreamed of "meadow in a can," summer wildflowers—pinks, bouncing bets, flea bane, butter and eggs, ox eye daisies, goldenrod (which caused hay fever, according to common but erroneous wisdom), black-eyed Susans, purple clover, and many others. At one spot along the edge of the woods, scarlet Oswego tea grew (I successfully moved

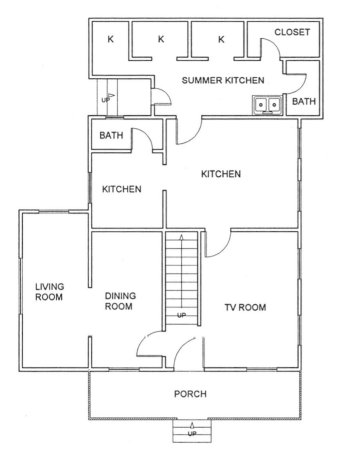

RICHMAN'S KUCHALEIN
First-Floor Plan, Phase II

some to our front lawn circle). On the way back, people would pick bunches of wildflowers to brighten their bungalows. The kids' favorites along the walk to the river were the many choke cherries that grew panicles of fruit, like grapes, which were marvelous ammunition to throw at our peers—or, even better, to use (when small) in homemade blowpipes. One summer, when we were in the midst of a Boy Scout inspired native dyes quest, we discovered that choke cherries make a good pink dye, albeit a transient one. Every summer was marked with different fads from vegetable dyes to radio transmissions.

You knew you were approaching the swimming place when you rounded a curve and saw a lone tree standing in the field—I never learned why that tree was allowed to stand in the meadow, but there it was. The whole walk was about one third of a mile. At last, you ducked under the final barrier—two high strands of barbed wire. After about twenty feet of woods you arrived at a sandy bank, where you took off your shoes and socks (yes, socks under sneakers), and you walked across the stone-bottomed shallows to "The Rocks," which formed our

73

beach. There were "the Little Rock," "the Big Rock," and "The Rock." The Little Rock and the Big Rock were flat enough to sit on. You could lean against The Rock. George Vantran, for a few years, rented Mr. Fox the right to have his tenants swim at this spot, too. When they showed up, they used the Little Rock and we used the Big Rock. Most adults found the river stones painful to walk across and negotiated them slowly or wore sandals or "swimming shoes." The kids ran across them quickly—this playground was ours.

At this location, the Neversink River was about one hundred feet wide. In later years, I often enjoyed the aesthetics of the spot. Looking upstream from The Rocks, there was a great vase-shaped elm, which I watched succumb to Dutch Elm disease, its skeleton falling away over ten years or so. The view downstream held nice rapids. Diagonally across from The Rocks was a real sand beach, the swimming spot for the Hotel Levbourne. A long, wooden stairway came down the steep bank and at the base an area had been cleared and converted into a sand beach. Sand was brought in annually to replenish the beach, which was for the use of hotel guests only. This, of course, meant that it was a point of honor for us to breach the beachhead, which was guarded by a lifeguard whose task was to watch over the guests and keep the bungalow kids away. This was as close as we got to class warfare. The hotel ran a rope across the river from their beach. This "lifeline," as it was called, was there to delineate the best swimming area, as well as to provide security for nonswimming bathers. We kids enjoyed underwater acrobatics in the deep. It's much easier to walk a tightrope underwater, and it's a cinch to do a somersault around an underwater rope. The lifeguard was always trying to chase us away, but his task was impossible. When he became too belligerent, we could always perform the ultimate dirty deed—splash the guests! This raised a commotion and would sometimes require that the hotel owners come down to calm their guests and shout at the bungalow kids.

When the Levbourne, feeling the pinch of 1950s competition, changed its name to "The Aladdin" and built a pool, the beach slowly disappeared. The swimming experience became less adventurous. No one cared if you swam across the river anymore. Much of the fun was gone, and the "lifeline" rotted away.

Each area of our river spot had its uses. Little kids and nonswimmers had to stay in front of the Big Rock. Here the water was shallow, ranging from a few inches to a foot or so. Beyond the Big Rock, toward the elm tree, was the place for practicing rock skipping. A lot of time was spent by the boys—few girls skipped rocks—to find the best skipper, or scaler, which was a round, thin river stone, about two and a half inches across. You could often get one to bounce two or three times before sinking, but a great scaler with a good arm could do almost fifteen bounces. As a teenager, in the late afternoon with no one else around, I witnessed friends standing on the Big Rock skip rocks that bounced across the Neversink and up to The Aladdin's beach.

In many ways, the river was much more interesting than pools. Minnows, tadpoles, and salamander newts were prey for even the smallest kids. One favored technique, not mother-approved, called for the cooperative effort of two kids. Take one towel and soak it. Spread it carefully on the shallow riverbed where fish fry congregate. Each kid squats down and holds two corners of the towel, netting the catch. Even younger kids were given an old kitchen strainer to use as a net. Most of the fry were released, some were kept in sand buckets or the jars we carried down to the river for this purpose. They, of course, died—and we wondered why and went back the next day and collected more. Store-bought toys, like sand strainers were also used as nets. We also liked to watch water bugs skim the surface and were fascinated by dragonflies, which we called "darning needles." Believing erroneously that they could inflict painful bites, we let them be.

Aquatic life, though, was always fair game, whether at our spot or somewhere else. My prize catch was a leech with young attached. Leeches were almost unknown in the Neversink—and it wasn't until years after I jarred the specimens that I found out what they were. When I was a teenager, we heard that fresh water clams were found upstream where the people from the Frank Villa and Abe Furman's swam. We went up to investigate and saw what was apparently a one-season flash in the pan. In early summer, we avidly explored drainage ditches and little stagnant pools for frog eggs and polliwogs. One especially exciting ditch, about a quarter mile up the road, had a reliable store of very large tadpoles.

Toy boats and rafts were important playthings. Store-purchased toys were fun—and at one time or another all of us had little, poorly made, wind-up boats that never survived many trips—but we repeatedly made primitive boats (including ineffectual, toy birch-bark canoes) rigged with crude sails. Our most successful boats were always raft-like and made from lumber scraps. If you launched them to the right of the Big Rock, the current would carry them slowly. As a little kid you had to make sure your boat didn't get away from you and get into the deep water behind the rock; a long cord was very effective for this.

When we were older and could be trusted to swim anywhere, we disdained the cords, launching our boats into the current so we could follow them.

As the Big Rock was our major beach, many adults never got beyond it. However, the river bottom on the left side of the rock was sandy and the water waist deep. This area was ideal for nonswimmers, and I remember very ample ladies in voluminous swimsuits standing and occasionally bobbing into the water and fanning water down their bosoms, exclaiming, *eh mechiah* (a pleasure). The river was not only a pleasure place, but also a washing place; kids, especially as tads, were washed with soap in the river in lieu of baths or showers. This saved gas used by hot water heaters. Later we were given cakes of soap (Ivory, of course—"It Floats!") and ordered to wash by ourselves. We loved this. Neversink water is very soft, and you could generate a lot of suds and play bathtub games with a new twist as you watched your suds float away. We had bubble contests—who could make the best bubble by getting a film on the loop formed between forefinger and thumb and blowing. Kids washed in front and to the right of the Big Rock, adults went downstream a bit. There were also a few men who went down to the river in the morning to wash and swim in privacy.

For the most part, the river water was clear as crystal, and you could easily see every stone on the river bottom. If you stood very still, fish fry would come nibble at your toes. The river bottom was alive with larvae, fry, and plants, as well as fish. When World War II ended and consumer goods became more plentiful, what we wanted the most for river time were first goggles and then divers' masks and snorkels so that we could really explore the river bottom. Around 1950, flippers also joined our paraphernalia.

Once you were judged to be a swimmer, you were given the right to swim in the "deep water," which was downstream beyond the Big Rock. Here you could join in the communal fun other than just Levbourne lifeguard baiting. A very few brave souls dived directly off the top of the Big Rock, which stood about five feet above the water at its highest point, but most of us lowered ourselves onto a rock ledge where the water came up to our ankles and dived from there. When we nonbrave souls went off the top of the Big Rock, it was "cannon-ball" style—a compressed jump designed to create maximum splash by hugging knees to chest—but this was discouraged as all the mothers on the rock were (1) concerned for your safety and (2) didn't want to be splashed.

When I was sixteen, I went to work at a nearby day camp that had a spring-fed pond where kids played pretty much as we did in the river. By the next year, however, they had a swimming pool, and I could see the whole swimming experience change. You couldn't tumble freely into a pool because of the danger of hitting the sides, and there is no interesting bottom life in a pool. Swimming time became much less social and less joyous, except for the most dedicated aquatics.

Swim time usually ended about half past four, when our ragtag group would reverse our earlier trek and head on home. It wasn't until kids were about fourteen that they were allowed to go swimming without parents present. When I was a teenager, friends and I went down to the river after everyone had left for the day, and we discovered that the local goyim were swimming. We had never realized that this occurred. I was reminded of this by the film *Sweet Lorraine*. In one scene, the handyman, a local, talks to the hotel owners' granddaughter and tells her "that the locals often would use the old pool at the hotel at night."[2]

We left the river by half past four so that everyone could be home by five and changed when Hymie Kanowitz, the milkman, came. Hymie and his brother, Joe, owned Kanowitz's Dairy in Woodbourne, and they were fixtures. In addition to milk, Hymie also sold Breakstone sour cream and cheeses. By order, you could get cream cheese or American cheese cut from Breakstone loaves. The small wooden boxes in which these four-pound cheese loaves came were highly desired for keeping things in, and Hymie only awarded them to his favorite customers—and always on the sly. Every now and then I see one of these boxes in an antique shop and become nostalgic, although not nostalgic enough to want to buy one—so far. Hymie would come into the colony at a quarter past five and blow his horn. Everyone knew the ritual, and all the women would descend on Hymie and his assistant to buy milk and other dairy products. In later years, as our clientele grew older and Hymie's business slowed down, he would often deliver newspapers to his long-time customers. When he died in the early 1980s, one of our oldest links to the halcyon days of the 1940s and 1950s was broken.

The kids cared about Hymie because he defined our swimming time. There were three other vendors we liked a lot more. It was great fun when the iceman came. While we always, in my memory, had refrigerators in "the city," as New York City was always called, we didn't get refrigerators in the country until 1946. Iceboxes were a bane to our mothers and emptying the water reservoir was always a mess, but in the summer the iceman would give the kids slivers of ice to suck on—and this was a real treat.

After World War II, Ruby the knish man would come around, irregularly, selling his hot pastry treats from a truck equipped with a multidrawer warming

77

oven. (In later years, when I worked at a day camp at a large colony, Ruby would arrive everyday after swim time—at "milk time"—to peddle his wares. He always offered me a free knish, and many day camp kids brought "knish money" with them.) More reliable was the ice cream man, who arrived about seven. This term doesn't relate to one person, but to a changing cast. Every kid 'had to have' ice cream, especially during those years when the ice cream man gave a plastic charm with each purchase. You needed a complete set of these—I still have mine.

Fishing was an important pastime, but it was generally discouraged during swim times. Fishhooks and crowds of bodies don't mix. Some kids, me included, did take rods or fishing lines along, but we had to fish upstream from the Big Rock. Really serious fishing began when you were old enough to get to the water by yourself. My first nonparentally supervised fishing trip was at age eight when my thirteen-year-old brother took me fishing down the road about a quarter of a mile toward Woodbourne, near the Godlins' home. Abe Godlin operated a local drugstore, owned much of the business district, and, of course, owned a bungalow colony, too. The fishing spot, reached via a rough path from the road, was across the river from Kassack's Bungalow Colony swimming beach. It was a foggy, damp August morning, with no noise to disturb us, or the fish. At this point, I should point out that my fishing equipment consisted of a drop line, which was purchased on one of my start-of-the-season one-dollar spending sprees. This tackle was green fishing line wrapped on a four-sided stationary reel and came equipped with hook, sinker, and floater. Perched on the steep, rocky shoreline, Seymour let me use his real fishing rod—all six feet of it, with a casting reel. I dropped the baited line into the water, and almost immediately caught a fish—a trout. I was so excited that after my brother took the fish off the hook, I fell into the water. Disgusted, Seymour walked me home. That was the last time he took me fishing.

By the next year, I was allowed independent fishing rights and the first of my own rods, little more than a toy. From my ninth to my sixteenth summer (when I needed a license and I started working), fishing was a major pastime for me and my buddies in our quest for chub, sunfish (or sunnies), and an occasional trout (or big sucker). Big suckers were especially annoying because, as you sat on the Big Rock in the morning or early evening, you could see them sucking along the submerged rocks right up to your baited hook—ignoring it completely. What frustration. Sometimes we hooked an unwelcome catch—a fresh water eel. No one would touch one of them—we simply cut our line off and let the creature go. It was only years later that I learned people ate eel, but, because the fish have no scales, they are not kosher and have no place in Jewish cuisine. Some of our fishing was done at the Frank Villa's swim spot, and occasionally at our narrow strip, but usually we fished from the Big Rock. The little, warm channel between the Big Rock and The Rock was great for sunnies, and the back of the Big Rock was good for chubs and an occasional sucker. Grandpa loved river fish. No matter how meager our catch, he always gutted the trophies we brought home, sautéed them with onions, and commended our pastime.

Suckers and chubs were caught using little bread balls as bait. Naturally we used rye bread. (In my family, white bread was allowed into the house very infrequently—"you get epilepsy from eating white bread.") You took a piece of the soft center, which you kept carefully wrapped in wax paper—if it dried and crumbled, you couldn't use it. You kneaded the bread between your thumb and forefinger into a dense mass and then further condensed it into a tiny ball that could be affixed to the tip of your hook. The trick was to get the ball large enough so it would fit on the barb, but not so large as to allow fish to nibble easily without getting hooked. We also enthusiastically dug for worms, but we much preferred to find them on the sidewalks and rocks after a rainstorm. Grasshoppers were the best bait for sunfish, and again we prized those of a certain size. We inserted the hook right below the head and pushed the hook through the soft body. We wanted insects that would fit the hook snugly to prevent the fish from stealing the bait. Grasshopper catching was an art. You waited for your prey to alight on a blade of grass so that you could swoop him into your fist from behind—usually grass and all. You had to be careful handling the bug. If you held it by one leg, it would leave you holding the leg. You needed to hold both legs, and you tried to avoid getting any of the brown sticky goo, which the insect extrudes to fend off would-be diners, on you.

While fishing and bait gathering were major time consumers, there was little wildlife we left alone. Trapping bumblebees in a jar was always considered daring. The technique was to stalk your prey in a nearby meadow, wait for it to land and start feeding on the nectar, and imprison it in a jar by slamming the lid shut over flower and bee. You always had punched a few air holes in the lid. Mayonnaise jars were preferred for this endeavor, which, like fishing, was limited very much to boys. Both boys and girls, however, enjoyed catching fireflies. These slow-flying creatures were easily caught in a hand and popped into a jar with a perforated lid. We often had contests for who could capture the most bugs. Both my brother and I had a certain cachet among the kids because, as the owners' grandsons, we had access to the tools and we became the official lid piercers. Using a board, a nail, and a hammer to provide ventilation to our short-lived captives—we wondered why they died. After all, we did throw some grass into the jars for them to eat. Alas, I now know the answer: Fireflies don't eat grass.

Butterflies were plentiful and often easy prey—especially Monarchs, the orange and black beauties that liked to feed on milkweed nectar. Again, you would stalk the butterfly and wait till it extended its proboscis and folded its wings, then you carefully pinched it by the wings and plopped it into a jar. The powdery surface of the insect's wings was disturbed, but you had your creature. As we grew older, several of us became interested in collecting butterflies. My first nets, and those of my buddies, were homemade; we stretched the neck of wire hangers and stitched nylon net around the hoop. I was eventually, after a few years, able to get a real butterfly net. On butterfly expeditions we also carried soft tweezers, brushes, and carbon tetrachloride to quickly end our preys' struggles. We would later mount our specimens.

In late June, we often found tadpoles in drainage ditches along the road. They were fun to catch. We hoped to watch one develop into a frog, but they, like the caterpillars we wanted to see turn into pupae, always seemed to die first. All of us enjoyed capturing frogs, and we made an unscientific distinction between frogs and toads: Frogs had smooth skin and toads had knobby skin. You handled frogs but were wary about toads because everyone knew they gave you warts. Here, too, the preferred domiciles for our captives were those trusty jars. When I was about six, I got the scare of my life when I stuck my hand into a hole in an old tree, and out jumped two or three big toads. Our local snakes were mostly garters and blacksnakes and generally we gave them a wide berth, but there was always one kid who went after snakes. In our crowd, it was an older guy named Jerry Dubofsky who was our snake hunter. He often carried a forked stick to be ready to trap a snake.

Mammals were rarer. Occasionally we'd see a rabbit or a squirrel, and we made all kinds of homemade traps, although we never caught one. We never saw deer. Now, in line with a national trend in deer population, we often see deer around the old place. They have become pests, eating Mother's flowers.

Swimming was the major pastime in the presence of parents, but the woods gave kids their most private amusement and adventure. The woods were our world. Virtually all bungalow colonies were built close to a road. It might be a remote road, but it was a road. And since Sullivan County is poor farm country, most colonies that lacked expansive grounds could informally borrow farmers' meadows and woodlots behind the colonies. We certainly did this. When we were prepubescent, we largely confined ourselves to our own woods. In later years, we would regularly penetrate beyond the barbed wire that separated our land from that of our farmer neighbor, George Vantran. What we did in the woods, of course, changed with age. As small kids, we played country store. The "storekeeper" had to find a product that bore a resemblance, often an unreasonable one, to some store items. And we played "Indian." Our piece of hillside had a regular set of paths that years of kids tramped down. On *The Brooklyn Bridge* episode that deals with selling "The Hollywood Country Club," young Natie asks his brother if the new owners will be able "to find the old Indian paths in the woods." Alan assures the younger boy that they won't. "Nah, only you, me, and Dad know about them."[3]

Our woods were second-growth hardwoods: maple, oak, beech, birch, and chestnut, with an occasional hemlock and white pine. Mountain Laurel and rhododendron and ferns abounded—and poison ivy did not exist. Our woodcraft included peeling a lot of bark from paper birch trees and trying to make miniature, water-tight canoes (it never worked). We chewed on the wintergreen-flavored inner bark of the birch, and we spent a lot of time making bows and arrows from sticks, twigs, and twine. We even shaped stone arrowheads. Although never a threat to Indian technology, we would spend countless hours on these weapons. As a teenager (at fourteen), I persuaded my parents to buy me a real bow and arrow and target. Once the novelty wore off, it was never as much fun as we had in the woods.

As small as our group of kids was, we always had gangs who were in, and those who were out. As the "farmer's" grandsons we were supposed to be angels. Seymour managed this as a by-product of the older-son syndrome. He generally kept away from those who bothered him—except me—and he was so outwardly intelligent that most people felt honored by his attention. About the only one who could regularly, and successfully, get under his skin was me, and we had many a fight. Because of this, mother wrung her hands and moaned or yelled, "Your children should only do to you, what you're doing to me!" When my lifestyle and that of a tenant's kid conflicted, that was another story. The kid's parents would complain to my grandparents, who would complain to Mother about her "wild Indian," and I would end up getting acquainted with well-placed whacks of a hairbrush on my butt. This merely slowed me down.

My mother still embarrasses me in public with a tale about an event I do not remember—allegedly that when I was three I gave a girl named Blossom "a shampoo" by urinating on her head!

While I have no memory of this, I do remember always being on the inside clique in the woods. One girl we ostracized, calling her "pigface." I took many whacks for that one. Today, I don't remember her real name at all. In the woods, you always needed an opposing group so you could defend "The Hut." The Hut was a small, natural clearing in the woods, enclosed by formidable bushes of rhododendron maximum. There were two entrances from major paths, and The Hut had to be defended at all times. We devised a number of defensive modes, including a very effective booby trap using "bull cactus," a Scotch thistle, which we swiped from the farmer's field across the road. It was hung, prickles down, in the trees and designed to fall when a trip cord was broken. As we grew older, The Hut lost some of its interest, and we would go further and further afield. We went under the barbed wire that separated our land from George Vantran's and explored the whole hill behind us, which had the remains of an old lumber road and several hilltop meadows embellished with marvelous glacial boulders.

The woods also served as a site of many a childhood game of doctor and some early adolescent sexual groping. The only intrusion into our private world centered around "the Big Rock." (Our terminology just wasn't very original.) This other, flat Big Rock was in a small, sun-drenched clearing, and it was here that a number of women, in fine European peasant tradition, would retreat to sunbathe in their underwear—or even topless. Naturally, when the women went into the woods, the kids were banished, but most of us managed to sneak into the woods for a look. All I saw were glimpses of naked flesh and long, pink underpants. Occasionally, we would be discovered and all hell would break loose. Watching Woody Allen's *Radio Days* brought the memories of these adventures back. They fit so well with the group of boys on a roof spying on a nude woman through binoculars.[4] But then, I'm around Woody's age and grew up in the same milieu and almost the same neighborhood.

The woods and meadows on the hillside were also great places for gathering stuff. We collected evergreen cones and acorns for weapons. We also liked to find white oak acorns with the caps intact and, as little kids, would spend a lot of time peeling off the caps and hollowing the nuts to make hiding places for treasures under the replaced caps. We also read that the Indians made meal from acorns, and we tried that, too, peeling, grinding, rinsing. We decided that the end product wasn't worthwhile. We also had contests for who could find the most cones or acorns or "wild radishes." Our ecological effect on the trilliums might have been a disaster if the birds and rabbits hadn't beat us to most of the ripe elongated fruits. Wintergreen berries were of interest—just by being red and scarce. Ink berries could stain your enemies more agreeably. Unusual fungus was also of great interest, and rotted logs were eagerly examined. We were all scared silly by the alleged poisonous quality of wild mushrooms, and our parents worked very hard to reinforce this notion.

Our most socially responsible foraging exploits were directed toward edible berries and fruits. In late June and early July, the meadows—especially the active cow pastures—were laden with wild strawberries, and picking these could keep you busy for a long time—although red hands and faces were more common than lots of berries for the larder. I don't recall ever bringing home more than a glass full. August was the time for serious berrying, for blueberries and blackberries were ripe. Everyone had a secret place to hunt berries. The best blueberries grew over the crest of the hill behind us—and, when the season was in, we went berrying everyday. We would pick blueberries into two- or four-quart milk pails, which we would first put on the ground when we were little kids. When we were older and big enough to support them, we hung the milk pails from our belts. When we expected an especially big harvest, we would carry a galvanized bucket or two along with us as well. The blueberries we went after were on high bushes, and I still remember the special pleasure of spying a tall branch laden with fruit and trying to pull the branch down to picking height while keeping my milk pail from tipping over.

More of a challenge was picking blackberries, which, of course, grow on thorn-laden canes. The costume here called for long pants and long-sleeved shirts. The nice part about blackberry picking was that the berries were large and you could fill your milk pail quickly if you found a good patch. The best blackberry country was under the power lines that ran along part of our hill. The power company cut a swatch of forest that opened up good blackberry terrain. On rare occasions, on the weekends, we would even go off the grounds to pick berries: to places tenants knew about from former colonies or such. The area where New York City was building a new reservoir, around ten miles away, was great blackberry country.

When we got home with the berries, we all ate a lot of fresh fruit, thoroughly washed. Blueberries with sour cream was considered a treat, and, when the season was at its height, there were also lots of blueberry pies, blueberry cakes, and,

83

of course, blueberry jam. My grandmother was a veritable pie machine, and she turned them out by the dozen—good or bad. Curiously, no one I knew ever made blueberry-filled blintzes, although many women made homemade blintzes in my childhood. Blackberries were used for jam. No one cooked with them. My grandfather liked to pack an old liquor bottle with blackberries to which he added sugar and rye whiskey, making a liquor syrup that he would drink with seltzer water, after it had aged awhile. Occasionally, we would also harvest choke cherries, which Grandma liked to use to color her applesauce.

Ruth Seltzer, a Long Island housewife, remembers being taken to Rubin's Farm in Liberty where they would pick blueberries, blackberries, and raspberries into "big straw baskets or tin pails." These were made into pies and jam. Rubin's was a *kuchalein* where guests "would eat family style at a table covered with black-and-white-check oilcloth. Whoever heard of linens in those days?"[5]

Calling kids in from the woods was always the noisiest time of day—as kids tested their parents' endurance. Grandpa had the good sense to make a game of it. He asked that I answer when he yelled, "Irwin, yoo hoo!" Many mothers were driven to desperation. One, Belle Schecter, was a hitter who had to catch her children first, never an easy task. Belle was famed for yelling, "Howard, Gerald, come now or I'll kill you."

Farm and Garden

Farm animals were a familiar sight in Sullivan County. Farming didn't really decline seriously until the early 1950s, and there were real Jewish farmers in the area, although they were not as numerous as the Christians.[6] The Rosensheins were our nearest Jewish farmer neighbors, and they also ran the *kuchalein* my parents went to years before. Like many farms in the region, theirs had river-bottom land and hillside land, which, in this case, was across Route 42. Many an afternoon we would walk up the road to watch the cows come home for milking. This activity took place after swim time. The Rosensheins' oldest son, Harold (the picture of a barefoot farm boy in overalls), would lead the cows down from their hillside pasture, cowbell on the leader clanging, along the road for about a tenth of a mile to the barn on the other side of Route 42; the berm was always well manured. The cows have been gone a long time, but I never walk along that stretch of road without watching out for cow flops. Harold was a little older than I, and we were always friendly, but not friends. Harold, in his early twenties, fell in love with the daughter of one of our tenants. Her name was Marsha. The romance continued on in the city after the summer, and Marsha and Harold wanted to get married. Marsha's father absolutely forbid the match, because he wouldn't have any daughter of his marrying a farmer! Being a dutiful daughter of the 1950s, Marsha stopped seeing Harold. Both had subsequent unhappy marriages to others, and Harold died young.

George Vantran was the farmer whose animals we saw most. He owned the land across the road from us and on the hill behind us. It had been from George that Grandpa had purchased his land. While the Rosenshein men were large and bear-like, George was taciturn and spare. A bachelor, he surprised everyone in town by marrying when he was fifty or so. Because Marge, his wife, was best known around Woodbourne's bars, it was a strange match. George's Holsteins were often pastured across the road from our place, and we could go down to the end of the driveway to watch them. His pasture was also bordered by blueberry bushes, so we often saw the cows as we berried. It was through his cow pastures that we would go on our way to swim; occasionally there was a bull in the pasture as well. George also pastured some of his cows on the hillside during much of the day, and he, like Harold, would bring them down and across the road. Sometimes while playing Indian on the hillside, we would meet with friendly cows.

George's barn, which still stands, is a variant bank barn, with a milking parlor on the ground level. After supper, I would often walk down the road with a summer friend or two to watch George milk his twenty or so cows. He used a pneumatic milking machine, but he always finished the cows off by hand. In the 1950s, he built a small, refrigerated storage shed outside the barn, when the government mandated refrigeration. But when I was a kid, he just let the milk stand in unrefrigerated milk cans. Grandpa liked raw milk, as did several of our tenants, and one of my enjoyable chores was buying this from George. I found the taste repulsive, but I enjoyed carrying the milk pails and watching George ladle the milk from his milk pails into ours (the same ones we used for berrying). A few of the tenants would also come down for their milk. When I was very small, I was a finicky eater and a skinny kid, which was an affront to any 1930s and early-1940s Jewish mother. My mother would go to almost any length to get me to eat. She took me to the river and got me to open up my mouth for food every time I threw a pebble in the water. She also took me to see the cows—and on many occasions she has told me about falling into the manure trench while coaxing me to eat.

George had bantam chickens that had free reign of the barnyard and barn,

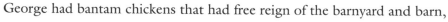

and he had a team of horses that he used to cut his hay until the mid 1950s. He also used them to haul his hay wagon. Only later did he use a tractor. His hay fields were really old-fashioned meadows with lots of wildflowers, a far cry from modern monocultures. George also kept a few pigs—which were certainly objects of curiosity in our little kosher circle—and his pigsty was appropriately muddy. In 1959, George sold the land across the road from our place to the Catholic Church, which soon built the Church of the Immaculate Conception and an attendant parking lot. The rest of that meadow has been converted into lawn and the site of a new social and recreation center.

Just across the road from our place, bordering on George's farm, was the Ampthor place. As a kid, I never realized how early into American history I was connected when I visited the Ampthors. When Mr. Ampthor died about 1950, he was near one hundred years old. The Ampthors (he was a retired farmer) lived in a green and white bungalow—a real bungalow, very much influenced by the craftsman movement—and the front porch was covered in rambling red roses. Along the side of the house there was a cottage garden, and behind the house there was a garage and workshop with an attached grape arbor, which fascinated me for its shade and rich insect life. Behind this little complex was the huge Ampthor vegetable garden, where everything was orderly and perfect. The Ampthors sold the ultimate in fresh vegetables to us and some of our tenants. If you wanted cucumbers, you would go out into the patch and they would find them for you. I liked to get carrots. I would watch one of the Ampthors dig around the top of the plants to see if the carrots were large enough to be picked. In addition, Mrs. Ampthor would tell us stories about the past, and why, when she was a girl, "No one ate tomatoes. They were poison." Every once in a while, Mr. Ampthor would make me a whistle from the stem of a pumpkin leaf.

Our own food raising was devoted to the small garden described earlier and our wartime chickens. When the war broke out, Grandpa built a small chicken coop and yard and each spring he would get a few dozen chicks. During the day, the chickens would be free to range. While I have grown up sentimental about grape arbors and vegetable gardens, I have no nostalgia about chickens. Though I will admit that I enjoyed scattering dried corn broadcast-style to feed them, I hated gathering eggs from their nests. It was quite literally a shitty job. As the summer drew to a close, each week a few chickens went to the *shochet,* or kosher slaughterer, to be killed. One year, we had a chicken with some personality. I called him "Whitey." To avoid upsetting me, Grandpa waited until after Labor Day to have him dispatched.

Noodling Around: Kids at Large

When we weren't doing chores, swimming, or playing in the woods, what else did we do? Diversions can be divided into two major categories: the eternal and the trendy. Swings and the see-saw were popular well into our teens; admittedly, the older we got, the more the aim of see-saw play was who could bounce the hardest and make the other kid fall off. We also had the big sandbox Grandpa made. Our toys included the usual, brightly painted, commercial tin pails, shovels, and sand strainers of the period, as well as toy cars and old kitchen utensils. As a little kid, I had a tricycle, which I peddled vigorously around the grounds—and was forced to share with the tenants' children: "Be nice to the customers." One day when I was five, I was displaying my prowess when I slammed into one of the whitewashed rocks lining our driveway, hit my mouth, and knocked out my front teeth. No more tricycle for anyone. We were never allowed to have bicycles because, "When your uncle had one, he broke his arm! Bicycles are dangerous." Of course, none of our tenant kids had bikes either due to the problem of transporting them from the city.

As we grew older, we wanted a Ping-Pong table, and finally Grandpa relented and built one for us out of boards. It was structurally sound, but the individual boards warped and playing was treacherous. The table, however, was always booked. Better players frequently proposed tournaments so they could dominate the table. During World War II, Ping-Pong balls were in short supply and a crushed ball was always a tragedy. We would try to remove minor dents from balls by boiling them. A basketball hoop nailed to a tree, sans backboard, was our only other built-in piece of equipment, and that came when I was ten. As kids, we always wanted what we saw at other colonies, but Grandma, who was especially conservative about money, was never amenable to *"nariskeit"* (foolishness). And what she said around the colony went. Other places had lawn gliders; we didn't. Other places had "tea houses," a 1930s term for small gazebos. These were taken over by kids for playing all manner of domestic games. Our neighbors, the Franks, had one, as did the Abe Furmans. I wanted one, but never got one. Nor did we ever get a handball court, complete with a real basketball hoop and backboard mounted on a post on the side of the cement playing area. That was the ultimate dream athletic center. The Franks had one and occasionally, but rarely, we would sneak over and use it. Before the age of the swimming pool, the handball court was the most common piece of athletic equipment that bungalow colonies adopted from hotels. After World War II, many bungalow colonies copied hotel casinos (or playhouses), and many handball courts became one wall of the casino.

Badminton and volleyball were popular sports because all you needed was a net and equipment—no court, no major expense. Baseball, softball actually, was played less often than we would have liked. The lawn was too small, especially as we got older. The other site was the cow pasture across the road—when it was empty of cows. The cow flop always made that a less than desirable option, but one we resorted to when we could. We also used the cow pasture to fly kites.

Water pistols, balloons, and cap guns were perennials. Rolls of caps had great noise potential, other than in cap pistols. You could put a cap on the sidewalk and slam it with your foot. In another popular form, you placed a cap in a nut between two screws and tossed it into the air over a sidewalk. Impact caused a satisfactory bang. My grandparents adopted a less than indulgent attitude toward this activity, thinking what this could do to their sidewalks—and so, for the most part, we only did it in the city where no one cared what you did at play on the sidewalk.

Airborne toys were always popular. Some kids, including Seymour, made model airplanes, cutting the structural elements of balsa wood patterns with Ex-acto knives, assembling them with airplane glue, and then covering the frame with tissue. This was always tricky in the crowded living conditions of summer, but it was managed. More of us made paper airplanes or played with store bought balsa wood gliders. Homemade parachutes made from handkerchiefs and cord were great favorites. You tied the cord to the handkerchief's corners and then tied the cord to a rock (or, rarely, a broken, lead soldier), rolled it up, and threw it as high as you could, enjoying it when the parachute worked as it was supposed to.

Bubble blowing was another popular pastime. For many years this meant using a bubble pipe and soapy water, which you begged your mother to mix up. In the 1950s, the appearance of commercial bubble mixtures, "magic bubbles," and wands made the old wooden and plastic bubble pipes obsolete. Other bubble entertainment included bubble gum, after it became widely available again following World War II. Father's drugstore in the city sold candy and gum. I recall one day in 1944 when kids walking along Eastern Parkway were blowing bubbles, "Where'd you get the gum?" I asked. "From your father's store." I ran as fast as I could the two blocks to Daddy's store, where he had two pieces left from a box of one hundred of "Fleers Double Bubble," the kind wrapped with comics. I wailed, "Why didn't you save me any?" Father was concerned at my behavior; he grimaced, "I didn't think of it." Another 1950s bubble craze was "plastic bubbles," which came in tubes. You took a glob of the stuff and put it on the end of a plastic straw and blew. If you positioned your glob right and made it the right size, you could blow quite large bubbles—and the stuff came in colors: red, blue, yellow, and green. These bubbles were more satisfying than soap bubbles because they lasted for a few days if undisturbed, considerably less if used as volleyballs. The fact that plastic bubbles disappeared from the market probably meant that they were toxic, but the 1950s were an innocent time.

We could spend hours looking at View Masters and exchanging reels. I was a real celebrity when I got a View Master slide projector in the late 1940s. I could actually project images! I had previously owned a little battery-powered gun that projected images, but you needed to be in a very dark spot and the projected images were only a few inches square. With the View Master projector, wall-sized images were possible. When I was fifteen, I was given a motion picture camera and a projector. I took many pictures at the colony and put on many shows for the guests who could never see movies of themselves too often. Today my only regret is that I didn't take more reels of film; they make a valuable archive resource.[1]

During World War II, watching the sky was very important. Whether in the city or in the country, we were very aware of aircraft, and we always attempted to identify planes that flew overhead.[2] We were also alert to "spy activities." We believed that Morse code messages were being sent from a distant farmhouse, but it was probably some kids hoping to make us think they were at an interesting locus. We practiced Morse code with flashlights whenever we could. Looking at the stars was always interesting—once we could stay up after dark. When I was thirteen, I was given a toy telescope, but I could never focus on anything more exotic than the moon.

You could play numerous games on our sidewalks, including potsie, which was a girl's game. Hit the penny was popular; you put the penny on the crack at the joint of two sidewalk slabs, and then, standing a slab away, you tried to bounce the ball on the coin. The first one to hit twenty-one times won. We also played box ball, a game like tennis, with the hand functioning as a racquet, no net, and two cement sidewalk slabs for the court. These games were also played back in New York City, where they were more interesting because the sidewalk slabs were bigger. Sidewalks were used for jumping rope as well. The girls jumped with two girls turning the rope and a third jumping. The boys used individual ropes for both exercise and competitive sport. We never sang, "My name is Alice and I come from. . . ."

We also played a full range of other informal kid games, including ring-a-levio, monkey in the middle, tug of war, War (Nazis vs. Americans), red light/green light, Simon Says, Cowboys and Indians, and hide-and-seek. Hide-and-seek was an especially favored pastime of which we had two distinct variants. The first was played exclusively in the woods (during the daytime) and the second was played with the woods being completely out of bounds (usually after supper.) The older we were, the later we played the game, which became much more interesting after dark.

Making things was always a part of summer, and I've already talked about boats, canoes, and bows and arrows in detail, but we would also spend hours shaping stones, both down at the river and in the woods. Whenever you found a rock outcropping with a sharp edge, you could use this edge to shape a soft stone. While hearts were the easiest forms to make, we also managed diamonds and occasionally clubs. I still have a box of these nonperishable mementos. Boys seemed to particularly like carving and whittling. Whenever we got our hands on a knife, not always easy as a kid, we would sharpen sticks for arrows, cut designs on saplings, and engage in other semi-antisocial behavior. For more artistic attempts, there were Exacto knives and cakes of Ivory soap (and you could always bathe with your mistakes.)

Plasticine modeling clay was a favorite, too, and mothers usually approved of it when it was used outside on the tables. They only objected when we messed up tables they wanted to use for card games. In the 1940s and 1950s, lots of us were intrigued by the little, circular, weaving/braiding devices that made "horse reins." Any thread could be used, and the aim was to make enough coil so your mother could make a rug. We were in the seven to ten age bracket, and all of us wasted a lot of time making bags full of the stuff, but no one I ever knew had enough to make a rug. It wouldn't surprise me to find my bag of horse reins in our attic. We also went through a potholder craze when simple looms and fabric loops became available in the late 1940s. On a more sophisticated level was Indian-bead weaving. Making plaster-of-paris molded figures was trendy in the early 1950s. You bought the molds, molded the figures, then painted them with watercolors after they hardened. Again, mothers favored this when done outside. Model making from kits—not only Seymour's airplanes, but boats as well—was widely practiced, too.

Of all the summer pastimes, nothing approached board and card games in popularity. We had the time for complete games of monopoly. And cards were as much a part of our everyday life as they were of our parents'. As little kids, we played the games of old maid and go fish, but very soon we grew into the adult games. By age eight we were playing poker. The chips we used were distinctive artifacts. Our milk, sweet cream, and sour cream (everybody used sweet and sour cream) came in returnable glass bottles with cardboard tops, in the center of which was a token-sized cardboard circle that read "Dairylea Pasteurized Milk." These tokens were our poker chips. Milk was one; sweet cream, three; and sour cream (the largest), five. They were forerunners of the pogs that have become so popular in the 1990s, except that, in the spirit of the times, they were free—self-made toys. At season's end, we would usually get together and burn our chips so that we'd start off even next year. Seymour and I were always at an advantage since Grandma and Grandpa saved their tokens for us in fall and spring. We didn't have to rely on the fruits of summer.

Knock rummy was probably next in line for adoption from our parents' world. From here we proceeded to gin rummy, which would remain popular through adolescence, as did our variant of pinochle. While both boys and girls played the other card games, pinochle was for boys only, as it was only the men who played pinochle at Richman's. Following fads, other card games came and went. These included, in order, Continental rummy, Michigan rummy, and the postwar craze, canasta. We played the quintessential middle-class woman's game, mah-jongg, as well. Cards were the mainstay when the most dreaded of normal summer disasters happened. The rainy day.

Remember how many people were packed into our main house or into each bungalow? Weekend rainy days were even worse because of the fathers being present. Every table was taken with card players, as were beds, and the youngest kids usually played on the floor. In the 1940s, parents were afraid of kids getting wet, which could lead to chills, which might then lead to the ultimate parental horror, polio. Parents were reluctant to even let kids go from the bungalows to the main house. Polio vaccine in the 1950s certainly liberated a lot of kids from being cooped up. Rainy days had a special meaning in the resort business. When you were trying to rent bungalows, rainy weekends were a disaster; most people stayed home, and those who came out were bargain hunters. During the season, rain was a catastrophe for hotels because guests would check out early. At bungalows you just suffered cramped quarters: families, guests, and mildewing wet laundry. Grandpa would joke with the tenants when they griped about the weather, "Well, you paid, so now go home!" This was only half in jest. Farmers liked the weather to turn cool and rainy before Labor Day—it might encourage people to leave early.

On one rainy day, a few post-toddler friends and I took over the downstairs bedroom in the Big House, moved a dresser in front of the door to block it, and proceeded to give each other haircuts. Despite subsequent trips to the professional barber the next day, we all looked funny for a few weeks, and we witnessed some first-class maternal hysterics. We had no difficulty finding time to engage in some kind of mischief, which mothers continually assured us would make their "hair gray before its time." (This attempt to instill guilt was often followed by the curse, "When you grow up, you should only have kids who do to you what you do to me.")

Then there was our run-in with the law. I was about five when I joined Philyne and Normy down by the road, throwing gravel at passing cars. Wonder-of-wonders, one of the small stones connected and broke the side wing window of a passing car. The irate driver, instead of driving into the colony where he would have been paid for the window (and my butt would have met the familiar hairbrush), went to Woodbourne and brought the local policeman back with him. Elmer-the-cop, as everybody called him, studied the situation briefly and, in 1940s-style justice, told the stranger to get out of town. But he gave us a stern lecture and, until the day he retired in the early 1970s, I could never look

Elmer in the eye again. Surprisingly, we got off easy. We didn't get whacked as we had "suffered enough" because of that "idiot of a driver." Forty years later, when my son Joshua and his friend pelted a neighbor's car with fallen apples, I had to bite my cheek while scolding him. "Your children should only do to you. . . ." I remembered.

Even "sainted" brother Seymour's halo slipped once in a while. There was all hell to pay when one night he and his chum hid behind the tombstones of the *goyish* cemetery between our place and town, before the days of street lights, and scared passersby. But, on the whole, there wasn't too much major trouble you could get into: some furtive smoking, perhaps, or a little teenage sexual misadventure. I am old-fashioned and reticent about the sexual hijinks. However, if one wants an account of condoms, erections, and sexual couplings at small resorts, follow the adventures of Harry Craft in *Summer on a Mountain of Spices*. His activities certainly ring true, but his frequency seems excessive.[3] Maybe I am just jealous.

Vandalism at bungalow colonies was relatively rare, and when it occurred, it was most often the result of unthinking boredom rather than outright maliciousness. Mell Lazarus, the creator of the comic strips "Momma" and "Miss Peach," remembers the summer in 1938, when he was nine. "We'd done all the summer country stuff; caught all the frogs, picked the blueberries, and shivered in enough icy water," he recalls. "What we needed on this unbearable boring afternoon was some action." The action he and his friends found was to use a long bench to smash the new Sheetrock walls in the casino, "the little building in which guests enjoyed their nightly bingo games and the occasional magic acts." The owner, Mr. Biolos, caught them in the act and told their mothers. It was Friday, and "by six o'clock Mr. Biolos was stationed out at the driveway, grimly waiting for the fathers to start showing up." When the fathers were shown the damage, they each reacted differently. Lazarus's father repaired the casino, replacing the Sheetrock himself. Artie and Eli, his sidekicks, were not as lucky. Artie's father "carefully took off his belt and—with practiced style—viciously whipped his screaming son." Eli's father "went raving mad, knocking his son off his feet with a slam to the head. As Eli lay crying on the grass, he kicked him on the legs, buttocks, and back." The onlookers, "an ugly crowd of once-gentle people," approved of what they saw. "They'll live, don't worry, and I bet they never do that again."[4] I witnessed occasional public outbursts like this, too. They made for vivid, unpleasant memories. I still shiver when I recall the mother of one of my Brooklyn chums who came after him with a *luchshen* (noodle) strap, a cat-o'-nine-tails. She used it with great vigor.

To Town: The Escape

One of the best antidotes to boredom was to go off the site. Going to town was always an exciting prospect. Seeing the same people day after day was a drag and the town offered the allure of stores, albeit with a limited range of choices. Sidney Offit, in *He Had It Made,* describes a fictional town that is clearly Woodbourne: "There was a sign that said. 'Woodmere, bungalows and hotels for your pleasure.' A movie house was on the corner and there was a large parking lot next to it. Then came a succession of small stores with big signs and plain window displays, merchandising groceries, meats, dairy products, and dry goods."[1]

In Woodbourne, the goyim shopped at the Victory Market, a small chain store later bought out by the Great American Chain (which is now returning its small stores to individual ownership.) The Victory Market sold ham! Today, it is an orthodox supermarket, a summer-only branch of a Brooklyn enterprise. A bar, Smiley's, continued the *shtetl* (small town) tradition of being owned by a Jewish family, the Smilowitzs. Smiley's clientele was almost exclusively *goyish.* Additionally, Woodbourne had two Jewish groceries, Dickin's and Herben's; two pharmacies, Godlin's and Lebed's; a five-and-ten, Bernstein's; a dairy, Kanowitz's; and a big market house that contained a produce seller, a grocer, and the local kosher butcher (Sitomer "the crook"). Dill's hardware store and a luncheonette—first Globerman's, then Malman's—rounded out the stores, along with a barber shop, a beauty parlor and a wonderful Art Deco movie house called the Centre Theater. Woodbourne had three houses of worship (as it still does): a Catholic church, a Dutch Reformed church, both of which were *terra incognita,* and a synagogue, B'nai Israel (Grandpa Richman's summer project).[2]

A trip to town was always thrilling. There were soda fountains, comic books, pinball machines, the five-and-ten, and the hardware store with its fishing supplies. On most trips, small kids served as mules for mothers' purchases, but they'd get a trip to the soda fountain. For years as a little kid, when we first came up to the country for the summer, Mother would take me to town and give me a dollar to spend. One could get fish hooks, floaters, and lures for one to two cents each, comic books for ten cents, and small toys or puzzles for fifteen to fifty cents at the five-and-ten. Of course, what kids really wanted was to be able to go to town alone, or with friends. My first solo trip was at about age eight; from then on we were permitted to make newspaper runs.

Summer haircuts were a downer; in those years boys had their hair cut every two weeks. One of my less pleasant and extremely vivid memories is having the barber's cloth around me on hot, pre–air conditioned days.

The major towns servicing the bungalow and hotel industry were Monticello (the Sullivan County seat) and Liberty. Monticello, as the name suggests, was laid out during the Jefferson administration, and Liberty, a town of the same vintage, had been a resort frequented by tuberculosis patients in the winter during the late nineteenth century. Up until the early 1920s, signs that read "No Jews or Tuberculars" were common in local stores.[3] Both towns had populations of several thousand.

Monticello has broad sidewalks; Liberty, squeezed into a valley and surrounded by steep hills, has narrow walks. In the summer of 1954, the valley configuration led to tragedy. The old Route 17 ran along Liberty's Main Street. On 24 July, "a tank truck out of control roared the mile and a half down White Bridge Hill, west of the village, and smashed into several cars. Three persons were killed and several injured."[4] People were terrified to go to Liberty, and everyone, especially the town's merchants, demanded that something be done about the situation. A few days after the tragedy, "the State Traffic Commission ordered erection of 'Trucks Use Lower Gear' signs along the hill," and, on 5 August, Governor Dewey gave "top priority . . . to plans to build a four-lane highway bypassing the village of Liberty."[5] This promise was soon carried out as the new Route 17 Quickway was speeded to completion.

Monticello was always the dominant town, but in both towns the streets were busy day and night with shoppers and seekers of the usually innocent pleasures that the area offered. Above all, each of these towns had two movie houses! Woodbourne and Loch Sheldrake—like the nearby, larger towns of South Fallsburg, Woodridge, and Mountaindale—had only one. Another major village in the region was the old canal town of Ellenville, in nearby Ulster County. Ellenville had two movie houses but, until the new Route 52 was built in the 1950s, few people from Woodbourne took the trip, although that area's resort business was virtually identical to Sullivan County's. One curious factor I noticed among tenants was that most preferred a distinct region. I knew of very few people who would spend one summer in Liberty, the next in Ellenville, and the next in Woodbourne. If they moved around from towns, it would tend to be a nearby town, such as from Woodbourne to Loch Sheldrake (three miles distant).

In the novel *Summer on a Mountain of Spices,* the narrator carefully describes a resort town through a New Yorker's eyes:

The town of Monticello, New York, had a vegetable quality. It appeared every spring from a stew of winter mist and mild sun. It came on Decoration Day, collapsed on Labor Day, and withered on Yom Kippur. During July and August, during full bloom, seeds were produced to ensure the species. The seeds were transported by cars, not bees, to the alabaster city a hundred miles away where they were fertilized by the pollens that came with the hope for better weather. . . .

There was a rumor that Monticello existed all year round. Believers could point to a school, a library, a fire department, a police department, the Broadway and Rialto theaters, D. Diamond's Market, two drugstores, a department store, the New York Deli and Burton's Sweete Shoppe. There were citizens, four churches, two doctors, a hospital, a graveyard, a ball field, even a small *shul.* Still, if the place had a winter life, Harry Craft never saw it. His own cousins, the Bermans, came to town in mid-May and went to school there, or said they did, until June recess. Could be. For all practical purposes, Monticello came and went with the leaves. . . .

Sullivan County was discovered by city-weary Jews early in the century. Some, with rural dreams, settled there to raise chickens and crops, good luck. . . .

How Monticello, WASP virgin, took the initial migration of green-horns and garment workers, plus the occasional doctor, dentist, lawyer was a mystery lost in time. To Harry Craft's memory, dating back to the thirties, the town was a willing whore to thousands of customers who came there to buy refreshments. Ex-Lax, souvenirs and postal stamps, shorts, sodas, movies on wet days, sun[tan] oil, dark glasses, Modess, iodine, bobby pins, rubbers, Chinese meals, BB guns from the Daisy Company that could remove eyes, milder toys for infants.[6]

Going into the village in the 1940s and early 1950s was serious business. Even as little kids, we would not be allowed in town in shorts. Shirtlessness was unknown except for an occasional *shicka* goy (drunkard).

Bernstein's was the source of novelties, toys, and puzzles—a dime could go a long way in the 1940s—before it perished in the flames of the great Woodbourne fire of 1964.[7] Globerman's was an old-fashioned, Norman Rockwell ice cream parlor with a white tile floor, ceiling fans, and original bent-iron ice cream parlor chairs. This was the place to go for treats. Parents could always be conned into an ice cream, although, as kids, we never ate out. For one thing, everything in Woodbourne was *tref* (not kosher), and for another, our family was part of a group that simply didn't trust restaurant food. "Don't you ever eat a hamburger out," we were warned. "You don't know what's in it!" This belief resulted in some people choosing bungalows over hotels for their summer resorts. I recall vividly my grandfather and his cronies (and Grandpa knew his way around hotels) talking about the dubious sanitary conditions in hotel kitchens (in the days before regular inspections) and food practices that included leftover food from guests' plates being recycled into tomorrow's soup. After eating Grandma's meals, Grandpa would often say, "A meal like this you can't get by a hotel, or by a restaurant." Stories, real and apocryphal, about hotel food abounded. Father liked to tell the story of a friend who checked into the Shawanga Lodge, a hotel near Wurtsboro, and was served the vegetable of the day, corn-on-the-cob, with his lunch. Jokingly, a tablemate said, "I'll bet we get corn soup at supper." When supper came corn soup was served, and the next morning the friend checked out. There is a scene in *Sweet Lorraine* illustrating a large quantity of coleslaw being made in a manner that would upset the faint of stomach![8]

All of these tales of the dangers of eating out only made the forbidden fruits more enticing, but for the most part, we stuck to Globerman's or the fountains at Godlin's or Lebed's for our cherry cokes, egg creams, ice cream sodas, malted milks, banana splits, and frappes (as sundaes were called). These were presumably nontoxic. It was at the fountain in Godlin's one day, after the end of the season, when, at age thirteen, I sneaked my first BLT.

The story of the subsequent history of Globerman's, which had been in Woodbourne since the 1920s, in many ways parallels the history of the bungalow business. In the early 1950s, the Globermans decided to retire and they sold the business to the Malman family from New York City, who renamed the place "Malman's" and had it remodeled into an up-to-date luncheonette-restaurant, with counter and booth service, serving a full range of nonkosher goodies that the less religiously observant could enjoy: BLTs, shrimp, and ham sandwiches. It was very much the "Ourplace" described in *Woodridge 1946*.[9] Malman's existed through the 1950s and 1960s. The business passed to daughter Selma and her husband. In the early 1970s, a great change came over the bungalow business, as the old order died out and the ultraorthodox Jews became the dominant order. Malman's closed, cleaned up, and reopened as "kosher" under rabbinical supervision of Nelson Laskin, the local rabbi. A few years later, it became "*glatt* kosher" under the supervision of a New York rabbi, to suit the ever more demanding orthodox clientele. Of course, this also meant that the store had to be closed on Friday night and Saturday, and Selma's husband had to wear a yarmulke. A few years later, they sold the luncheonette to ultraorthodox proprietors. Unable to support the owners year-round, the business has undergone another transformation and is now a pizzeria. Selma and her husband run a summer-only amusement arcade next door.

Aside from the fountains, candy bars, and comic books, Godlin's and Lebed's greatest attractions were their pinball machines and jukeboxes (a nickel a play, six for a quarter). As little kids we looked up to the teenage masters of the machines, although we were regularly admonished about the evils of playing pinball and were semiforbidden to play. It was sheer pleasure to sneak a nickel for a play and to wonder at the kids who could play to their heart's content—especially those who had enough skill to win free games. The pinball areas would regularly fill up with kids who were *kibitzing* or quietly watching, but not spending money. At this juncture, the never overly kind proprietors or their nastier employees would chase the nonplayers and nonspenders out. I still remember the humiliation, but it was short-lived at the time. Joey Adams recalls that "*kuchalanes* were mostly for older folks and children. Young adults or teenagers could skip down to the village and hang around the ice cream parlor and listen to the jukebox or go to the movies."[10]

The most delicious treat of all was the movie theater, the Centre, which usually changed its bill twice a week. Every week the theater sent A. Richman's a poster, and a free pass for displaying it. Seymour got the pass, which I inherited after his death. Before our teen years we didn't see many movies because, "You'll miss the sunshine." Night shows were out, so rainy days were our chance. The Centre was glorious; built around the same time as Radio City Music Hall in New York City, the auditorium was very high-style Art Deco, with wonderfully styled murals. Over the years, I've been in virtually every Borscht Belt movie house and, while many have Deco touches, none approached the Centre's interior. The theater has had a mixed history. Always seasonal, it opened the last week in June and closed the Sunday after Labor Day. It was part of a small chain until the late 1960s, when it was sold to the hippie son of a New York businessman who painted the Deco lobby in psychedelic colors and changed the theater's name to The Peace Palace. A few years later, it reverted to the mortgage holder who found an elderly couple who ran it until 1989. One of the few movie theaters in the Catskills that has a stage, it was used a few times for Hasidic entertainment and then boarded up. In 1996, it was purchased as the new home of Sullivan Performing Arts, a theater group founded twenty-three years ago and previously housed at Sullivan County Community College.[11] The Strand Theater, renamed The Hippodrome, in Loch Sheldrake still operates thanks in part to the existence of the nearby Sullivan County Community College. The Rivoli in South Fallsburg became the leading cheap movie theater in the area. Owner Sam Rosenshein, whose father-in-law built the theater, pioneered the one dollar admission in the area in the 1970s.[12] The Broadway in Monticello was revived in the 1980s, only to fold again. One of Liberty's movie theaters became a multiscreen; the other is closed.

Once we entered our early teens, the movies became very important. We could walk down to town, go to the seven o'clock show, and then patronize Lebed's or Godlin's and hope they'd let us hang out by the pinball machine. Usually the movie was filled at night, and, when the show ended, the stores would be jammed full and you'd have to stand in line to get to the fountain.

Life changed after I got my driver's license in 1956. When I got access to the car, I could frequent distant movies and eat at the hot spot of the 1950s: Herbie's Restaurant in Loch Sheldrake. Herbie's created a sensation by introducing the Chinese Roast Pork on Garlic Bread Sandwich, which was served with a spear of sour pickle. Lines fifty to seventy-five deep were common at Herbie's after movies in Loch Sheldrake, Woodbourne, and even Liberty let out.

There were downsides to the pleasures of town. One was being expected to be a pack mule on the way back. As a teenager, I'd try to sneak away to town because not only was it fair game for my mother and grandparents to ask me to pick up something for them in the village, but, as the "owners' grandson," I was a public utility as well—fair game for anyone who needed "five pounds of potatoes" or "a few peaches."

Other than going to town, we left the place relatively rarely; this was typical of the times. Larger places, those with casinos, often had special events, games, and dances to keep the kids and teenagers occupied. A circus or carnival coming to town, as they often did during the 1940s and 1950s, was another special event. Once, in the early 1950s, a circus actually set up for a three day stay on George Vantran's land—toward Woodbourne, beyond the barn. Each day we walked down, watching everything and getting to see two performances. In addition, twelve miles up the road, every summer for almost a hundred years, there was and is The Little World's Fair, which we never went to because, "It's just for goyim." From my driving years forward, I've gone to it periodically, but then I was always destined to be an American Studies person. Times have changed; today, you even see *Hasidim* looking at the animals and watching the tractor-pulling contest.

A special kid treat was a hike or a cookout. These usually took place on cool August days. For us a hike meant going two miles up the road to the little town of Hasbrouck, or taking the prison road to Old Falls in Fallsburg, New York, two miles the other way. When Seymour was thirteen through fifteen, he and his buddy Lenny would sometimes take a few of us younger kids, especially sibs, to Sandy Beach—a river beach that was truly rocky and remote. There, Seymour and Lenny could show off their Boy Scout lore. We would make a camp fire and toast marshmallows and hot dogs. We could have done the same thing in our outdoor fireplace at home, but it wouldn't have been the same.

A few of our activities in the summer may have been unique to Sullivan County, but most of what we did and how we spent our time was very American and familiar to vacationers in other resorts. Our parents and grandparents *shepped naches* (beamed with pride) at our increasingly American ways. The penultimate compliment that parents would bestow on a son was, "He's an all-American boy." A girl could aspire to be a "real princess." Remember that in the quintessential middle-class middle-American sitcom *Father Knows Best,* Robert Young's character always called his daughter "Princess." Only later was it derogatory for a girl to be a "JAP" (a Jewish American Princess), with the implication of her being spoiled by over-indulgent parents.

Everyone waited for mail deliveries, which came twice a day in 1941 when this picture was taken. Mailbox snapshots are a very common summertime genre. To city dwellers, these rural delivery boxes were an exotic artifact that spelled summer. (Photo: Unknown)

Bayle (Grandma) Richman was camera shy, and there are very few pictures of her. In this circa 1946 photograph, she poses with a plant in front of the big house. (Photo: Seymour Richman)

Bertha Richman on the side lawn in 1950, before the Richmans got their first power lawnmower. The grass was much weedier because it was cut less often. Note the heavy wooden lawn furniture and the peegee Hydrangea in full bloom in the back. The picture was taken after Labor Day. Bordering the lawn are fruit trees. Grandpa Richman always white-washed the trunks to keep insects off.

Grandpa Richman poses with the new lawn mower, 1952. The new bungalows are in the background. Note the table and the benches that Grandpa built. This photo was taken during the week; note there is only one car visible in the parking lot.

Grandpa Richman (on the right) and Mr. Cantor, the house painter, circa 1955. They are on the side lawn near the outdoor fireplace. Probably photographed on a weekend. The parking lot is filled. The new bungalows are in the background.

Grandpa Richman dressed up, 1957. He is posing on the porch of 1485 East 34th Street in Brooklyn. In the winter, Grandma and Grandpa Richman lived with their son and his family in Brooklyn.

"Watch Harry's belly button go in and out!" Jack Cowan said, just before the photo was snapped. Silly laughs and smiles were the result as four of the Richmans and many of their tenants gathered for a group photograph in 1951. Jack, who was the proprietor of an elegant Manhattan dress shop, is fifth from the right in the back row. His stylish wife and business partner, Eve, sits in an Adirondack chair. The crowd was middle class to upscale. The woman with the striped dress, two rows behind Eve, was the Mann's maid. Lou and Kate Mann (holding their young daughter) owned a chain of ladies specialty shops in Brooklyn. Grandpa Richman, in his typical summer outfit, is the first man on the right. Taken on a Saturday in August, several Sabbath-observant guests are absent. (Photo: Harry Stern)

Irwin and Seymour at the well in 1943. The hand pump provided cold, delicious drinking water for the table. It was also used to fill the *chinik* (kettle) that Grandma Richman always kept on the stove to provide hot water for tea, dishes, or laundry. (Photo: Abraham Schwebel)

Miriam Damico and her handyman, 1993. Despite the friendly pose, he was a seasonal hire and typically wouldn't last the whole summer.

Playground equipment was homemade and scarce. The Richmans only had one swing, and it was tough getting a turn when the older kids wanted to play. Irwin Richman had his chance to pose on the swing, at rest, because his Uncle Abe wanted to take his picture. The aim of standing on the swing was to enable you to pump and make the swing lift to dangerous heights. High-top sneakers were summer footwear. You seldom wore them in the city, and in 1943 you were not allowed to wear them to school. (Photo: Abraham Schwebel)

Irwin and Blossom, 1942. The granddaughter of a tenant, Blossom Friedman, like many little girls of immigrant background, often went topless until about age eight. They stand in front of one of Grandma's circular flower beds lined with white-washed river stones. One of Grandma's dahlias blooms over Irwin's left shoulder. (Photo: Unknown)

Out of the woods where he had just practiced his 'Indian crafts,' Seymour, circa 1940, holds a homemade bow and arrow as he poses in the front of the big house porch. Note the rockers on the porch. (Photo: Alexander Richman)

The family group snapshot in the Neversink was mandatory. Here Seymour, Bertha, Irwin, and Alexander pose in 1947. Alexander seldom went swimming, and he is wearing his wool bathing suit of the 1930s. Bertha is in a modish satin two-piece suit, and Seymour and Irwin are in the newly fashionable boxer-style swimsuits. (Photo: Unknown)

Enjoying life upstream from The Rocks, in 1948 Irwin uncharacteristically lounges in an old inner tube. Inner tube races and battles were more typical.
(Photo: Alexander Richman)

The Hotel Levbourne, which became The Aladdin, was the Richmans' nearest hotel neighbor. You could see it across the river. Irwin and Seymour often trespassed on the Levbourne's swimming beach and faced the wrath of the hotel's lifeguard who had to guard both his guests and his turf.

HOTEL LEVBOURNE, Woodbourne, N. Y.

Daily Life: Mostly Adults

After paying for accommodations, the most traumatic part of the summer for most adults was getting packed and traveling to the mountains. How families arrived varied with time and economics. The trip could be quite luxurious or a crowded and uncomfortable ordeal.

Joey Adams remembered an early mountain experience, a summer at Boxer's Dairy Farm near Ellenville. Even more vivid were the memories of preparing for the trip. His family was to go to the country 15 June: "About the middle of May my father brought home the burlap sacks. Who had luggage?" They also borrowed valises. And "anyone who had a valise that closed without a rope was a millionaire." When you went to a *kuchalein,* you took your clothes and everything needed for housekeeping, except furniture, right down "to pots, pans, dishes, silverware, hammocks, and toilet paper." Joey's mother carefully packed all of the household goods. "Pots and pans were expertly stashed between pillows and blankets so they wouldn't rattle." Among other essentials were "umbrellas and seven pairs of rubbers for the rain, fly swatters, . . . netting for the baby, [and] a jar of Vicks (just in case)." The filled burlap sacks were sent ahead by Railway Express.[1]

On departure day the family, laden with valises and boxes and paper bags, took the cheapest way to the mountains, the train. Getting to the train was an unpleasant adventure in itself: "We took the trolley from Brooklyn . . . to 42nd Street, then the 42nd Street cross-town to the Hudson River. There we grabbed the Weehawken Ferry," a steamer, "which blackened your face and nostrils for a week." Arriving at the New York, Ontario, and Western terminal, and not being able to afford a redcap, the family dragged their luggage down along the train to the Ellenville car. "Of course, the damn ropes always broke and nightgowns, bloomers, and hot water bottles were always lying all over the train."[2]

Once settled aboard the train, the family started to eat the food they'd brought along. Their mother always proclaimed that it was "better to die from hunger, than you should eat from a lunch counter. Poison they give you." Along with many of her generation, like my grandparents, Adams's mother believed "restaurateurs were on a par with thieves, robbers, and dope peddlers." Lunch usually included canned salmon salad sandwiches, hard-boiled eggs, and "whatever was left over . . . from the night before . . . clamped between two pieces of bread. Maybe cold, rubbery calves' liver on rye ain't exactly a taste sensation, but who could afford to waste food?"[3]

After the long journey, which always took at least six hours, the family would be met at the local railroad station by the "farmer," often with a horse-drawn wagon. The farmer was not necessarily there out of the goodness of his heart, rather he made sure you arrived at his place. His presence guaranteed you didn't yield to the blandishments of other farmers, less fortunate, who, if they had vacancies, would even offer to give back your deposit money if only you'd stay at their place instead, at less money. "Farmers" had to be early and aggressive when meeting their tenants.

Buses were a bit more expensive, but they eventually helped drive the passenger trains out of existence. They were also more convenient in that they left from Brooklyn and the Bronx, as well as from Manhattan. But the trip along the poor roads of the time was long, and pre–World War II buses were often "smelly, gassy, cracking vehicles [that] had to detour hours out of their way." Midway on the trip there was always a stop at "The Red Apple Rest or at [Orseck's] 999," where "the restaurants, the restrooms and lunchrooms usually looked like a battle scene in *Quo Vadis*."[4]

The best public transportation to the Catskills was via hack, which, while it was more expensive, promised portal-to-portal service. While the train cost under two dollars a person, the hack was upwards of five dollars well into the 1920s and 1930s. If you had a lot of luggage you might be assessed another dollar. The hack was a large sedan that had room for seven passengers and the driver. You paid a premium for a window seat; you paid a reduced rate for children if you kept them on your lap. Hackers promised door-to-door service. "And he kept his word, he went door-to door to door-to-door until he picked up everyone."[5] Luggage was packed in the trunk, tied to the hack's sides, and lashed onto the top. Bungalow colony fares would take everything, "even ironing boards. It was like they were going to Europe." Hackers were adept at packing. "We'd get the stuff into the car any way we could—hanging out of the trunks, tied on the roof rack with ropes. It took hours to get everything strapped in and ready to go."[6]

From the passenger's perspective, the dream trip was to be picked up last and dropped off first, for the driver it was simply to make it. "Wurtsboro Mountain was always a pain in the ass," hacker Billy Feigenbaum recalled. "We were always so loaded down with crap that the Checker couldn't get over five miles an hour." In the 1950s, hacks, such as Goldy's Limousine Service, charged ten to twelve dollars for a seat in a ten-passenger stretch Buick.[7] Joey Adams describes a hacker as "a symphony in rags, his livery a pair of torn pants, and underwear, shirt and a handkerchief around his neck . . . [which] soaked up perspiration." He often smoked "a black stinky cigar."[8] This might be an extreme description, but drivers were a harried lot who worked long hours with uncomfortable people packed into a car with strangers.

Joey Adams also recalls a trip when his mother reserved the backseat of a hack for Joey, his sister Yetta, and herself. "The rest of the car contained an elderly lady and a young man who were squeezed together with the hacker in the front seat. A tubby bleached blond sat on a jump seat with most of her belongings." The other jump seat was occupied by a bald-headed man "reverently carrying a jar . . . [of] garlic pickles" that stank up the air.[9]

Since hacks were most crowded and expensive on the weekend, mothers and their children would often come up during the week with the father following on the weekend. It was not unusual for wives arriving at Richman's to say, "My husband will pay you on Friday"—and they always did. The most affluent non–car owners would rent an entire hack, and they had a quicker, safer, less crowded, if more expensive trip. Hacks still exist, although today they are usually large vans and they charge thirty-five to forty-five dollars per person. My mother uses one when she needs to go into the city to see her doctor.

If you had your own car, transportation was easier. Many first-time renters would bring a load of household goods up with them when they rented. Others might do the same on Memorial Day weekend. By the mid 1950s, as competition got fiercer, many larger colonies would allow tenants to come up for the long preseason holiday weekend. As people became more affluent and possessions multiplied, many people had trailers put on their cars or had much of their baggage delivered by van. At Richman's we had several well-to-do tenants who would arrive by car, usually a Cadillac, followed by a truck with their belongings, usually driven by an employee of the family business.

No matter how you traveled, when you arrived you had to unpack. On the "last Sunday in June, . . . Hector's Pond Colony, a pocket of ranch-style cottages, was undergoing heavy assault. Suitcases, cartons, bundles of bedding, groceries and assorted necessities [were] flowing feverishly into the clapboard frames."[10] At all colonies, arrival times were frantic as everyone unloaded, often helped by well-tipped handymen. On more than one occasion while working around the place, I was mistaken for a handyman by new guests. I usually helped them, but I had to decline a tip. Old-timers would mostly be embarrassed to ask a "Jewish college boy" to do such menial work. Owners hurried around attempting to resolve last minute crises and making themselves available to receive payment. All of this frenzy would, of course, be repeated in reverse in ten weeks. Once unpacked, summer was ready to begin.

A photo montage in *A Summer World* shows hotel activities and a group of people playing cards at Cutler's Cottages in South Fallsburg in the 1940s. The caption calls this "the slow track," but card playing was the single most important daytime activity at most hotels as well as at bungalow colonies.[11] During the many times I visited hotels as a kid and a young adult, I was always fascinated by how little the athletic facilities were used. This has probably changed in our fitness-conscious era, but empty swimming pools and mostly empty tennis courts are an indelible memory. On a visit to someone at a hotel or a colony, a sightseeing trip around the place was *de rigeur*. The visitor would see that card playing predominated all, and if a pool had a true function—it was to allow you to play cards next to it.

The hotel goers were truly differentiated from the bungalow people by the everyday chores of life. Hotel goers could avoid doing anything but dressing and eating, both done many times a day. *Kuchaleiners* had to literally "cook for themselves," but life went on at a more casual pace than in the city. Quarters were smaller and more simply furnished, daily dressing was informal, there was less laundry, and, with husbands gone much of the week, cooking was simpler. At Richman's, the rhythms of everyday life changed after the halcyon years of the 1940s and 1950s. Our clientele differed, or in most cases, just aged. We went from lively families to retired folks, the week and the weekend melded together, and eventually our clientele literally died away.

The world of more rigid standards of proper appearance (and no permanent press!) made for a lot of work for women. Not only were sheets and towels ironed, but usually all of the kids' clothing, as well as adult attire. Most women ironed on the kitchen table, but a few would bring their own ironing boards. Others borrowed my grandmother's. Several older women joined my grandmother in using "sad irons" (irons that were heated on the stove). At least two of these, ideally three, were used in shifts. But most women had electric irons. I also remember the postwar joy that came with the development of the steam iron. A few fortunate women would use the services of Mrs. Hill, a Christian lady up the road, who did laundry. Friday was for cooking and going to the beauty parlor—or at least walking around all day with one's hair in curlers. "You could always tell when it was Friday at a bungalow colony," Joey Adams recalled, "out came the curlers, the bleach and the nail polish, and the lawn looked like a fire drill at Elizabeth Arden's."[12] Friday, like every other day, began early because for the most part the kids had been outside by nine—even though mothers had made a determined effort to keep them in. Why? Because in the mountains the grass was often wet with dew, and mothers didn't want their kids to get wet feet.

As noted earlier, all mothers feared polio, and Jewish mothers especially connected wet feet and colds. It was a revelation to me when I married a Lutheran girl that getting wet feet was not viewed with horror by her or her family. This fear of wet feet was institutionalized among Jews. Any mother who saw wet feet felt free to admonish anybody's kid about the perils he or she faced. This was perhaps the only unanimous childcare tenet in the mountains.

A child becoming sick could be bad for business. We always prayed that no infectious disease would break out, and they didn't at Richman's—blind luck—although I know of several large colonies that had epidemics of measles or chicken pox during the season. An owner's worst nightmare was an outbreak of polio. There were rumors of cases, but everything was very hush, hush. When a child or an adult got sick or wounded themselves and needed a few sutures, they found that Woodbourne was served by two doctors. One, Dr. Jack Rubin, was also a prison doctor who had been in Woodbourne since the late 1920s, and the other, Dr. Leon Small, was a Holocaust survivor. Most small towns in the region had several general practitioners, a pattern that, reflecting a national trend, began to change dramatically in the mid 1960s. After both Drs. Rubin and Small retired, Woodbourne was served periodically by other physicians, including a Latin American-born doctor who was murdered, gangland style, with his nurse—not during the season, of course. The case has never been solved. Today, many local physicians continue to be from Third World countries or are orthodox Jews with summer-only clinics often housed at bungalow colonies.[13] When our tenant families were young, visits to the doctor and house calls were rare. In later years, when most of the tenants were older, physician appointments were a regular part of the routine. In one of the few bungalow anecdotes included in *It Happened in the Catskills*, a New York attorney, Dick Kittrell, recalls his wife's efforts to get her sick child to the doctor's office.

Everyone was talking about the Nevele the summer of 1966, when President Lyndon B. Johnson visited the Catskills to dedicate a hospital in Ellenville. His helicopter landed on the grounds of the hotel, and he spent the night. Security forces were stationed all around the area to guard him. Traffic was halted along Routes 209 and 52 from Ellenville all the way to the towns of Kingston, Wurtsboro, Walden, and Woodbourne.

At that time, my wife, Miriam, and our son, Gary, were in Woodbourne, where we used to spend the summer when the kids were little, and I remember that summer as the time Miriam overcame the resistance of crack army troops and passed through their ranks at Neversink River Bridge.

Our son, who was four years old then, wasn't feeling well, and Miriam decided a visit to the doctor was in order. Undeterred by the sight of men in uniform, she bundled the boy into the car and headed off toward Dr. Martin Rubin's office on the far side of the Neversink Bridge. At the edge of town, she was stopped by troops standing guard by the foot of the bridge. Miriam got out of the car and engaged the soldiers in a heated discussion which was accompanied by much hand waving and finger pointing and ended with a summons to the captain commanding the force.

After conversing briefly with Miriam, the captain signaled his men to allow the vehicle to pass, whereupon Miriam got back in her car, and breaking through army lines, drove across the bridge to an old two-story building just beyond to keep her appointment. Gary recovered quickly.

Miriam was vindicated. Everyone at Kassack's Bungalow Colony remarked on her dauntlessness and courage. President Johnson, upon hearing of the captain's action, commended him publicly for his humanitarian gesture. And I never did believe the rumor that persisted all summer that the President, enraged at the breach of his security, secretly ordered the captain to be sent to Vietnam the next day.[14]

A mother's typical day would begin when the kids woke her up. She made breakfast, cleaned and did other chores, made lunch, fed the kids, and was outside in time for the walk down to the river. When the family came back from the river, it was time to change and get the kids changed (young kids had already been changed before the walk back), shop when Hymie the dairyman came, and then make supper for the family. Meals tended to be simple. Few Jews ate meat at each meal, especially since many kept kosher—and drinking milk (believed to be very important for children) and eating meat at the same meal is not kosher. Breakfasts of cold cereal, canned juice, and milk were very common, as were eggs and toast. Smoked fish—the bagel, cream cheese, and lox feast—was usually a weekend treat. Lunch was often a sandwich—peanut-butter-and-jelly and American-cheese-and-mustard-on-rye were favorites. Tuna fish and canned salmon were often served. A quirky kid, my favorite sandwich was cream cheese, lettuce, and caviar on a seeded roll. As a special treat, we might get spaghetti (overcooked and served with ketchup) or Aunt Jemima pancakes with syrup. All sandwiches were accompanied by milk and cakes or cookies—usually store-bought treats. Yankee Doodles and Oreo cookies were favorites. Dinners featured broiled or fried meat in big portions: hamburgers, steaks, lamb chops, and liver. Potatoes, canned vegetables, and fruits rounded out the meal. In our house, we often ate more elaborately at dinnertime, even during the week, because Grandpa really liked to eat and Grandma was a very obliging cook. She would make traditional dishes throughout the week, but even with Grandma, Friday was the major cooking day.

After dinner, the kids would have their last chance to whoop it up, while mothers cleaned up the kitchens before beginning the nightly ritual of rounding up the kids and putting them down for the night. Bedtime varied with age, and I remember hating going to bed while it was still light outside, as it was in the summer until nine o'clock or so. Mostly, the preteenage group were put down by nine; for older kids, ten to eleven was the usual time.

When the kids were in bed, the women would play cards. They'd meet in

107

Daily Life: Mostly Adults

various bungalows or in the small kitchens in the Big House where they were within earshot of the children. Gin rummy was very popular in the 1940s and early 1950s—later canasta became all the rage. Occasionally, most of the women would come together in the kitchen of the Big House to play Continental rummy or Michigan rummy. Our women seldom played poker, but it was commonly played at other colonies. All the games were penny ante, and even at that many of the women, including some of our richest, hated to lose "unlimited" amounts of money that might go to a dollar fifty or two dollars if luck was incredibly bad, so they played with twenty-five cents or fifty cents "pie." After you lost that amount of money in an evening, you could play gratis, and you could still collect winnings.

Children vanished from the scene as our crowd aged, and cards became increasingly important as a time killer. Afternoons were spent playing cards, usually rummy or canasta, and in the evenings, most of the women would gather in our Big House kitchen to play cards or kibitz. Games that whole gangs could play, such as Michigan rummy, were especially valued. Although our place was small, there were always cliques, and in larger places this was even more evident. At Richman's in later years, one clique centered around our neighbors, the Puttermans and the Yustmans. Both were very affluent and both owned their own small houses. They had friends among our tenants, whom they would invite over to play cards at their houses. Increasingly, when "the 400," as the rest of the tenants called them derisively, had their card parties, mother felt obliged to see that the other tenants were happy and so she organized card parties for them—canasta was a favorite here, too.

In larger places with day camps and freer-spending crowds, cards were played more often and for higher stakes. It was not unusual to see games that went on all day and night. Bridge, that normative middle-class pastime, was rare in Sullivan County. I only remember one group of our guests ever playing it. It was played at some of the larger places, but poker and gin rummy were much more common.

Another game, moderately popular at our place but extremely popular at the larger places, was mah-jongg. Played with tiles rather than cards, mah-jongg became a national craze in the 1920s. Considerably more expensive than cards, the sets themselves cost thirty to a hundred dollars or more. The depression put an end to this national craze, but postwar Jewish women took to the game with a vengeance. A day of major importance came each July when the National Mah-Jongg League issued its annual new card, detailing that year's permissible "hands" or tile combinations. The click, click of tiles and phrases like "five bam" and "two cracks" filled the air many an afternoon at the large colonies. Mah-jongg was a gambling game. The stakes were usually higher than cards, and there was no "pie." In the city, my mother played mah-jongg with her group of five. As only four could play each game, one sat out each hand on a rotation basis. That way the game never had to stop for bathroom breaks. The women would meet in each others' houses on a rotation basis and see who could outdo whom in the preparation of snacks: cakes, pies, and other goodies. Other women, more fanatical about the game, belonged to several groups and could play afternoon and evening. At the larger places, a number of cliques were based on these winter mah-jongg groups whose members rented together and played the game morning, noon, and night. Emulating their mothers, teenage girls often played serious games of mah-jongg as well. Apparently, mah-jongg is still played. After not hearing of Jewish mah-jongg for years, I was mildly surprised to see an advertisement in the Lancaster Jewish Community Center newsletter announcing, "It's Time to Order Your 1997 Mah-Jongg Card!"[15]

Mothers at large colonies had the opportunity for "a real vacation," with freedom to pursue their own interests, especially in the postwar years. Day camps could make the kids disappear all day, laundry services processed their linen and clothes, and cleaning help was also available. Ann Cutler in *Bungalow Nine* complains of being tired from all of her chores. Looking to the future, she tells Jason that hopefully "you can treat me to a full-time maid like the Millers have":

JASON: Up here?

ANN: Even the Krinskys have a woman twice a week.

JASON: What would a cleaning woman do even once a week in these small matchboxes?

ANN: The Krinsky's irons one day and cleans the other. Whenever I tote our laundry to the machines, I run into someone's hired girl.[16]

Summertime help could charge a premium. Even at Richman's, while most women did their own work, several had cleaning help and a few had full-time maids.

Bingo was another diversion. In the 1940s, bingo was mostly a kids' game. Five or six kids played, taking turns at calling. By the mid 1950s the adults had started playing, and by the end of the 1950s Richman's even had a professional cage with balls for number selection. While it was extremely rare to see colony-wide card games of any kind, bingo was always integrated at our place and even "the 400" joined in. At first everyone took turns calling but, little by little, this chore fell to my mother. Bingo, thankfully, was only played once a week, and in later years it was in our garage, which doubled as a casino. By the 1950s, professional callers were common at larger places. Some callers ran the whole operation and owned the equipment. At Richman's, bingo was played with a fifty cent pie. It could be considerably more expensive to play at other places where you typically paid for each card used and the game was a profit maker.

Women also had their "girls' night out" when they went to the movies in town. During the 1940s and 1950s, this meant walking to town—sometimes they took a cab home, but most of the tenants were in their twenties or thirties and the walk was fun. Often, they'd go on two nights, with one half watching the other half's children. Before coming home, a stop at a soda fountain for a frappe (one syllable) was a necessity. As the Richman's crowd aged, the women went to the movies by car. After my father died, Mother learned to drive and would often shuttle the ladies down in two or even three trips. In 1993, when I interviewed her, Miriam Damico was still ferrying her ladies around.[17]

Beginning in the postwar years, first hotels and then bungalow colonies started to show movies one or two nights a week—sometimes outside, but often in the casinos or playhouses. Some owners, such as the Kassacks for whom I worked in Woodbourne, owned their own projectors and showed films themselves, renting the films from catalogs. Others would hire projector, operator, and film as a package from one of several film entertainment companies that operated in the county. In the summer of 1959, Dave Burcat, who worked with me as arts-and-crafts counselor at Kassack's Day Camp and who became a life-long friend, moonlighted as a projectionist. If he were showing something interesting, I might go see the film—that summer, I saw a lot of films, and a lot of bungalow colonies and small hotels. Dave was married, had two kids, and was finishing dental school at the University of Pennsylvania. If it could be arranged, I would pick up his wife, Jessie, who ran the day camp's nursery, and take her along to see the film—then we'd all go out later. The car I drove was a very distinctive, very ratty old Chrysler. One evening, Jessie and I were riding up to see Dave, and a film, when I noticed a car following us as we turned into the hotel driveway. When the occupants of the other car saw us, they zoomed away, but not before I caught a glimpse of them. They were other counselors from the camp where we worked, and they thought Jessie and I were up to no good. After the movie, we came up with some dream scenarios, including having Dave "shoot" me at flag raising the next day. We didn't go through with it, but the next day everyone was very solicitous of Dave and very cool to Jessie and me.

The entire dynamics of the colonies changed when the men came up. For most people this was Friday night. While there was a train that ran until the early 1950s, I don't recall anyone using it—the heyday of the train had apparently been the 1920s. Most of our tenants arrived by car or bus. As Harvey Jacobs noted, most likely they had made a pit stop at the Red Apple Rest or the Orseck brothers on the way:

> On the south side of Route 17 was The Orseck Boys. On the north side, the Red Apple Rest. Two restaurants practically identical.
>
> Both oases had outdoor stands that sold hot dogs, hamburgers, lox and bagels, Cracker Jack [sic] candy, Life Savers, postcards. Both had gas pumps and plenty of sanitary toilets with signs proclaiming them inspected safe, boiled against any kind of bacteria. Both had lines of buses parked in their lots, indication [sic] that the food and comfort stations were trusted by big companies with plenty to fear from the law.
>
> Both had multitudes of identical customers, families, young studs, old ladies, girls in shorts, teenagers in shirts that said Taft or Thomas Jefferson in block type, occasional loners who sat chewing and watching, clusters of humans from this or that bus with an eye on the driver who could pull out without them, smaller groups from the hacks, all in motion. Inside the restaurants were huge cafeterias where everybody was his own waiter. If you had time, if you could find a table, you sat. Tables were shared with strangers, as at the Automat in New York. The difference was that here the strangers were interchangeable. A father could go and support the wrong family, or a mother nurse the wrong kids, and it might never be noticed.
>
> All were Jews on the move to and from vacations, all except those who worked behind counters or took plates and flatware from the tables. They were locals with a pale, puzzled look of overwhelm. Their faces contrasted with the pure colors of Jell-O in tall cups, mountains capped with whipped cream peaks, the favorite dessert.[18]

Stop or no-stop along the way, the men were tired on arrival, but most were also young. Dinner was waiting on the table for them. Curlers were out

111

of their wives' hair, and they would often go out to see a late movie—and it wasn't unusual to have eleven o'clock movies on Friday nights. But the next night was the biggest entertainment night—in many ways, Saturday night was the culmination of the entire weekend. Friday night was foreplay. By the end of the 1950s, some of the bigger colonies were even offering live bands on Friday nights. Some tenants didn't go out, but played poker and gin on Friday nights.

Joey Adams's view of Friday night was that "after a little sex and a big dinner the husband took over the seat vacated only a few hours before by his wife . . . to play gin."[19] Actually, sex was reserved for late at night, after the children were asleep. I remember hearing people grousing about how late the kids were up the night before and how that hampered their plans.

When the men came up with cars, many brought food, especially fruit and vegetables from the city. With cars available, some people went shopping, some went visiting, but most stayed put and played cards. The men's game at Richman's was three-hand pinochle played with two decks. Often two games or more went simultaneously, one featuring folding money and the others, change. Some men preferred to play rummy. At my father's pinochle table, it was not unusual for several hundred dollars to change hands during the weekend. The regulars could all afford it, but I remember when a new guest joined them and lost heavily. His wife came to the regulars and berated them for taking advantage of the poor guy. They never played with him again, and his family didn't return the following year.

The fathers at Richman's were not very sports-minded, although most of them went swimming on the weekend if it was hot enough to drive them from the card tables to The Rocks. At many of the larger colonies, especially those with younger crowds in the late 1950s and 1960s, sports were very important on the weekends, and fathers took full advantage of all the facilities—except for the swimming pools, which tended to be mostly used by the kids, with parents playing cards at the poolside.

Some men also enjoyed fishing. Most went to the Neversink, while others drove to a nearby lake. Morningside Lake was especially popular in our area. Nightcrawlers were especially favored for bait. Mother's cousin Sidney, then our tenant, told a tale of bait-gathering woe from his previous colony. Anticipating Saturday fishing, Sid and a pal went out with a flashlight on a rainy Friday night. The worms were out in abundance, and as they collected them near the bungalows they enthused, "what a beauty" and "boy that's a big one." The next day an irate tenant-friend berated them. "Don't you guys have any shame?" He, perhaps egotistically, thought they were voyeurs.

After the 1950s completion of the Neversink Dam as part of New York's watershed program, and the ensuing impounding of its waters, the Neversink River became unswimmable because its flow was changed. Formerly free-flowing for many miles, the water warmed up in the summertime to a temperature in the seventies and eighties. Now, water from the bottom of the reservoir was released in a restricted flow just about nine miles above our swimming spot.[20] Water temperatures are usually in the fifties, except in the midst of a heat spell when they may rise to the low sixties. With a restricted flow, the water level was also radically lowered, rendering many swimming holes too shallow. New York City compensated those resort owners who owned riparian rights for the loss of the swimming use of the river, and many bungalow colony owners used the money to build swimming pools.

Before World War II, only hotels had swimming pools, and many of these were spring fed and so had algae in the water. I vividly remember going swimming at the Raleigh Hotel pool during the war—in a large green tank. While most tenants cheered the antiseptic blue and white modern pools, some people were nostalgic for the messier early ones. In the film *Sweet Lorraine,* the granddaughter and the handyman met at the site of the "Old Pool," which the girl "always loved."[21] But progress was at hand. Shortly after the war ended, the building of blue-painted, chlorinated pools began in earnest. Hotels advertised "Hollywood" pools, and some of the larger bungalow colonies followed suit. The river's demise as a swimming alternative stimulated the rush to pools, and, by 1960, most colonies whether they could afford it or not had a pool. The demand for nice, sanitary-looking pools was so overwhelming that even hotels and colonies on good swimming lakes put in pools. The anomaly of a pool right at lakeside became commonplace. Many of my grandfather's mortgage loans during the 1950s were made to pay for swimming pools. If you decided to go ahead with the pool, your next decision was whether to have a pool less than seven feet deep, or a deeper one capable of allowing for a diving board. Any pool under seven feet, by law, didn't require a lifeguard—deeper pools did. While lifeguard lore at hotels often involves romance, bungalow colony lifeguards were usually teenagers whose parents were staying at the colony—and the job really lacked cachet and glamour. Sometimes parents only agreed to rent on the condition that a son be made the lifeguard. It was usually the lifeguard's job to check the chlorination level of the pool, to skim leaves off the surface, and, most particularly, to remove any dead creatures—frogs or small mammals—before the guests used the pool. City people were especially squeamish about sharing their water with animal corpses. At many colonies, the pool became what one observer called an example of "conspicuous nonconsumption,"[22] where tenants, even nonswimmers, would not rent in a pool's absence. On the heels of the pool trend came the demand at hotels for indoor pools. Hotelman Carl Gilbert ruefully noted in the 1970s that, "A person will call and ask if we have an indoor pool. They may not use it, but if you don't have it, they won't come."[23] The indoor pool mania never hit the colonies, although at least one colony, Mason's in Monticello, had one. Indoor pools tended to be used even less than outdoor ones, but they were and are symbolic.

Richman's received almost fifteen thousand dollars for our riparian rights, and Grandpa and Father debated putting in a pool. I naturally wanted one. There was discussion with our neighbors the Yustmans and the Puttermans about sharing the cost, but that went nowhere. Pools were costly, not only in their structure, but because of the elaborate, massive filtration systems then used. Sensibly Grandpa and Father decided against a pool, but with the loss of swimming facilities, we could only attract a crowd not interested in swimming—that is, mostly older people or people with very small children who liked the lower rates we had to charge because we lacked a pool. Today, the Sullivan County landscape is littered with abandoned pools built for small colonies that were simply not economical.

At large colonies, athletic men would play water polo and the whole colony would stage water shows that were mock emulations of Esther Williams movies. A water show illustrated with home movies made at Lansman's is in *The Rise and Fall of the Borscht Belt*.[24] But mostly the pool was a background.

Handball courts were common and were used to play both handball and racquetball. Basketball courts—incorporated with the handball court's paving or separated in the larger colonies—were also very popular, especially with American-born fathers who had played the game in school. By the 1960s, some colonies even had tennis courts. But the single most popular game was baseball. Many of the larger colonies were league members, and the big games against other colonies were on Sunday mornings. Saturday was practice day. Women and children were expected to show up and cheer. Lansman's, our local Goliath bungalow colony, usually dominated the play. Jason Cutler, the hero of *Bungalow Nine* who is hung over after a night of partying, is rousted out of bed by other active tenants of Hector's. "Hey Cutler! Yo Cutler! The visiting team is on the field."[25] Dressing quickly and skipping breakfast and even coffee, goaded by his wife ("Musn't be a poor sport, Darling"),[26] he drags himself to the field, and—as a first-time bungalow tenant—is astounded by what he sees:

> The ball field was a human beehive. The visitors had the diamond. Along the fringes the local team was limbering up arms, batting fungos and capering about with vigor Jason found demoralizing. Hector stood by importantly wearing blue pants and a blue cap mounted rakishly over his left side tic. He was ready to umpire. The men of the colony were out in force. They had more than enough for a team; light-footed Al Miller, hoarse-voiced Buddy Berg, florid Milt Krinsky, big Jack Rappaport, smiling Joe Alfelder, Abe Barsky prancing about . . . and plenty more. The heavy drinkers, heavy dancers, and good-time-Charleys until three in the morning were out en masse, behaving as if Saturday night had never been.[27]

If sport intensity varied from colony to colony, with some colonies almost ignoring strenuous physical activity, food was another story. Meals and noshing are part of the Catskill culture. "Eating was done on an almost continuous basis—breakfast around eight, coffee and maybe a piece of cake or toasted bagel around ten-thirty, lunch at twelve-thirty, fruit, coffee and cake in the mid afternoon, dinner around six-thirty," recalls *New York Times* food and restaurant critic Mimi Sheraton of Catskill summers. "Then after card playing and other evening activities, some herring, more cake, a little of this and that around eleven, just before bed."[28]

Cramped as most bungalows were, many people had weekend or weeklong guests. (At larger places, owners tried to discourage this by charging a per-night guest fee for the use of facilities, but enforcement was difficult—short of a bed check.) Hostess gifts were expected, and "whoever came up from the city brought food, as though my mother hadn't stocked up for the new arrivals," Sheraton remembers. "The customary gift was delicatessen," and there were always "towering boxes of cake."[29]

Weekend food was different from weekday fare, with some of these differences tied into religious observance. Neither Richman's nor most other bungalow colonies were particularly observant. Ours, with a higher proportion of older people than most in the 1960s and 1970s, was perhaps more religious

115

than some. At Richman's, most people kept kosher, but not all. Most people also lighted Sabbath candle, and my mother stopped lighting candles when she stopped having tenants. Friday was the traditional day for cooking in the Jewish tradition because of the prohibition of cooking on the Sabbath. Many younger Jewish women in the 1940s and 1950s, while not observant, cooked up a storm on Friday so that they wouldn't have to cook during the weekend when the men came up. What was cooked was governed by individual preference, with older-generation women more likely to make the time-consuming Jewish specialties, such as gefilte fish and blintzes. Most people seemed to agree on roast chicken and some version of pot roast.

Grandma cooked and baked on a scale beyond all of our tenants. She had a full kitchen—albeit one where the cooking and baking was done on a wood- and coal-burning stove—and the kitchen was hot as hell in summer. Our dinners always ended with soup: beet borscht, cabbage borscht, beef barley, and split-pea soup were usual. All of these soups were cooked with large cuts of beef, often flanken. Chicken soup was a must on Friday night. Dessert—several pastries—would follow.

Fridays always began with a trip to the live poultry market in Woodbourne, where Grandma and the other *balabusters* (real housewives) would go to select their chickens (Richman-raised, in Grandma's case, which she took to the *shochet,* or ritual slaughterer). The live chickens were displayed in barred chicken crates. After the bird was selected, the poultry dealer weighed it, and then handed it over to the *shochet* (you paid him directly). Then you could pay the resident chicken flicker (plucker) to pluck it, or do it yourself. Fat chickens were especially desirable because women would render the fat to make *schmaltz,* the purified chicken fat that was used in many Jewish dishes, as well as spread on bread as a butter substitute during meat meals, usually salted and topped with onion. When the schmaltz was rendered, little *gribenes* (Jewish cracklings) were left. These were fired crisp and were delicious. Women bragged about who had the fattest chicken, which would, of course, yield the most schmaltz. Also special were chickens that had unlaid eggs. These were highly prized little yolks that were boiled, often in chicken soup, and given to kids as a treat.

When chicken soup was served, it had to be accompanied by noodles, matzo balls, or *kreplach* (Jewish won ton). Every Friday evening meal had to include chopped liver (made with schmaltz), gefilte fish, roast chicken, or pot roast, accompanied by *kugel* (potato or noodle). If vegetables were served, they would be heavily disguised, such as carrots cooked with honey and prunes. Pickled cucumbers, tomatoes, and peppers were usually on the table, as was sauerkraut when in season. Dessert was yeast cake or cookies and canned fruit. Plain vegetables were never served until after my father developed diabetes and had to watch his diet. Salad was introduced at that same time. Grandpa never changed his diet. When offered plain vegetables or salad, he invariably replied, "Wait, I'll go ask the horse what he wants!"

Among Grandma's specialties were stuffed *helzel* (chicken neck, stuffed with a meat and potato), *lungen* stew (stewed lung and spleen in an onion gravy), and *p'cha* (calves-foot jelly made with garlic and red pepper)—usually eaten only by Grandpa. The penultimate treat was *kishka,* which took an incredible amount of time to prepare. The cook started with the large intestines of a cow (the gut, or *kiske*) and cleaned it of its content (it came mostly cleaned) and its fat. Any holes had to be sewn with thread, and then the *kishka* was stuffed with a mixture made of oatmeal and beef fat, flavored with salt and pepper. Next the loose end was sewn up, and the *kishka* was boiled for several hours before discarding the water. Then, the *kishka* could be cooked further in the quintessential Saturday dish, *cholent,* or baked in the oven to brown. In later years, we would cut it in slices and broil it to get it crispy and get rid of a lot of the fat. Grandma's other accomplishments included making her own pickled herring, which was a distasteful and stinky job. She would also make blintzes in large quantities. After Grandma died, my mother followed the tradition for many years. The credit sequences of the film *Mr. Saturday Night* are a marvelous visual recreation of the preparation of traditional foods.[30]

While Grandma made her own *challah* for Fridays ("the only white bread that didn't give you epilepsy"), she didn't make bread for ordinary eating—that came from the local bakery. Every town had at least one purveyor of rye bread (seeded or unseeded), pumpernickel, corn bread (which was mostly rye), and seeded and unseeded rolls. The old bakery of Woodbourne, which was in business until about 1960, was very old-world-like, down a little dirt road set off by itself. The sales counter was just that—a counter in front of the bread, in bins and ovens. After 1960, Woodbourne's bakery changed owners, moved to Main Street, and became very normative (like a New York City neighborhood bakery), featuring a salesroom with glass and metal display cases for a large pastry assortment, greatly expanded from the few and basic pastries offered prior to the move. The baking area is completely closed off. Once a year-round operation selling to year-round residents (many of whom started to winter in Florida), Woodbourne's bakery since the mid 1960s has been a summer-only operation, although Madnick's in nearby South Fallsburg, renamed Country Kosher Bakery by its new owners, still operates year-round. Katz's Bakery in Liberty—widely celebrated as the Catskills' finest—has, alas, gone out of business.

Bread was eaten in enormous quantities in our family, and by most Jewish families with first-generation roots. Anything eaten without bread was considered a "nosh," a snack. In the midst of our enormous meals we were admonished, "Eat bread! Don't nosh," and "*Ess broit; broit est stark*" (eat bread; bread gives strength). Bread was usually purchased daily. I bought many a "large, seeded rye" (two pounds) for our family of six. On Sunday morning, bagel was the bread of choice for many—and bagel came in just one variety, with or without poppy seeds. Unlike other bread products, they were not made at the local bakery, but in a special bagel bakery and distributed in the early morning on Sunday. Our bagel bakery was in Monticello. You could buy bagel (we never used the plural) at different places. You went to buy "six bagel and five rolls" at the bakery, of course, but also at Kanowitz's where you bought your lox and cream cheese. The *B'alystock pletzel* or the *bialy,* a specialty bread usually available only Sunday mornings, is the Jewish answer to the English muffin. Sunday mornings saw long lines at bakeries and dairies and appetizing stores as bungalow residents gathered their breakfast ingredients.

Table beverages varied by generation at dairy meals: tea or coffee for adults, milk for children. Meat meals always called for a pitcher of cold water pumped up from our hand pump—all of our tenants shared this treat, using it as a substitute as we did for the seltzer that we used at every meal in the city. Grandpa, who always claimed that "water rusted his pipes," drank beer or red wine, homemade by a friendly Italian. At Richman's, eating out was unknown during this early period. Woodbourne didn't have Chinese food until the mid 1950s, and pizza didn't come until later. Eating out generally meant eating deli sandwiches in South Fallsburg. These delis closed, as did Singer's in Liberty and Kaplan's in Monticello. We can't buy a good deli sandwich in the county today, except, perhaps, in an ultraorthodox restaurant where we would not feel particularly welcome (and where we might be suspicious about the sanitation). At the larger colonies, with their younger clientele, eating out on the weekend was a way for the adults to escape from the children and for the wife to escape from cooking. Sullivan County has never been a gourmet's paradise, but it has several long-lived restaurants, including a good steakhouse, The Homestead, in Bridgeville. My family's favorite quintessential Catskill restaurant is Frankie and Johnny's in Hurleyville, which continues to serve huge portions of red-sauced food at very reasonable prices to appreciative herds of well-fed summer visitors and year-round residents. Frankie and Johnny, father and son, run the kitchen. Mother, Maria, greets guests, runs the dining room, and watches the register.

At the colonies, as elsewhere, one witnessed the well-documented phenomenon of the acculturation of Jewish-immigrant group food practices. Today, with a great cultural dichotomy in the Catskills, and with the rise of orthodox dominance, it is interesting to see the proliferation of kosher restaurants, but these do not usually feature traditional "Jewish" foods, rather barbecued chicken and kosher Chinese food and kosher pizza.

We had a ritual as guests left at season's end, which I learned was also observed at other small places. Everyone, owners and remaining tenants, would give the departing folks a loud sendoff. Banging pots and pans with spoons, we would sing "We hate to see you go; we hope the heck you never come back; we hate to see you go!" Everyone had a grand time laughing as the overloaded car pulled out of the driveway. Grandpa always observed, "*Der shtetl kumpd ein dorf,*" which translates, "The town becomes a crossroads."

The Quest
for Entertainment

Entertainment was always very important to Sullivan County. The list of performers who got their start in the Borscht Belt is long and legendary and their stories have been told to death. While live professional entertainment came to the bungalow colonies in the 1950s, prior to that much entertainment was home grown or stolen—that is from the perspective of hotel owners who often looked at bungalow people as *schnorers* (beggars) or *gonifs* (thieves).

In the matriarchal world of the weekday bungalow colonies, card games and the occasional movie were the primary nighttime entertainment. The weekend was another story. This was the time to *hule* (party)—and party everyone did. Saturday night was the night of the bungalow community. This community was alive and united and did something. The "something" could be a simple cookout, homemade entertainment (reviews, games, dances), going to the movies en mass, or the ultimate—getting into a hotel to see a show.

At Richman's, parties changed radically over the years. The first parties were organized by the tenants, and Grandpa would donate five dollars to the party fund. The guests would kick in a quarter a person, and a self-appointed committee would buy marshmallows, hot dogs, rolls, mustard, and relish. Notice no ketchup: It was years before I saw a kosher hot dog dressed with ketchup.

Soda was also supplied, but never beer, although Grandpa would sneak off to help himself from his private stock. Kids liked these parties because we could attend and gorge ourselves. We had parties two or three times a year. The parties during the Fourth of July weekend and the Labor Day weekend (on the preceding Saturday or Sunday night) were fixtures; another during the middle of the summer was optional. These events were informal and cooperative. When kids heard a party was coming up, we took to the woods to gather the perfect marshmallow toasters, long greenwood sticks. Older kids would whittle points on these skewers. We were also pressed into scouring the woods for dead brush to be used for the ritual bonfire. As a matter of fact, building a bonfire was something done almost every Saturday night. These regular bonfires were early in the evening and smaller than those related to a party. At first fires were built on the ground, then in the mid 1940s Grandpa built an outdoor fireplace. When the fire was at its height, the kids delighted in toasting marshmallows, chasing each other with pointed sticks, and fencing. "Don't run with the sticks," parents admonished, "You'll put out an eye." Fortunately, we never had any wounds worse than a scratch.

When the fire burned down to the bright-ash stage, the hot dogs were grilled. First a grate was laid down across the ember area, then the hot dogs were placed in wire grill cages and cooked. One tenant always appointed himself grill chef. The hot dogs would then be dumped on a platter and everyone helped themselves. No paper plates, just packages of buns. And during the war, people brought their own glasses for soda. Most people were not as germ conscious as they are now it wasn't until later that parties used paper cups. Everyone cooled a bottle or two of the party soda in their ice boxes, or later in their refrigerators, and no ice was served with the drinks. We played games such as musical chairs, adults and children together. After the kids were put to bed, the adults would sing, tell risque jokes, and generally horse around.

The Fourth of July weekend was always considered the official start of the season and was a cause for celebration. Some of our tenants had firecrackers (which were, and are, illegal in New York but could still be bought in New Jersey), and a few tenants even had cherry bombs and an occasional rocket. The kids were limited to sparklers purchased in Woodbourne. They were a letdown from the glamorous (and more dangerous) fireworks, but you could run with them (until caught by a parent) and swing them in arks. We also watched the sky for rockets set off at other colonies and hotels and by the goyim as they celebrated the holiday. All of the party activity took place on the side lawn, which had one major drawback: In the mountains the dew wets the grass early and people complained of wet feet and slippery ground. We needed another place to have parties.

Mother started a campaign in the 1950s for Grandpa, who knew cement work, to build a patio. During my sophomore year in college (1954–1955), Grandpa went on a trip to California to visit his brother and sister who lived there. Later, one of his nieces wrote to my mother, telling how much they were enjoying the patio "Uncle Abe" had helped construct. Grandpa was defeated, and he agreed to build a patio. Once on a project, Grandpa was a demon—a demon who didn't believe in modern equipment. That summer when I arrived in Woodbourne, I had more action than mowing and raking grass. First I helped dig the foundation area for the patio and spread the crushed stone. Then my roommate, Alan Marks, arrived to spend a few weeks with us, and Grandpa promptly impressed him as a laborer. We mixed every bit of cement in a trough Grandpa built, mixing sand and cement with water with a broad-edged hoe. It was one of the hottest June weeks on record, but we were forced on. Father even lifted a few shovelfuls of cement, almost as a ritual. That season, our guests were surprised with a new patio. In 1952, we added another improvement—an outdoor speaker for our phonograph, so people could have music on the lawn. With the completion of the patio, dancing became a regular event at the Saturday night parties, and parties became more frequent. Home movies show our group performing the Bunny Hop and playing musical chairs. Prizes were awarded at games—our movies also show mother having won a yo-yo. Our place wasn't unique; in *The Rise and Fall of the Borscht Belt,* the narrator recalls that bungalow social life revolved around "the patio or the outdoor dance floor."

Nineteen fifty-four marked a new era in our parties. One of our tenants was my father's cousin Florence who, with her husband Murray, operated a very successful hardware business in Queens. Florence decided to give my parents, whose anniversary was 28 August, a surprise wedding anniversary party. Florence and Murray collected money for the party from the tenants, and a committee was set up to collect money for a gift—a silver-plated tray manufactured by our neighbor, Max Putterman.

While earlier parties were outdoors and informal, this was in the house and dressy. (My parents had been taken out to dinner so the surprise could be sprung when they returned.) I was seventeen and had my new movie camera to record the event. The table had been moved out of the dining room so everyone could dance there, and I brought in my pet white rabbit to help us learn the Bunny Hop. The following year, Florence and Murray organized another, less surprise, party. Again the time was the Saturday evening a week before Labor Day.

My parents' twenty-fifth wedding anniversary was in 1956, and they decided to give their own party. Mother cooked up a storm: chopped liver, potato and *kasha* knishes, *kishka*, and her excellent potato salad. In the postwar years, people would take turns adding dishes—potato salad, cole slaw, and so on—to the Saturday night parties. Mother's potato salad had its reputation. One of her proudest moments was when a tenant filled a plate with potato salad, tasted it, declared, "This isn't Bertha's," and dumped the remains, unceremoniously, in the fireplace. At the Silver Anniversary, the potato salad appeared alongside Mother's less widely acclaimed, but excellent, cole slaw. Sliced corned beef, pastrami, and tongue were also served. For dessert, Mother baked honey cake (her mother's recipe) and a wonderful carrot cake, always called "Bubble Cake" after the name of the lady who provided the recipe.

I picked flowers and ferns to decorate the food tables that were set up in the summer kitchen, and I sculpted the chopped liver into a chicken. In the 1950s, that was haute cuisine at Jewish weddings and bar mitzvahs. In the film *Goodbye Columbus,* they introduced the wedding sequence with the decapitation of the chopped-chicken-liver bird.[1] I also carved a basket out of watermelon—this was filled with balls of watermelon, honeydew, and cantaloupe, another 1950s craze.

The Silver Anniversary was the biggest party we had since Seymour's bar mitzvah party in 1946. In addition to the tenants, we had a number of relatives and some of my parents' city friends in attendance. Everyone was dressed up to 1950s regulation. The party set a precedent; from this time forward, my parents gave their annual end-of-summer party, and the guests gave them a gift. At first, the parties were given on Labor Day weekend, but later my mother gave them a week earlier. The menu, except for the chopped liver and the *kishka,* remained fixed. Soon my mother assumed the Fourth of July party, as well. The menu was similar to Labor Day, but a bit simpler. The search for good-quality cold cuts at the most reasonable cost was perennial. In 1960, the folks found a butcher who sold the cold cuts reasonably priced—if you'd slice them yourself. My father learned that Meyer Lebed, one of the town's pharmacists, had an electric slicer at home left over from the days when his store had a lunch counter. He offered us its use. So twice a year for twenty years, I was responsible for slicing twenty pounds of deli, a job I remember as hot, greasy, and generally distasteful.

By the mid 1950s, parties provided by "the farmer" were a regular part of the summer season at most places. All those I knew of, however, were less personal than the ones my parents hosted. At most of the parties, especially at larger places, cold-cut platters were prepared by the local deli, or by the "concession" if there was one, and commercial sour pickles, potato salad, cole slaw, and rye bread were served. Another difference was that liquor and beer were provided along with soda at many places. I remember from the years I worked at Kassack's how much the owners, Leo and Sophie, who were very nice people, hated to put out money for liquor. Despite the fact that most Jews drank less than society in general, there was a lot of drinking at many of these parties. As a counselor, I was invited to the parties and could go into the casinos on special occasions and Saturday nights, and I witnessed a fair amount of drunken and lewd behavior. As I came out of a Labor Day party at Meyer Furman's colony, one of my campers, a boy of about twelve, asked me, "How's my mother?" I had seen her staggering from man to man but said, "Fine." His response was, "Thank God. Last year she took off all her clothes and danced on the roof of the casino."

In *Bungalow Nine,* Ann and Jason watch as their neighbors the Krinskys do a wildly exhibitionist Lindy. The whole casino watched and egged them on when "in a frenzied break Julia wiggled out of her skirt and sent it flying into the crowd. More cheers as her blouse followed. . . . From all sides the chant came. 'Take it off!'" As the band played ever louder and faster, she "began a movement of fingers on her slip straps; . . . the slip fell to the floor." Things weren't as naughty as they seemed: "Julia Krinsky, hands high, posed in all her glory in a skintight flesh-colored leotard."[2]

Naughty entertainment, as well as food, was often a part of summer fun for adults. In *Bungalow Nine,* there's a description of a quintessential Labor Day party at a large colony. After the music stopped,

they took the plastic covers off a mammoth buffet display of refreshments on tables crossing the end of the casino. Dominating the spread were two huge platters of chopped chicken-liver, sculptured into roosters. There were platters of antiseptic-looking gefilte fish slices, trays of cranberry sauce slices, a gargantuan salad bowl, dips and spreads of every sort, giant jellied fruit molds, doughnuts, crumbly, short roggalach, and gallons of cider. At the other end of the room, behind the bar, the coffee urn was steaming its fragrance into the room. The mob closed in and went to work.[3]

The after-meal entertainment featured what were then called stag films. These black-and-white silent films were a far cry from slick modern porn and were often shown in what amounted to an average fraternity party atmosphere. The folks at Hector's were first treated to "Buster Ball in a Turkish Harem," complete with subtitles, "He's All Man!!"[4]

While I never witnessed one of these bungalow colony naughty nights, I certainly heard about them from tenants at various colonies, as well as from some of Grandpa's clients who bragged about being able to get the films to show their tenants and how much fun the tenants had watching them. Miriam Damico's eyes glazed over with pleasant memories when she told me about the belly dancers and strippers who were hired to entertain at her Moonglow Inn. "Everybody had such fun," she recalled, "and the teenagers tried to see in. We had Venetians [blinds] on the windows of the casino." Miriam, who ran a store at the colony, also fondly remembered that kids often came to the store on Sunday morning for "a bagel and cream cheese" while their parents slept. "I would just put it on their tabs," Miriam said.[5]

Flirtations and affairs among tenants happened. In later years, my mother would often tell me in a conspiratorial voice," You'd never believe who was fooling around with who. You don't know, but I know everything." Larger places were more fertile; some places had faster crowds: The Boris Bungalow Colony (owned by novelist Martin Boris's father) advertised "No Deadheads allowed." While many flirted, it is hard to imagine that many affairs were actually consummated "on the premises"—in crowded, very public surroundings. Most Jews of the time were comfort-minded so the woods were out, and motels didn't reach Sullivan County until the postwar years. And, of course, there were affairs that lasted into the city, and some, eventually, resulted in the scandals of divorce and remarriage.

When casinos were built at the larger and mid-sized colonies, one of the first rules established was that kids, and especially young teens, were banished from any Friday or Saturday festivities. To compensate, many colonies had "Teen Night" parties on Wednesday or Thursday nights. There was record music or a jukebox. The refreshments, if any, were simple. These events are remembered by interviewee Dorothy Gittelman in *The Rise and Fall of the Borscht Belt:*

My husband-to-be came in, with a bunch of friends. They were imported, because men were hard to come by. We had lots of women all over the place, lots of girls. You had a specific ritual, because you'd walk along and you couldn't speak to anyone too long, because you couldn't waste the weekend. You had just a certain amount of time, and if they didn't take your number it was totally wasted. So quickly you went in, and you didn't sit down. Because I was tall, so if I sat down, they wouldn't know how tall I was. So for the entire evening I stood up. Now also you didn't stay with five or six girls, because boys don't like to walk over to a group of giggling girls. So we separated. And they immediately would come over, or whatever it was, and we'd dance, and you were successful if they took your number.[6]

As our clientele aged during the 1960s and 1970s and fewer people had the stamina to go out, there was a demand for weekly parties, and we entered what would become a time warp. Grandpa still donated his five dollars, and someone collected fifty cents a person from the others. People would take turns arranging for food—usually hot dogs or bagels with cream cheese and lox, coffee, and store-bought cake. At first these parties were held on the patio, but soon they moved into our garage. Grandpa put down a big linoleum rug and strung extra lights, and Mother tacked on the wall machine-made tapestries that a cousin had given her. When the weather was mild, the garage doors were open. If it was cool, the garage doors were closed and everyone entered from the side door. The parties were routine. They started at about half past eight, when everyone danced. There was some social dancing and at least one Russian *sher* or a *hora*. At about half past ten the food was served, and an hour later the party was over. As the years went by, the party cost remained fifty cents per person and increasingly the burden fell on my mother; the menu became schmaltz herring and potatoes, purchased cake, and coffee. Since most of our older guests were European born, herring and potatoes was the soul food of their childhoods.[7] Older American-born children could also enjoy the dish; I found it repulsive, although I have always liked pickled herring and herring salad. By 1965, my mother was collecting the money and doing the shopping. By 1975, everyone was sitting around waiting for the food to be served. Increasingly, my mother resented being caught in this net of service. She lived for *Tish A' Bov*, a Jewish holiday (of which I had not been aware), which usually fell in late July or August, when she could call off her parties for religious reasons. The "parties" became increasingly dreary—especially with all the talk about why they shouldn't eat herring "for *mein* pressure." But they did. Mother and Grandpa did their best to trap me to help at these parties, but I usually had other plans.

Amateur theatrics was a delightful part of summer. Kids were encouraged to perform at parties, but entertainment was an adult concern. At least once at Richman's, we had the quintessential Catskill entertainment, a "mock marriage"—where the bride, always pregnant, is played by a man and the groom, always hesitant, is played by a woman. The "rabbi" character, especially, is to be as raunchy as he can be. A mock marriage performed lakeside can be seen in *The Rise and Fall of the Borscht Belt*.[8] We also performed burlesque skits that were similarly risque. I worked the lights, which were my photo floods. Several of these skits are recorded in the book *Summer on a Mountain of Spices*.

> *Joe Kamin is a rabbi. Zalik Boulak is the rebbitsin [rabbi's wife]. The rebbitsin is in bed. She wears a kerchief on her head. Her chest is bare with blankets pulled up to her shoulders. The rabbi is dolling himself up.*

JOE: Get dressed my pet. It's Shabbos. On Friday the congregation sends a delegation of honor to escort me to the synagogue.

ZALIK: I got time, honeycake. Keep your tzitzits on.

> *The sound of the delegation in the hall.*

JOE: Gottenyu. They're coming. Quick. Put my yarmulke over your most sacred part, they shouldn't see you naked.

> *Zalik takes the skullcap and slips it under the blanket.*

ZALIK: Hide, pussycat. I'll make believe I'm sleeping, they'll go away.

> *The delegation enters. Barry Guerfin, Mr. Rifkin, and Morty Popkin look around.*

BARRY: So where is our beloved rabbi?

MORTY: Lookee here.

> *The delegation sees the rebbitsin in bed. She is prodded. No reaction. Mr. Rifkin pulls back the blanket for a quick peek. He puts his hand in and comes out with the yarmulke.*

THE DELEGATION: Help! Help! We have lost our beloved rabbi!

Curtain.

A quickie.

Joe Kamin in the spotlight.

JOE: How are Yidlach different from Cossacks? I'll show you.

Joe unbuttons his fly.

Screams are heard.

Joe pulls out the tail of his shirt.

JOE: Who else but the Chosen could get such a shirt for two twenty-five, tax included?

Lights.[9]

At larger colonies with casinos, the tenants often put on elaborate shows, complete with costumes. At Lansman's, the tenants did a French chorus scene, complete with the exhibition of decorative underwear. Marty Lansman, the last private owner, remembers these times fondly—when tenants created the entertainment and spent all evening at the casino, staying until three or four in the morning.[10]

A casino, according to *Webster's* dictionary, is "a clubhouse or building used for social meetings, having rooms for public amusement, gambling, dancing," and so on.[11] The bungalow colony casino fulfilled all of these functions. Like "bungalow," "casino" is a word that had upper-class associations. Newport society played tennis and amused themselves at the Newport Casino designed by McKim, Mead, and White in the 1880s. By the turn of the century, many Gilded Age estates had casinos of their own, which served as guest houses and recreational pavilions. The casino commissioned in 1902 by John Jacob Astor, IV, for his Hudson Valley estate "Ferncliff" exists today. It has a French facade and contains a white marble swimming pool, a skylighted tennis court, a billiard room, and five guest bedrooms.[12] Clearly, the word has European origins and was widely used in society news.

Architecturally, bungalow colony casinos were very unimpressive. They were typically large frame buildings with gabled roofs, and, as noted earlier, many had one gable wall modified to serve as a handball court. The entrance door to the casino was usually in the middle of a broad wall. Some had bathrooms, others did not. Some housed a luncheonette, or a "concession." At larger places, a stage was very important, as was a dressing room and some kind of kitchen facility (if there was no concession). In the years before air conditioning, the casino needed many screened windows for ventilation. Interiors were spare. The walls might be unfinished or, at more pretentious places, covered in plywood (plain or fancy) or Sheetrock. When the Cutlers see the casino interior at Hector's Pond, they see a thousand others: "A low-lying flat ceiling of composition squares blotted out the rafters and gables. Ann pouted at the long rows of fluorescent lights." Surprised, she "whispered to Jason. 'This doesn't look the least bit rustic. It's dreary and functional.'"[13] But the casino was filled with life. Parties were held here and, on rainy days, card games often filled the hall. Also, Monte Carlo nights were held; these gambling events were illegal, but no one complained.

By the early 1950s, large bungalow colonies were emulating hotels in offering bands on Saturday night. The workweek shrank and better roads made it possible for people to reach the mountains earlier. Friday night bands were added. Soon colonies were offering paid performers, as well. The advent of television, having a well-understood deleterious effect on amateur home entertainment, was another potent force leading to the professionalization of entertainment. Advances in television technology and better telephone service went a long way toward breaking down the sense of community that existed in colonies.

Early on, telephone calls for anyone were a matter of community interest. Dorothy Gittelman remembers what this meant to a dating teenager:

And the excitement when they called up a bungalow colony! There were no such things as phones in every bungalow, they would announce it over the loudspeaker. They would say, "Dorothy Gittelman, wanted over the telephone." What was happening to me! I was being called, and the whole bungalow colony knew it. I got prestige. And sometimes you'd have a stranger call you, just so you could run down to the phone, and "Look how popular she is, she's just running down all day long." And you would go from the top of the hill all the way down, and you'd pick up the phone, and by the time you got all the way down there, you didn't care who it was, it was just a wonderful thing. That's how we met, that was the ritual we went through.[14]

At Richman's, the telephone paging routine was simple. The coin telephone was wall-mounted in the summer kitchen. Mostly it was one of the family who would answer, "Hello, Richman's" or in later years, "Good afternoon, Richman's." Then we would simply open the door and yell, "Mrs. Rabinowitz, telephone," or "Marsha, telephone." Anyone on the lawn felt the obligation to shout as well, until they saw the caller's recipient running to the main house. And run they did, especially when the call was announced as, "Mr. Goldberg, long-distance calling." Our home movies show teenage Valerie Stern running to answer the phone, looking very much like "the morning after." Privacy of communication was unknown, as you answered your call in earshot of five kitchens. At larger bungalow colonies, this system was slightly more refined, if not a lot more private. The phone would ring in the office (often there were several lines) and then, in the postwar years, a loudspeaker was used to announce the call. "Cynthia Macklin, telephone," would blare over the colony and beyond. At our place, which was at least a half mile from any loudspeaker, we heard the distant cacophony of other people's messages from at least three or four bungalow colonies and hotels. The response at the big places was similar to that at ours—you ran to the nearest phone down the line. These phones were usually located in little sheds or on the porch of the casino. As the postwar world became more affluent, the larger hotels installed phones in their rooms and consequently stopped paging. It was only a matter of time that some of the larger places like Lansman's put in a switchboard system and telephones in all units—at an extra charge, of course. The fictional Cutlers shared a four-party line, and "Ann envied the amount of time the others spent phoning back and forth."[15]

It took a very long time for modern telephone equipment to come to the mountains, and it wasn't until the early 1960s that dial phones were installed. Prior to that, making a telephone call was an experience from another age. Our telephone number was Woodbourne 1159, and when you wanted to make a call, you picked up the receiver, put in a nickel or a dime (depending on the era), and waited until an operator came on the line, asking, "Number please?" In prime times during the season, you could wait up to forty-five minutes to get through to an operator—Saturday night was the worst. On the plus side, you seldom needed to know the number if you were calling a popular spot, such as a movie house, or a hotel. "Give me the Flagler" was an acceptable answer to "Number please?" if you wanted that South Fallsburg hotel.

Most colonies had coin telephones. Contrary to popular belief, these were not public phones, but private lines with coin boxes. The bungalow colony owner paid a rental fee for the line and the phone and was given a percentage of the coins collected in the coin box. At a small place like ours, the telephone often cost us money. At larger places, you would make money on the coin boxes, especially if you were isolated enough.

Conventional wisdom would suggest that it would be easy to find out how many bungalow colonies existed at any given time by counting "bungalow and apartment" listings in the telephone book—but these listings cost extra and most small places, like ours, were simply listed in the white pages under the owner's name. We were always listed as "Richman, A., Woodbourne." A *New York Times* article claims that in 1953 Sullivan County had 528 hotels, 2,000 bungalow colonies, and 1,000 rooming houses. Colonies and rooming houses each averaged about twenty-five units. Neighboring counties had additional resorts.[16]

When my parents decided to give up their home in the city and make Woodbourne their main base of operation, they had a new telephone line put in the old kitchen, which had heat—the summer kitchen has never been heated. For years thereafter, we had one number in the summer/season (the coin box) and one in the winter/nonseason, Woodbourne 1189, with service suspended on the appropriate telephone. By the mid 1960s, many tenants, even at our place, started having private telephones installed for the season, and the news and spectacle of the 'telephone dash' lessened. Eventually, so few people were using our telephone that, in the mid 1970s, we discontinued the coin box and just had the one private line. But the voice of the loudspeaker is not dead yet. You can still hear it at camps and at surviving colonies where it is used for announcements.

Television was ultimately more divisive. My family was very conservative, and we didn't even have a television set in the city until 1950—and only then because it's what I wanted as my bar mitzvah present. Watching television in the Catskills was frustrating. Television reception was awful—worse than radio. The familiar rooftop antenna was not enough to bring in a decent signal in our valleys, and images were snowy to say the least. In the electronic blizzard, there may have been an image.

In the late 1950s, we finally got television in the country. My folks and our neighbors, the Yustmans and the Puttermans, went in as partners. Getting permission from the local farmer, George Vantran, they had cable (about two thousand feet of wire) run up to the top of the hill behind our house and, on the hilltop, a seventy-foot antenna was erected. That first summer, reception

131

was spectacular, and the $1,500 cost for the system ($750 for us) was well worth the price. In subsequent years, the system was less satisfactory. Over the winter, storms would deflect the antenna, and we could never find anyone to adjust it for us. So we lived with "ghosts" and mild snow storms until the mid 1960s when Woodbourne got CATV. Colonies less fortunately situated than ours had to wait even longer for CATV before they could have tolerable television. Once our house had heat installed and the cookstove was idled, we seldom ate in the dining room, and this became the natural place to put the TV. As a result, the dining room was no longer available for card playing. In places with casinos, TVs were installed there for use on nonshow nights. Smaller places might put TVs in small sheds facing the lawn where tenants watched *al fresco*.

Now people had a choice, they could play cards at night or watch television, and soon a routine developed at Richman's. In the afternoon a small contingent would watch television soap operas, and in the evening the television was on from eight to eleven. Which show was on was chosen by consensus, and only family could change channels and controls. Mother and Grandpa especially had visions of tenants wrecking things. God forbid a plastic knob might break. "Who could have been touching this?" If in our history even some minor mishap had befallen us as a result of tenant malfeasance, it was never forgotten. When I brought friends home, I was instructed to tell them not to try to flush cardboard toilet paper tubes down the toilet. This had happened once.

Within a few years of the coming of cable, the companies started offering the service to tenants. By the mid 1960s, several tenants had their own hookups, and, by the 1970s, individual hookups became common. With the increased availability of television, local movie theaters in small towns declined and nighttime business in the towns followed suit. Woodbourne's movie house, The Centre Theater, closed in 1989.

In recent years, there has been a renaissance of movie-going with the development of mall cinemas in Monticello and with the efforts of a few enterprising owners of older theaters, like Sam Rosenshein owner of The Rivoli in Fallsburg, who started showing dollar movies and filling the house. Although the price is now up to three dollars, the crowds are still coming, but it is largely an older group and most of South Fallsburg is still closed tight at night.

The advent of television had a dramatic effect on the larger places that offered shows. The demand was for better acts. The customers were not content with young entertainers breaking in their material. They wanted entertainment you could compare to television, and if they didn't care for what was being presented in the casino, they could opt out for TV. This also had a great impact on what movies people would watch at the colonies—they wanted only films of recent vintage.

Most of the writings about the Sullivan County phenomenon concern its entertainment. It was the spawning ground for dozens of greats, from Danny Kaye to Jerry Lewis, and certainly by the late 1920s most hotels offered some kind of entertainment. Most of it was not star quality, nor did it always spawn lasting talent, but it was *leiberdich* (lively).[17] Hotel entertainment began informally, and the neighbors were all welcome. Crowds made everything *freilich* (happy), but as entertainment became more professional, and cost money, the attitude of hotel owners changed and a long-raging battle ensued. People from the *kuchaleins* and the bungalow colonies wanted to continue enjoying the entertainment. Joey Adams recalls the period when "the great activity was . . . sneaking over to the big hotel." Bungalow colonies located near hotels would command premiums even though it was no guarantee that you'd be able to get in to see the shows. Barron's in South Fallsburg charged prime rates because it was next to The Flagler and within walking distance of at least five other hotels.[18] The Flagler is now the Crystal Run School (for retarded adults), and Barron's has become a run-of-the-mill Hasidic colony.

Most hotel owners tried to keep the bungalow people out. This basic war phase ran from the 1920s through the late 1950s, when many owners realized, rather belatedly, that they could make money from the bungalow people. From the 1920s, however, there have been hotels (including The Flagler) that arranged with nearby colonies to let their tenants in for a flat summer fee. And there were also hotels, like the Tamarack Lodge in Greenfield Park, that owned their own colonies and rented the bungalows with "full hotel privileges."

Sneaking into hotels was a sport brought to a high level of sophistication, and basically hotels really only cared about exclusion on the two show nights—Friday and Saturday—when crowds were largest. A few hotels, such as Grossinger's, had fences all around them. Others, such as Chester's in Woodbourne, were on dead-end roads where guards had access to arriving cars. However, most were open and freely accessible; these had guards at the casinos who were assigned to keep all but the guests out. They tried. All kinds of techniques were used. Family connections were important. The password to the guards might be "my father, the salad man," or "my son, the busboy."[19] At least one hotel owner, "Pop" Nemerson of South Fallsburg's Nemerson Hotel, used to challenge would-be-casino-enterers with the question, "What did you have for dinner?" Some hotel owners gave out tickets in the dining room or stamped the guest's hand. In the late 1950s, invisible ink—visible only under black light—was popular. Generally, the only legal way to see the shows, aside from being a guest, was to be "a guest of a guest." And it was a part of Jewish middle-class etiquette that if you were at a hotel and had bungalow friends, you'd invite them over to see a show. Most hotel owners grudgingly went along with this, although a few charged a small fee. The largest hotels, like Grossinger's, said no.

Each type of defense erected by hotel owners had a breaching point. It was like war. Hotels with fences: Hitch a ride with a guest and drive through the gate. Once in the gate there were no further controls. One year I had an arts-and-crafts counselor who had never been to the Catskills before and didn't know you couldn't get into The Concord, and he and his wife simply wanted to see it. He had just had periodontal surgery and was using an ice pack. He parked his car in one of The Concord lots and walked in, holding his ice pack to his face. No one challenged him. Busy times were always good—if you mixed with a crowd you could slip in. Also, fenced hotels had large grounds. I went to shows at both The Concord and Grossinger's by crawling under the fence. (This tactic was not good after a rain.) You could generally find areas where more enterprising people had breached the fence with wire and bolt cutters. It was a good idea to bring along a piece of old sheet to protect your clothes.

My first visit to The Concord was in the company of Irving Rabinowitz, the son of one of our tenants. When his mother met me she said, "Oivin, your name is just like *mein* son, Oiving." Irving was one of the most accomplished inter-lopers I ever met, as well as the most talented hunter. He scored within twenty minutes of our arrival. Irving had built-in radar. I saw him in action several times. He zeroed in on his target, she would be nibbling on his ear within min-utes, and they'd disappear. He would be back on the dance floor about an hour or so later. "What did you say?" I asked. "I just had to meet people." And so on to the next.

A place at the end of a road was easier. You reconnoitered during the day, and at night, with the help of a muted flashlight, you found your way around the guards. Again, this was not something to do shortly after a rain. Chester's was the only place I frequented that had this type of location, and for the most part I went there during the week, when no one ever stopped to check. Chester's, no longer in business, was sold to an orthodox girls camp and is now an orthodox hotel, but it was still legend among bungalow kids for its wild reputation. I was always too young for Chester's, which suffered the fate of most resorts: They never attracted a younger generation. The wild things who went there in the 1930s and 1940s were the same people (now less wild) who went in the 1950s and 1960s. I did discover, however, that many of the Chester people didn't go there for the hotel's vaunted "intellectual" entertainment. As one female guest said to me when I asked if she was going to the show later, "I never go to hear that junk." The promise of romance was clearly the hotel's commodity.

Guarded casinos were the most difficult. I might add that we were allowed to visit nearby hotels alone when we were about thirteen. As I look back, the innocence of the times always amazes me. Until I was fifteen, getting into The Aladdin was easy. I was friendly with Kenny Komito, whose parents owned the place, and he'd get me in, even though he himself seldom saw a show. (I never understood that then—I do now. It was his sister who would marry Sidney Offit and who would be the model for the hotel-hating daughter in *He Had It Made*.) Kenny's early death put an end to that, but every now and then his father would let me in for old-times sake. Again, the best adult technique was to blend with the crowd, so you timed your arrival for when guests were pouring into the casino. Frequently paying guests were not too happy to have to hand over tickets or flash their stamped hands.

Often a friend-of-a-friend was a busboy or a waiter who could get you tickets. Sometimes one of them could borrow a stamp. I had a very good friend, Ben Perchik, who worked at the Tamarack Lodge. When I wanted to get in for a Saturday night, he would go to the lobby and get his hand stamped and then zip out quickly, and we'd roll the backs of our hands together so that I'd have an image, too. It worked every time.

As a teenager and in my early twenties, I would go to hotels often during the week. You never had to sneak in to see the movies or the plays put on by professional troupes, or to dance. But most people just looked to the hotels on weekends. Interestingly, while many hotels tried to keep out bungalow crashers, real farmers were usually welcomed. But then the nature of farming, with early morning demands from chickens and cows, discouraged farmers from going to the hotels very often.[20]

Summertime was a good time for a Jewish girl to find a husband. In *Radio Days*, Woody Allen's celebration of the 1930s and 1940s, Aunt Bea, who wants to get married, asks her married sister whether she should go on a cruise or go to the mountains: "The men are richer on a cruise, but there are more of them in the mountains." "I found my husband in the mountains," the sister replies. "Go on a cruise."[21] Dorothy Gittelman found her future husband at her own bungalow colony.[22] But many a *kuchalein* girl tried the hotels as well, "although they hated having to sneak in like second-story men. . . . More daring kuchalane girls," Joey Adams continued, "would put on walking shoes and trudge . . . to the hotel carrying high heels." They'd hide their everyday shoes in the bushes, "don their sleek pumps, and pass among the anointed as one of them. When and if they were caught, they were thrown out."[23]

The quality of music at the hotels varied greatly. My brother, Seymour, played the trumpet, and when he was sixteen, he and three friends formed a band and got a job (fifteen dollars a week, each, plus room and board) performing at the Ulster Lake House, where they played six nights a week and "cut" a show on Saturday. Other places were much more professional.

My strongest memory of hotel sneaking in the 1950s was how hot it was. Casinos were not air-conditioned, and men always wore a tie and jacket. Mink stoles for women were *de rigueur* from the mid 1950s. The show would start, depending on the hotel, at nine or ten o'clock. In later years, some hotels presented shows in their now air-conditioned cocktail lounges at midnight, one, or even later. After the show, the folding chairs would be cleared from the center of the room and there would be dancing until the wee hours. The shows in the 1950s invariably were three acts: first a novelty or a dance act, then a female singer, and finally a male comic. Over the years as talent became more expensive, most places cut acts back to two or even one. By the 1970s, a single hour-long act became standard, and dance and novelty acts virtually disappeared. When bungalow colonies got into the business, they couldn't compete with hotels, so their schedules were the reverse of hotels. Dancing began at 9:00 or so, and the show went on at 11:00 or 11:30 or 12:00.

Charlie Rapp was the best known of a number of agents who supplied acts to the mountain resorts, and at the height of the season decent acts would often be booked at three or four places a night. It was not uncommon for an act to do a hotel at 9:00, a second one at 10:00, a bungalow colony at 11:30 and a late or a late show at a hotel at 1:00 or even 2:00 A.M. Henry Tobias, employing hyperbole, "estimated that from July first to Labor Day, he [Rapp] was responsible for 98 percent of the lavish and expensive shows put on in Sullivan County." Rapp wasn't a mere "10 percenter" who was content with a commission. Usually, he hired entertainers by the week and sold their services a la carte. He even acquired two small hotels for the sole purpose of housing his acts. "I've got a big worksheet that tells me where everyone is appearing, who has to pick up whom, how many shows are scheduled for that night—everything," Rapp explained. But human error had its part. "The girl in my office once sent three top names to a bungalow colony. They played before an audience of eighty people." Lucky colony! "It had a name similar to one of the top hotels, where they should have gone."[24]

Charlie's nephew Howard Rapp started, as a kid, collecting money for entertainment from hotel owners and bungalow colony "farmers." Too young to drive, he had Mendel, a locally famed Fallsburg taxi driver, take him around. In the course of many trips, Rapp learned all the back roads. Acts would always ask the kid geographic questions like: "Can we triple Kutsher's, Pullman's Bungalows, and the Nemerson?"[25] There were other agents as well. Hy Einhorn and Aaron Topper were the leading bookers of small hotels and bungalow colonies. One of their acts, comedian and Yiddish theater actor Feibish Finkel who played many a colony, would only achieve wider fame in the 1990s as the lawyer on the TV series *Picket Fences.*[26]

In *Broadway Danny Rose,* Woody Allen is portrayed as a marginal agent peddling his bizarre clients—a one-legged tap dancer, a one-armed juggler, and "Eddie Clark's Penguin"—to a skeptical but frugal hotel and bungalow colony owner, Phillie. "The Penguin skates on stage dressed as a rabbi." Phillie is unimpressed: "Weinstein's Majestic Bungalow Colony is a classy place and I need a classy act."[27]

Bungalow colonies providing their own entertainment cut down on the hotel crashing, but did not eliminate the problem. Older teens and adult children who wouldn't be caught dead in the casino with their parents still stormed the hotels. And adults still liked the prestige of going to a show at a famous place. On *The Brooklyn Bridge,* the characters recite the whole litany of big hotels they crashed in a prideful reminiscence.[28]

Most entertainers didn't really like to play the bungalow colonies, but it was money. They especially didn't like playing the colonies late, at "one or two in the morning." As performer Hal Richardson recalled, "you'd walked in through those torn screen doors. There'd be a bottle on every table." Bungalow colony facilities were often the pits. Hot dressing rooms; no air-conditioning. "You change in the back. People peek in through the broken window [shades]." The heat on the stage was oppressive, and in most colonies there were no spotlights, only ceiling lights." Richardson remembers working the SES Bungalows: "[and when I] opened my mouth to sing, a giant moth flew in. I almost choked. I spit the moth out. 'That moth,' I told the audience, 'does that every week. He loves that song.'"[29] I remember seeing the same

137

thing happen to a performer at The Aladdin Hotel. Moths were regulars in casinos, drawn by the lights.

By the mid 1950s, the hotel casino was on its way out and the air-conditioned nightclub was coming in. A whole new pattern was emerging because nightclubs have tables, and table seating is controlled by a *maitre d'*. While you could still sneak into the hotels, you couldn't sit down, except in the bars or the cocktail lounges, which were usually separate from the central action. Most hotels built their new nightclubs on the large side as a hedge against future expansion. Since they had extra room, especially when they had a slow weekend, hotels encouraged people to pay at the door and attend shows. Many hotels in the 1960s and early 1970s even started advertising on the local radio stations and in the newspapers, inviting the public in to see the shows. This revenue was pure gravy, since the fixed costs of overhead and talent were in place. The hotel owners would not only collect an admission fee (at first from three to seven dollars depending on the hotel), but they would also sell a drink or two. My favorite part of hotel nightclubs was that, in the spirit of making everything easy for guests, all of the big hotels had children's drum sticks on the table. You could simply bang the stick on the Formica tabletop to make appreciative noise and spare your hands the arduous task of clapping.

Hotels also started to push for people to buy a package deal—dinner and a show. The most popular of these evenings were Saturdays and holidays, such as the Sunday before Labor Day, when a cocktail party and an *hors d'oeuvre* buffet were also included. The abundance and the ambience of these evenings were very much like those in a Jewish wedding of the period, and this atmosphere is caught beautifully in the wedding sequence of the movie *Goodbye Columbus*.[30] By the mid 1960s at Richman's, going out to the hotels was a regular part of the season. Mother, by popular demand, started giving her Fourth of July party a week before the Fourth and her Labor Day party a week before Labor Day— because Mother, her second husband, Sam Levenstein, and most of our guests formed the silk-suited, mink-stole-clad Richman contingent, who tramped off triumphantly to The Flagler, The Pines, Brown's, or one of the other once-haughty hotels where lines had formerly been drawn between guests and bungalow people. I vividly remember when Molley Rabinowitz, Irving's mother and the last of our long-time crew to get a mink stole (an *Hadassah tallit*), announced proudly in her richly accented English while modeling her new acquisition on the lawn: "Look everyone! Now I've gots what all the ladies has gots!"

Several of our guests would occasionally join the neighbors, the Yustmans and the Puttermans, who fairly regularly went off for Saturday night at The Aladdin—a less gala and less expensive treat. I went along on several of the major holiday forays, and I always remember fondly the time my old college roommate, Dr. Alan Marks, came to visit from Boston. Mrs. Yustman turned to Mrs. Putterman and whispered, "Look at him! A doctor, and he eats pickles with his hands!" The poor woman didn't know that Alan, a psychiatrist, could read lips. "That's right, ladies," he said, waving his pickle spear. "I eat pickles with my hands." The arbiters of taste were very quiet for the rest of the evening. Today the large hotels still welcome outsiders, but it's been years since we've gone. Certainly we have not gone since my mother retired from running the colony in 1980. We have, however, once a summer, just gone over to The Aladdin to see the show for Mother's sake. On one of the last trips, we heard the Yiddish *klezmer* great Dave Tarras (1897–1989) play. He was sensational and it was just months before his death.[31]

My favorite hotel remembrances derive from one of our most unforgettable tenants, Mary Cohen, who manufactured "Baylen Corn Plasters," was her own saleslady, and sold wholesale drugs on the side. She had learned the business from her husband, who, before I met him, had a stroke and could not speak. The Cohens met my father through his business, and one thing led to another and they became our tenants. Mrs. Cohen, as everyone called her, was a marvelously flamboyant woman who wore flashy clothing, outlandish jewelry, and carried everything off *con brio*. She was a superb raconteur of slightly risque jokes and a wonderful singer of traditional Yiddish songs. She had style. One summer's end, when she was preparing to go home and the back of her car was crammed and looked unsightly, she spread her mink coat over the load to make it look more attractive. No one, by the way, thought it was unusual that she had a mink coat with her in the summer.

Mary Cohen had two daughters. Both were at our place on occasion, and one, "Jeannie Reynolds," is an entertainer who played the Catskills until two years ago, as well as New York and Florida. We always tried to catch Jeannie in one of her shows. Over the years, we've watched her change from a blond sexpot singer to a Sophie Tucker-style singer-comedian. With Jeannie as a tenant we also got an insight into the life of the show people who worked the Borscht Belt in its most active period.

Young Jeannie would wait each day for calls telling of her bookings for that evening, which was the customary way that all but big star performers were treated. Very often she did three or four shows a night, with a bungalow colony pushed in there at about eleven. The shows at colonies were usually late starting, because performers got paid less and it was always less prestigious to play the colonies. Jeannie was a freelancer and not a Charlie Rapp contract player.

A couple of times, I went along with Jeannie and her husband, Hal Schleifer, on an evening's work, and it was impressive. They went from hotel to hotel to bungalow colony to a hotel—all at close tolerance—often driving five to twenty miles between shows at breakneck speeds on back roads. They had just enough time for Jeannie to get out of the car and change her sweaty dress, and for Hal, who was her accompanist, to distribute her music to the band. After an evening with Hal and Jeannie, I understood the significance of the ritual you'd see while a band was playing for a dance act—folders of music would be passed out. This meant that the singer had arrived. While the dance act was taking their bows, their music was already being collected so that they could be ready to go on to the next place.

At the places that had full-time bands and classier production values, Jeannie and Hal rehearsed in the afternoon. At other places, like the colonies, it was purely sight-reading. Jeannie's work was made easier by Hal who, as her accompanist, took care of the musical side and could fill in when the band stank. He also went to beautician school to learn how to keep her bleached-blond hair looking right. A few times Jeannie and Hal led my father and mother and a few other brave friends on a whirlwind caravan from place to place on a Saturday night.

It was interesting to see Jeannie, the glamorous creature at night, doing her laundry the next day, looking pretty much like most housewives—albeit with a better figure. Jeannie and Hal had a very successful, if uncelebrated career, which paid for nice homes in the Catskills and in the New York area and Florida. Along the way they raised a family, and Jeannie, today, loves to talk about her grandkids. Some of her entertainer friends came to visit Richman's—they looked so ordinary off the stage. The greatest contrast between performance and real-life appearance was evident in performers who relied on a lot of make-up. When I worked at Kassack's one weekend, they had a troop of female impersonators— "The Jewel Box Review." When the performers came to rehearse, I was around out of curiosity, and I never saw a drabber looking crew, except for clowns. When I ran a day camp, we would often rent a clown for our July Fourth party— and here, too, a drab person would show up, ask where he could make up, and emerge with an entirely different personality—even when off stage.

One performer whose stage persona was very close to her ordinary self was Mother's friend, Lucille Blackton (*née* Schwartz). Lucille was a frustrated would-be-opera-star, who I knew as a great mountain of a woman with a glorious voice. She had done bit roles on Broadway and in road companies, most notably as Mrs. Pomerantz in *Fiorello,* when she met her future husband, Henry LeClair (born Cohen), who had originated the role of Declaration signer Robert Livingston in the Broadway play *"1776!"* In downtime they toured the Catskills. He weighed at least a hundred pounds less than she did, and it was an unforgettable spectacle when they sang "Sweethearts." In later years, Henry and Lucille moved to Florida where Lucille sang in the professional choirs of a synagogue and a Methodist Church. "You can't make a living from one God," Lucille lamented. A phone call from Florida alerted us to what was the last time we saw Henry perform. He was on the short-lived *Mary Tyler Moore* comedy revue as a member of the comedic "Lew Grant Dancers."

When I am feeling nostalgic for the hectic Catskill era, I put my copy of *Jeannie Reynolds Remembers* on the phonograph and hum along to her performance of Hal's arrangement of "Mama." Hal and Jeannie sold the albums themselves after their shows.[32] Other acts also peddled their own records and tapes at the back of casinos and nightclubs whenever they could.

The Borscht Belt has been characterized as low-brow in its entertainment and cultural values, and mostly with good reason. A high point in a movement to bring culture to the Catskills, and to hotel and bungalow colony guests, was the establishment of the Empire State Music Festival in Ellenville, which had just been connected to the heart of the resort industry by the opening of the new Route 52. Bill Rose, a local gentile banker from Ellenville, was the principal mover behind the festival, and he attracted money from several, prominent, local Jewish families, including the Resnicks and the Slutskys. A festival tent was built, and soon "the new Route 52 was jammed with guests from Monticello, Liberty, Fallsburg, Glen Wild, . . . and all the other resort towns that were, on the new road, only half an hour from Ellenville."[33] I was there and attended events for the life of the festival. People came that first season to see *La Boheme* and *Madame Butterfly* and symphonic performances. The first season came to a premature halt when the hurricane destroyed the tent. Rebuilt for the next season, the festival tried for larger gates with Broadway musicals, as well as high culture. There was a third and a fourth season, but "ticket sales could not raise enough revenue" and the Civic Association, the festival's parent association, never got expected state support. Perhaps most devastating was Bill Rose's arrest. He was helping to support the festival by very creative banking. There was no fifth season and Ellenville never became a second Tanglewood, as hoped.[34] Over the years, various summer theaters have been in the area, however, while they draw some bungalow people, theater has never been important to the region. The oldest and most successful theater in the region, now approaching the age of fifty, is at Forestburg. Sullivan County Community College, which opened in the 1960s, also brought to the region some cultural opportunities that appeal to a small audience of summer visitors.

More in line with Catskills' taste has been the Monticello Raceway, a harness track that opened in June 1958. While never the success its supporters had expected, the raceway has continued to attract bungalow people.[35] I remember groups of people from many colonies going out to the track during the week. Still in operation, it also hosts a large flea market very popular with people from the bungalows on holidays and Sundays. Today, many in the Catskills want gambling to help their resorts. In a grotesque move, county leaders are now trying to reconfigure the raceway into an Oneida or a St. Regis Mohawk Indian Reservation so a gambling casino can be built there.[36]

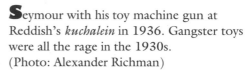
Seymour with his toy machine gun at Reddish's *kuchalein* in 1936. Gangster toys were all the rage in the 1930s. (Photo: Alexander Richman)

Irwin in a canvas chair, 1941. These folding chairs were very popular in the 1930s and 1940s. The cloth at the top was part of a canopy that could be opened for shade. (Photo: Alexander Richman)

Irwin and Seymour on the gravel and crushed-stone driveway, circa 1942. Note the white-washed stones that lined the driveway. Very labor intensive, you had to move them when you cut the grass. While riding his tricycle, Irwin hit one of these stones, went flying, and knocked out his front teeth. (Photo: Alexander Richman)

In 1943, World War II was on and kids wanted to be soldiers. Ida Miron, "*der alte* Miron's" sister, is on the walk. (Photo Alexander Richman)

Clowning around on the lawn, circa 1945. Normy and Philyne Roth were good friends and their parents long-time tenants and friends of the Richmans. Bertha Richman and their mother, Zena, met when they were both new-lyweds. (Photo: Seymour Richman)

Baseball was an important time filler, as was trick photography. In 1947, your camera was a simple Kodak Brownie, so you pinned the ball to the bat. No one was allowed to play baseball so close to the bungalows. You played in the farm pasture across the road where you always had to watch for cow patties. (Photo: Leonard Roth)

The front porch (1948) on the big house was always a popular place to play, except from one to four in the afternoon when Grandpa Richman took his nap in the parlor-bedroom behind the windows.
(Photo: Seymour Richman)

The most common of all childhood pastimes at bungalows or in New York City: Siblings fight siblings. Lenny Roth has just subdued kid-sister Philyne, circa 1946. Irwin and his mother have many vivid memories of fights between Irwin and Seymour. Seymour always tried to drown Irwin in the Neversink. Unfortunately, for posterity's sake, no one ever recorded any of these bouts, and they were too busy to do it themselves. Irwin was usually gasping for breath.
(Photo: Seymour Richman)

Seymour and Lenny box on the side lawn, circa 1947. The old bungalows built just six years before are nicely nestled in among the trees. Note the white-washed rocks that edge the driveway and the newly planted plum tree on the right.

The three Tobachnicks, children of a tenant, play wheelbarrow on the side lawn, c. 1948. The aim was to see how far the group could get before they tripped over each other. Note the Adirondack chairs, which were painted red and pale green.

Irwin and Seymour sit on the river rocks in 1945. A hike down to stony 'Sandy Beach' along the Neversink was a summer treat for the kids. The abundant river rocks allowed for building a fire place. The campfire was used for grilling hot dogs and toasting marshmallows. (Photo: Leonard Roth)

Main Street, Looking East, Woodbourne, N. Y.

Woodbourne, circa 1950, before the disastrous fire. On the left are Kanowitz's Dairy, Bernstein's Five-and-Ten, Smiley's Bar, Lebed's Candy Store, and Herben's Grocery. The building with the shed roof dormer housed Dominion's Barber Shop. The old Woodbourne Bridge is visible in the background.

Religion

Before Joey Adams's mother would rent at Mrs. Boxer's *kuchalein* in the 1920s, she insisted that the place be strictly kosher. The *"farmeka"* assured her, "We have two stoves—one for dairy and one for meat, and even our iceboxes are kosher."[1] These concerns weakened as New York's Jews acculturated. By the time traditional bungalow colonies were in their heyday, 1940–1965, the vast majority of American Jews were essentially secular. They were more likely to be cultural or gastronomic Jews than observant ones. Even among the hotels, only a few were religiously observant—and these were clearly talked about as being bizarre.[2] "The Pioneer Country" in Fallsburg emerged as a very orthodox hotel after World War II, and I remember my father and some tenants talking about this strange place where they put a chain across the driveway on Saturday. Were there ultraorthodox bungalow colonies? Possibly, but I didn't hear of them until the late 1950s. Now, in the 1990s, the orthodox form is dominant; I discuss this variant in "An Age of Change," Chapter 14.

My time spent around large bungalow colonies indicated to me that they were usually very secular. The occasional orthodox or even observant tenants kept quiet about their practices and kept to themselves. As I indicated earlier, the weekend, especially Friday night and Saturday, was dedicated to fun. Those who were religiously observant simply faded into the background. Colonies that had luncheonettes or fountains usually sold *tref,* and on-site stores often sold nonkosher foods as well. Many households did keep kosher, but it was not a prevalent concern. In my years of working in and directing day camps, I never encountered any parental concern about religious observation. For example, to the question, "Was the ice cream the kids had for snack kosher?" I have no answer now. We simply were not concerned about the issue. It never came up.

At Richman's, our religious history is something I know intimately, and here I witnessed many changes over a period of forty-some years. Grandma and my mother kept a kosher home and Grandpa was a leader of Woodbourne's Jewish community and the long-time president of Congregation B'nai Israel, an orthodox congregation. Like many facets of Grandpa, his religious practices were unique. When he was in Woodbourne, he went to synagogue every Saturday, a practice he maintained (with my mother's nagging in his later years) until he was in his early nineties. In the winter, he spent his Saturdays with his cronies, eating, drinking, and playing cards at a Turkish bath, or as he would say, "*ein bord.*" Religion was a summer thing for him. Occasionally, a half-hearted suggestion was made to Seymour and me that we should be quieter on *Shabbos,* but there was never any real follow-through.

No one else in the family regularly went to religious services, and Father was actively indifferent about going to *shul* (synagogue). He worshiped at the card table from nine in the morning on. Grandpa, to my knowledge, never ate *chazar* (pig) or seafood (pork of the sea), but he had no qualms about eating *tref* outside the family circle. I remember, however, the outrage when we went to New Jersey to visit relatives in the late 1940s and were served nonkosher steaks by cousin Sadie. Grandpa didn't say anything there, but for months thereafter the insult was a recurrent topic of conversation. Grandpa had no compunction about riding on the Sabbath or turning on the lights. As a matter of fact, after he came home from *shul* on Saturday, he would have his lunch, take his customary nap, get up, shave again (he was meticulous), and emerge in his usual country attire of shorts—no shirt. When it was cool, he put a kerchief around his neck! While we always had a traditional Friday evening menu of chicken soup, gefilte fish, and roast chicken, we never observed any ritual with it. The same was true of Saturday. None of the rest of us changed out of our casual clothes.

There are all levels of observance of the injunction against work on the Sabbath. Our long-time tenants the Dubofskys were orthodox. Mister Dubofsky said his prayers every morning and put on his *tefillin,* or phylacteries. He wore a yarmulke when he prayed and ate, but not at other times. On occasion, he would join our neighbor Mr. Yustman and Grandpa on the walk into town to *shul*. The Dubofskys were older than most of our tenants during the 1940s and 1950s. During World War II, both of their sons served in the military. Most of our other tenants had young children. Mister Dubofsky didn't ride or turn on the lights during the Sabbath, but, thankfully, he did flush the toilet. Conversely, we occasionally had tenants who fried bacon, whose pungent odor is easily recognized and was familiar even to most of those who kept kosher homes.

In the 1950s, we had a colorful religious character, Mr. Menaker, who was our tenant on an almost involuntary basis. He was the second husband of Mrs. Miron's sister. "Old Man Miron" was one of Grandpa's millionaire buddies. The Mirons and Mrs. Menaker liked being at Richman's, and, clearly, Mr. Menaker's concerns never mattered much. Menaker stories became part of our folklore.

Because I worked at camp Monday through Friday, I did my lawn and garden maintenance on Saturday and was regularly excoriated by Mr. Menaker. He would loudly proclaim to others within my earshot, "Look at him, he works on *Shabbat,* like an animal." He also assured me that anything I touched on Saturday would die. Years later, when I told this story to my colleague Dr. Nancy Tischler, a woman brought up in a different religious tradition, she said, "Funny, I was told that about Sunday."

Most people gave Mr. Menaker wide berth, they just didn't want to hear him. One weekend, one of our tenants had a Christian visitor. On Saturday, the hapless woman sat down on the lawn near Menaker and lighted a cigarette (everyone else knew better—no one stopped smoking; they just didn't do it near him). Menaker fumed, *"Zee nor! Sie schmuked en Shabbos vie ein goyite."* ("Look! She smokes on Saturday like a Christian.") It never dawned on him that a Christian could be in his compound. The visitor's hostess vindictively, with barely suppressed glee, informed Menaker that the woman was not Jewish.

One Sabbath, Menaker was railing about impious dress on *Shabbos,* and especially the way women dressed. While people would walk away from him when they wanted a smoke, they were not willing to change dress patterns. This was the age of shorts and halters for women. "Look," Menaker pointed at a tenant, "if my wife dressed like that, I'd kill myself." Menaker's wife, a very portly, good-natured lady perked up. "Menaker," she said, "if I thought you meant it, I'd go out and buy some shorts today."

Many of our families lit *Shabbos* candles even if they followed no other observances. My mother always lit candles in a five-light *lecht,* or candelabra. When she went out of the bungalow business, she stopped. "I don't have to anymore," she said, when I asked her why. Most of our tenants brought inexpensive glass or brass candlesticks with them. Some simply used flat river rocks as a candle base, adhering the candles with melted wax.

My brother Seymour's death had a traumatic effect on the family. Such tragedy can either strengthen faith or weaken it. In our family, it weakened it. Mother seldom lit candles in the city afterward, and slowly, the rules of *kasruth* (keeping kosher) became less important to her. In both country and city we had separate dishes for meat and dairy, but as the years went by I noticed more defilement of dishes as they were indiscriminately used. Our guests either didn't notice or didn't care. No one ever questioned the kosher nature of the food served at parties. I know, and knew then, that the meat we served was religiously tainted, because the slicer we used at Lebed's had been in the luncheonette. It had been used to cut *tref* of the most egregious sort.

My maternal grandmother kept to religion a bit stronger than most. At age seventy, we finally lured her to a Chinese restaurant. "Don't tell me what I'm eating, but it's delicious." During the last summers of her life, Grandma Schwebel (then remarried to Jack Nashofer) summered at Richman's in one of the old bungalows. As a treat, I would bring her an order of shrimp in lobster sauce, her favorite, which she always ate on the screened porch from a paper plate with a plastic fork. No overt *tref* was going to enter her house.

The most religious activity we saw was on those years when Rosh Hashona came the Thursday and Friday after Labor Day. Most people stayed on the extra week, and on Rosh Hashona, everyone dressed up. Even my father went to *shul* for the last hour of each day's service—a custom in which I joined him. I have some wonderful home movies taken during such a Rosh Hashona in the 1950s. About six of the men (including me) went to *shul.* On the return trip, I walked quickly to arrive ahead of the others. When they came back, I was ready to photograph them as they walked in the driveway. Then I stopped the camera, and most of the colony, in their holiday finery, went out on the road and I photographed them again, appearing as if they were all coming from *shul.*

By the 1960s, our clientele had shifted. Because we lacked a pool, only our older tenants stayed with us. Most of them were European born, and as they aged the religious practices of their youth became more important. With most of the men in retirement, they had more time on their hands. Cards and TV couldn't fill it all. It was in the late 1960s that I learned that the holiday of *Tish A' Bov* existed. A holiday of commemoration, you were not to indulge in idle entertainment. My mother seized on the festival as an excuse not to have tenant parties. A few tenants, as mentioned earlier, used the holiday as an occasion to go to a hotel, since only the super orthodox hotels ever observed the holiday. Mother also took advantage of *Tish A' Bov* by joining with her hotel-hopping friends.

Overt or public religious observances at our place were rare before the 1960s. Some had very special personal attachment, like Seymour's bar mitzvah party. This event was planned to be on the lawn, but it rained, so the massive event was shifted into the house. There were tables and chairs everywhere, and during the day about two hundred people trooped through the house to feast on Grandma Richman's and Mother's cooking and baking. The most common celebration was less elaborate. It was a *kiddush,* which is a ritual celebration of bread and wine that follows religious services on Saturday. A simple *kiddush* was rendered virtually every week by the Yustmans in their house for a few fellow worshipers, but at Richman's elaborate *kiddushim* were given by individuals to celebrate an impending or past bar mitzvah, an engagement, or some other happy event. In my mother's golden-age club today, they celebrate a completely secular *kiddush*—when someone's family marks a special event, members buy cake and ice cream for all. I have home movies of a 1950s *kiddush* celebrating an engagement. While a few men, including Grandpa, are wearing shirts and ties, everyone else is in informal attire. The outdoor *kiddush* used our Ping-Pong table as a buffet. Wine and liquor were served as well as *challah,* cake, herring, and gefilte fish.

Woodbourne and most other small and large towns in the Catskills have or had a synagogue. I had considered writing about the synagogues, when I learned of a very ambitious study being undertaken by Dr. Maurie Sacks of Montclair State College. A portfolio of these synagogues and a list of past and present synagogues is included in Oscar Israelowitz's *Catskills Guide.*[3] Many are in trouble today, others have vanished. Fewer winter people care, and the very orthodox prefer makeshift synagogues of their own—usually in the former casino of their colony. Most synagogues had a *kiddush* every Saturday, given by a happy congregant or the congregation as a whole. In *The Rise and Fall of the Borscht Belt,* a former Loch Sheldrake hotel owner reminisces about elaborate *kiddushim* at the local synagogue (on the lake) to which local hotels, including her own, sent trays of fish, herring, and other traditional delicacies.[4]

147

The religious history of small town synagogues is interesting. Most are orthodox, even long after most of their congregants have left orthodoxy. Why? Because orthodox rabbis are in ample supply and they work more cheaply. In Woodbourne, the increasing orthodoxy manifested itself in the 1960s when the rabbi demanded a separate women's section in the *shul,* to be surrounded by a curtain. Prior to that, most women sat in the back, but no one said anything if a woman chose to sit with her family.

As the local *shuls,* with few exceptions, remained orthodox because of finances or tradition, more and more families with children moved their memberships to reformed and conservative congregations in Liberty, Monticello, or Ellenville. The more generous and affluent would often continue to belong to their local *shul* as well, but their major commitment was elsewhere. In a unique move, the synagogue in Livingston Manor came under the influence of a group of history-minded, liberal Jews who restored the synagogue to its original appearance, with a center *bema,* while converting it into a reformed congregation.

In the 1960s, our more religious tenants organized evening prayers in our garage. To have these prayers, one needed a *minyan,* ten Jewish men. At our small place, it was sometimes hard to get ten—at such times I was a tempting target. I tried to plan my days so I'd be long gone before sundown, but occasionally I was forced into one of the meetings—sitting there fuming, rather than praying. By the 1970s, there was always a *minyan* before the Saturday night parties. While I am sure there were similar observances at other small colonies in the 1970s and into the 1990s, I doubt that any such practice existed at large secular colonies. I know that I never witnessed one.

Summer Emergencies and Other Unforgettable Events

For the bungalow colony owner, the summer season was a series of disasters waiting to happen. Providing you rented, what could go wrong? Plenty. Would your tenants show up? After all, the only assurance you had was a deposit of twenty-five, fifty, or a hundred dollars. At larger, very popular colonies, most renting was done at the end of the summer and they had a payment schedule that would guarantee the owner at least 50 percent of the rental before summer started. At Richman's, we never had a "no show," but we did have one case of an unstable woman who "hated" the place two days after arrival. Since she was the sister-in-law of a friend, and we knew that she had, indeed, just come out of a mental hospital, her husband was given his money back. Although we never had a "no show," we did have several late cancellations. In this case the deposit would be given back if we could rent at full price, but I know of many colonies that would not, under any circumstances, give back a deposit—it was considered extra income. This was especially true during the halcyon postwar years.

Weather was always a problem. "The country's no good if the sun doesn't shine," Grandpa always said, and to this day my mother takes a rainy day as a personal affront. A dry summer could spell disaster if your water supply failed. A wet summer could also be a disaster, albeit a lesser one, because people would feel very cooped up. Bungalow colonies brought together a lot of people in small areas, as is remembered by Alvin Fertel, a junior high school administrator whose family escaped from the Bronx to a rather primitive colony during his early years.

> I went back about twenty-five or thirty years later to show it to my children. The building was still standing, even though it was abandoned. They couldn't get over the smallness of it, I mean the actual tininess of it. The entire bungalow wouldn't fit into a normal-size living room. The bedrooms were just big enough to accommodate two double beds with a space for one person to stand between them. The living room—there was no living room. There was just a very tiny kitchen, a three-burner stove, a wooden icebox, cold water. No shower. You took your shower in a community shower. The women washed their clothing in a community washtub.[1]

Overcrowding was not what he remembered the most, rather a "tremendous spirit of comradery. Plenty of kids my age."[2] But when weather stayed foul for long periods and kids were confined indoors with their mothers, comradery often gave way to irritation and then enmity. Kids' fights were common, but adult fights were not unknown. Bad weather could bring irritations over invaded kitchen space or some other real or imagined infraction to a boiling point, followed by name calling and occasional hair pulling. Fortunately, fathers were up during less of the summer. Their fights, though rare, were more violent.

Then there was the fear of disease. Chicken pox, measles, and whooping cough outbreaks were not unknown, and a few colonies in the 1940s and 1950s even had a polio case or two. This completely destroyed the summer, and usually the colony as families fled. No one would rent at a colony that had polio. With the coming of swimming pools, pinkeye infections were common, but manageable.

When I was six, I contracted bronchial pneumonia—a serious ailment in prepenicillin days—right before Memorial Day, and I was still suffering from lingering effects of the illness when the season came. I wasn't allowed to go swimming, so my grandparents devised an elaborate rouse to keep me from the water. They told me that every twenty years or so big monsters came to the river, and this was the year. Grandma would whisk me away on walks when everyone was going to the river. I, of course, not only wanted to go swimming, but wanted to see the monsters, too!

Tenants could hold the owners liable for personal injuries. Liability insurance was a must, and resorts generally had special seasonal policies by the 1960s, when America was becoming increasingly litigation conscious. Bigger colonies took other steps to protect themselves from a catastrophic judgement. One common ploy was to incorporate the colony and rent the operating rights to another corporation. Both corporations, of course, had the same shareholders. The operating corporation had no assets, and therefore there was no reason to sue it. The ownership corporation was protected by a massive first or second mortgage against the property held personally, as individuals, by the owner or owners. Neat, legal, and protective, this arrangement was explained to me by the operator of a large, successful colony.

In the course of having a lot of people around, injuries occurred. Occasional broken limbs and heart attacks were par for the course, especially at larger places. If they assumed epidemic proportion, they could put a pall on the summer. I was in Kassack's casino one evening when a visiting grandfather had a heart attack. Fortunately for the Kassacks and the other guests, the man walked out of the casino and then collapsed. The show went on and most people were unaware of what happened. Luckily, the grandfather survived. In a few weeks, he was back in the casino.

The most unusual accident I witnessed was at Kassack's Day Camp. A kid was sitting, watching the rehearsal of a play. His elbow was resting on the edge of the stage, and his head was cradled in his hand. When his elbow slipped, the kid's face hit the stage and he broke his nose. The boy's parents were upset that the insurance company would only pay the doctor's bill, plus a few hundred dollars, but eventually the claim was settled. Most injuries were more prosaic.

We were very fortunate at Richman's. The only time we had to file an insurance claim was when an elderly woman with high blood pressure climbed on a chair to change a lightbulb and fell. She claimed the chair was defective. The insurance company quickly settled the claim for the nuisance it was. More serious was the woman with undiagnosed uterine cancer who began to hemorrhage one night. Her mattress was ruined and, of course, she couldn't finish the season. Our most traumatic occurrence was in the 1970s when one of our long-time residents, an elderly gentleman, died of a heart attack while playing cards.

Beyond the major calamities, there were less cosmic events, like breakdowns in utility systems. During storms, electricity would often be cut off, and part of every well-equipped bungalow colony owner's larder was a supply of candles. One advantage of being Friday-night-candle-lighters was that most of our tenants had their own candles and candlesticks. Gas was another problem. Tenants with individual gas tanks would come running when their gas was out. "Get the gas man here right away!" Often it seemed that this happened on Friday when everyone was especially hyper. A telephone call would solve this problem, but not quickly enough for the lady who expected the gas to be delivered within fifteen minutes.

After we installed central hot water, there were breakdowns—usually one per summer, and usually early in the summer—when the long-idle system was cranked up. Owners would get complaints about every five minutes while waiting for the plumber to come. Naturally, all the plumber's customers were without hot water at that moment. So you waited. Waiting for plumbers was a way of life, not only for heating problems, but also for pump problems and those occasions when a kid dropped a toy down the toilet.

Then there were the septic tanks and the drainage fields. Would they hold up? This was a recurrent nightmare. Garbage disposal was another concern. Until the late 1950s, there was no public trash collection system in much of Sullivan County. Large and small colonies with a lot of land solved the problem by having their own dumps. Some large colonies hired trucks to haul their garbage to the county dump. At Richman's, Grandpa burned the trash in a bottomless, forty-gallon drum set up on cinder blocks. This primitive incinerator was hidden behind a copse of trees. Tenants would put their trash in the barrel and Grandpa would fire it up every afternoon after his nap.

Noncombustibles (broken glass, cans) were shoveled up once a year by a goy who hauled them to the dump. Fortunately trash was generated in relatively small quantities then, before the packaging explosion. Once we had regular outside collection, we built a small garbage shed or "house" near the road and the tenants would dump their trash into cans there. At a number of larger colonies, the handymen collected trash from each bungalow so that tenants wouldn't have to carry it themselves. Garbage collection was very unreliable, and recurrent questions were: Would the garbage man show up? Was the garbage house too full? Did a skunk or raccoon get into the garbage house?

City folks and country insects are always a mismatch. Wet summers were especially bad because of all the mosquitos that hatched. Tenants frequently complained to the owner, who could generally do nothing about the problem until the DDT years, when lots of larger colonies had their grounds sprayed regularly with the insecticide. Ant infestations were common, and we, like many places, often resorted to an exterminator if home remedies didn't work.

The worst problem of all, prior to the DDT era, was flies. The insects would appear in droves and perch on screen doors, drawn by the scent of food. Fly killing was a major occupation for all ages, and prowess with a fly swatter was highly applauded. "Flit," a popular pre-DDT insecticide, was used periodically. It was applied using a piston-driven "Flit Gun," or sprayer. Food was covered and tightly sealed and little kids shooed away from the "Flitting." As older kids, Seymour and I were Flit appliers, which gave us a sense of power. During the war, drugstores and hardware stores featured Flit signs, which promised that Flit destroyed bugs and showed a Flit Gun aimed at mosquitos and houseflies with the faces of Tojo Hideki, Hitler, and Mussolini.

Every indoor space was adorned with strips of flypaper hanging from lighting fixtures. Watching flies getting stuck was always worth some time. Unfurling and hanging fresh flypaper was treacherous. Would the paper come out right, or tangle? Would you get it hung without getting caught in it? Flypaper was especially unpleasant for kids. It could interfere with your paper airplane, or if you jumped inside the house during a rainy day you might brush against it. Worst of all, you might pull it down and have it wrap around your face and hair, transferring gobs of sticky residue. Ceilings were often low, and flypaper is a good thirty inches long. A lot of kids liked to catch flies by hand and pull off their wings to make "trained flies" who could walk!

Screens were part of the defense against flies, and the walls reverberated with the calls: "Make sure the screen is closed!" They were referring to the door that had a spring-closing mechanism, which made a very satisfying bang when slammed. Running kids enjoyed slamming screen doors, and parents reacted automatically, "Don't run! Don't slam the door!"

The most dramatic natural catastrophe was the flooding that resulted from the torrential rains caused by Hurricane Diane in August 1955. This was the storm that destroyed the Empire State Music Festival's tent.[3] The *New York Times* reported that "large sections of southeastern New York State, including heavily populated resort areas, lay under swirling flood waters."[4] In the Monticello area, eight inches of rain fell in twenty-four hours, ending 19 August. The deluge came as part of the twenty-one inches that had fallen since 7 August of that wet summer.[5] The worst-hit Catskill town was Ellenville, in nearby Ulster County, where Mayor Eugene Glusker reported "chaotic conditions" with hundreds homeless and "several streams flowing through the town."[6] "In Sullivan County, an emergency was declared as farmlands and villages along the Delaware and other streams were flooded."[7] (Our Neversink River is a Delaware tributary.)

The terror and anguish of a bungalow colony being caught up in the midst of a disastrous flood is conjured graphically in *Bungalow Nine*.[8] I remember the rain vividly. I was eighteen and cooped-up as a day camp counselor with howling kids all day. The camp grounds were muddy, and a small, usually placid, stream near the camp house was a raging torrent. I also remember going to town to see the river. The water was so high that you could touch it from the bridge, which was normally twenty feet above the water level.

Most Woodbourne resorts were spared flood damage because the Neversink in and around Woodbourne is generally much lower than the developed areas. This was not the case with a new colony built down the road from us, whose inaugural year was 1955. Before he built the place, the owner of the new River Haven Colony was warned by many people, including Grandpa, that the farmland he had bought flooded. He interpreted the warnings as jealousy and countered that 'the state engineers in Albany had informed him that the site would not flood.' Early Saturday, 20 August, at two in the morning, men in boats had to rescue tenants from the two lower double bungalows. The next year, normal spring floods hit the lower bungalows again. The owner then moved them to higher ground. As you pass the colony, now a well-kept co-op, forty years later, you might wonder about the two bungalows up near the road, situated so that they have no relation to the rest of the place.

Two events of major historic importance happened in summertime during my bungalow years. One was the dropping of the atomic bomb on Hiroshima and Nagasaki, and the other, following in due course, was the end of World War II. The images of both events are still vivid. Their accounts reached us on hot August days. The news of the bomb was awesome. The second section of the novel *Summer on a Mountain of Spices* is entitled "First Steps in the Age of the Atom."[9] At the time, I was younger than the novel's young protagonist, Harry Craft, who had previously learned about the atom in chemistry classes at New York City's elite Stuyvesant High School.[10] But that day as I sat, at age eight, in the dining room in Woodbourne, I conjured images of a mushroom cloud and tried to imagine the "rain of ruin" brought by the new weapon, just as Harry did as he sat in the Card Room of the Willow Spring Hotel near Monticello. President Harry Truman announced a new age. "It is a harnessing of the basic power of the Universe," he reported. "The force from which the sun draws its power has been loosed against those who brought the war to the Far East."[11]

I did not consciously realize the way in which this event would impact upon my life. In the Cold War years, I had a special reason for wanting to go to the country—the Russians weren't going to bomb Woodbourne. While I was growing up, many a thunderstorm gave kids reason to believe that New York had been bombed. Loud thunderclaps without rain evoked a special terror. We, the children of the Atomic Age, were being bombed! In a 1950s publicity piece, "Published by the Sullivan County Board of Supervisors," you read the usual reasons for visiting a vacation area—sports, shopping, scenery, entertainment, "no mosquitoes," and so on. You are also tempted with an extra incentive: "Sullivan County hotels, bungalows, and rooming houses are far outside potential atomic bomb blast areas; as emergency housing, they form a vital part of the Civilian Defense Program."[12]

The end of World War II, following the bombing by a few days, was a rare time. Most of us were playing in the woods when the news came, and when we heard about it we wanted to go to town to mill with everyone else, but the mothers had their own plan. No going to town! Too many people would be there. We would have a big victory party on Saturday when the men came up. While visiting town was out, the sounds of victory were in the air. Hotel loudspeakers blared, sirens wailed. The Woodbourne volunteer fire department truck clanged up and down the road. People from other colonies stopped by on the way to town—whether they knew us or not. Everyone wanted to talk about the end of the war. Strangers hugged strangers.

In the ensuing days, food rationing or no, by hook or by crook, each woman went to the kitchen and cooked her specialty in a unity of effort I never witnessed before or since. Delicious odors redolent of onions, garlic, cinnamon, paprika, and bay leaf enveloped the whole colony as the women chopped, stewed, and roasted. *Kugels*—noodle and potato—and *kishkas,* roasts and *tzimmes,* chickens and stuffed *helzel* poured out of the bungalows and the main house on platters and in pots; proudly and joyously carried—all to be followed by *rugelach,* cookies, cakes, tortes, *mandelbrot,* pies, and even *taiglach.*[13]

On the day of the party, unique in my memory, all of our outdoor tables plus a few carried out from the bungalows were set up on the shady lawn between the main house and the old bungalow. The whole colony and weekend guests sat down together to feast. Kids milled around, Grandpa was free with his liquor, and soda flowed. While only the Dubofskys had sons in the war, everyone else had a parent, a brother, an uncle, or a fiance in the military. People joked, danced, kissed, ate, and drank. They made toasts, but nobody offered up any prayers. We were all too happy. In later years I have talked to many bungalow people. All of them remember V-J celebrations at their colony. It was the supreme event.

On a less global scale is Woodbourne's greatest trauma, which started at 4:30 A.M. on 3 February 1964.[14] A newspaper deliveryman from Port Jervis saw flames, and he and Sidney Goldstein, a Woodbourne insurance man, "roused the sleeping families" in town. "Saved by the alert duo were Sam Smilowitz, asleep in an apartment over his bar, . . . and Mr. and Mrs. Eddie Chertkoff," who lived over the Lebed's drugstore. The flames moved quickly: "By the time Goldstein emerged from rousing those over Lebed's, his car was trapped by falling utility lines and was destroyed." The flames went from side to side and wind sent flaming embers across the street. "The fire destroyed Smiley's Bar, where it apparently originated, and leveled a Laundromat owned also by Samuel Smilowitz." Other businesses burned out or ruined included Lebed's pharmacy, Godlin's drugstore, Frank's Taxi Stand, Kanowitz's, and "the recently remodeled Sylvia's Beauty Shop."[15] Five buildings and eleven businesses were destroyed. While everyone rebuilt, and, indeed, "a modern shopping plaza" did "greet summer visitors when they return[ed] to Woodbourne,"[16] the town of my childhood was gone. The town of the heights of the tourist industry was gone. Young Jeffrey Chertkoff's parakeet "Whitey" was the fire's only animated victim.[17] Jeffrey, who had been my camper at Kassack's Day Camp for several summers, was an unlucky person. In the 1990s, after having moved to New York City, Jeffrey became one of Woodbourne's first victims of AIDS.

In the late 1980s, New York State would further change Woodbourne by demolishing the steel-truss bridge that crossed the Neversink where it bisects town, replacing it with a standard highway bridge. A landmark was gone forever. The new signs that welcome you to Woodbourne ironically bear images of that now destroyed icon.

The Day Camp

In 1953 when I first worked at a day camp, my salary was one hundred dollars, payable at the end of the summer, plus tips. My first paycheck from Meyer Furman's Day Camp bounced, returned for insufficient funds—Meyer soon made it good. I worked for him for two more summers because I liked the head counselor. When he left, so did I.

Like much in the bungalow business, the day camp concept was developed by the Catskill hotels, which quite early recognized that mothers would especially enjoy their holidays if the kids were out of sight for at least part of the time. By the 1920s, the larger hotels had children's dining rooms separate from the adults'. The day camp was a post–World War II introduction.[1] Which bungalow colony had the first day camp will probably never be known, but the time of the first one was probably 1950, because it was a very new field when I entered it in 1953. Day camps were offered to tenants as a premium service, that is, on a pay-per-child basis. However, at most places it was required that your child attend camp. At the onset, the fee varied from $35 to $75 per child, but this increased steadily, and by the end of the 1960s the fee was over $250 per child.[2] Like much else about the bungalow business during that period, the day camp was not usually a lush profit center. Although the largest camps could be very profitable, most owners could hope for no more than a modest profit and were happy if they broke even on the operation. The camp's purpose was to help rent bungalows. Day camps were an annoyance. Some owners tried to farm out the camps as concessions, and a few small companies ran day camps for various colonies for several years. However, the only way these companies could make any money was to skimp on everything from arts-and-crafts supplies to toilet paper. Parents rebelled, and colony owners generally ran their own camps by the mid 1950s.

Owners watched salary expenses, insurance, and supplies. Staff endured campers. Central to the camp was the "head counselor," or "camp director," who was usually a New York City school teacher or—more rarely—a suburban school teacher. The head counselor was paid a salary and provided with accommodations. This job was highly prized by those who wanted an affordable way to have their kids spend the summer in the mountains. The other more or less adult positions at the camps were the nursery counselor and the arts-and-crafts counselor. Apart from a smattering of college freshman and sophomores, who didn't really need money but were in the country for one reason or another, the counselors were high school students, with a minimum age of fifteen so that they could have legal "working papers." Some of the counselors were children of tenants—the terms of employment were tied to their parents' rental contract. There were also CITs, counselors-in-training, thirteen and fourteen years old, who were tired of being campers. They were always children of tenants and often excampers, going through that rough transition from paying customer to paid employee. Many CITs never made it through the summer. Most large colonies also had a lifeguard who was expected to give campers swimming lessons as part of his duties.

My first head counselor was Sol Ellman. He and his wife, Una (nursery school teacher and all around piano player), introduced me to camp work. They were among the very few gentle folk who went into the business. After four seasons, they left it. Their backgrounds had been in sleep-away camps, but now with two young children, they tried day camping to have family togetherness. They lived in an apartment on the ground-floor level of the barn that served as our camp house. Usually head counselors were housed in units on the grounds, and owners resented having to give up rent on these units. At some places, such as Kassack's, the owners rented accommodations for staff at less expensive colonies nearby.

I became a head counselor when I was twenty-one, and I was heartily disliked by many of my peers who looked upon me as a kid who was taking the food out of the mouth of a fellow teacher. Many places changed head counselors every year, a few kept the same ones for many years, and at a few, such as Damoshack's Woodland Colony, the head counselor was also the owner's son. Generally, I enjoyed working best with owners' sons on cooperative ventures. They didn't fear for their jobs and could make their own decisions. Brought up in the family that I was, I never thought of myself as exactly an employee and I never argued over resources with my employers, the Kassack's; they trusted me. The first year that I was an arts-and-crafts counselor, also my last year at Meyer Furman's, I was very disappointed with my tips. When I got home, my grandfather brought over to me a dish of grapes with two fifty dollar bills tucked into the fruit. He was implying, 'Why be concerned by cheapskates! You don't need the money!' In my camp career, I was a counselor for two years, arts-and-crafts counselor for three years, and head counselor for three years.

The camp season was eight weeks long and began the Monday after the Fourth of July and ended the Friday before Labor Day. Camp ran from nine to five, with an hour lunch break from twelve to one. At most places, the kids went home for lunch, although at a very few camps the kids were served lunch. Most camps welcomed "outside campers," and these kids carried their lunches or ate at the concession. Counselors took turns on lunch duty. Most resented this assignment, but the outsiders needed supervisors. Camp was Monday through Friday. Mothers were freed for extensive sessions of playing cards or mah-jongg and time at the pool. Pool times had some limitations for campers, however. While several colonies had camps large enough to support a separate, dedicated pool for campers, most others reserved specific pool times for camper use. At most camps, two swims a day were planned, eleven to noon, and two to three-thirty. Morning swims were especially popular with the counselors since kids could be dismissed for lunch right from the pool. Most day camps began with a flag-raising ceremony (at which we took attendance). We sang, "The More We Get Together," recited the Pledge of Allegiance, and sang "The Star Spangled Banner." I always insisted that my campers be lined up by groups, a useful technique I learned from the Ellmans. Every once in a while, a smart-mouthed kid would ask, "Why do I have to line up? Is this a concentration camp?" My answer was always direct: "Get in line for your number." Everyone in the 1950s knew the implication of that answer.

The campers were divided up into groups according to age and sex. Campers started at age three, and all preschoolers were in the nursery group. Most camps used a theme for naming the groups. Some used Indian tribes, others used plants or sports teams. At both Kassack's and Meyer Furman's, we used a western motif. The nursery group was the Papooses. Here we had a nursery teacher, one counselor to every six kids, and a CIT or two. Next came the Tenderfeet Boys and Girls, ages six and seven. The Cowboys and Cowgirls were eight to eleven, and the Ranchers and Rancherettes were twelve and thirteen. Group sizes varied, as did camp sizes. When younger kids were in larger supply, we could add other groups like the Buckaroos (ages ten and eleven). The minimum economic size for a camp was about 40 kids, the maximum I knew of was about 200, and the normative was 75 to 125. Smaller colonies often struggled for a few years with 20 or so kids, but they were doomed to failure.

No camp I ever saw was quite as gung ho as that at the fictional "Hector's Pond Colony," where little Toddy couldn't wait to get to camp on opening day:

> Toddy bounced across the grass shaking Mollie Cottontail into a frappé. As she broke into the circle of children at the flagpole before the casino, bugle call sounded. She was still breathing hard when a tall spare young man in his middle twenties addressed his forty-odd campers in tones fraught with drama. "Welcome to Hector's Pond Day Camp. I am Uncle Billy Weiss." He indicated a petite, pretty contemporary at his side. "This is Lois Weiss. I am your Chief, Aunt Lois is Senior Squaw of the Heckawah Indian Tribe. And you . . ." He motioned to his hearers with both arms spread. "You are the Heckawahs." After letting that fact register, he continued. "Each sub-tribe will have its own name. Your mission will be the winning of honors for your sportsmanship, swimming skills, arts and crafts, best camper, dramatics, singing, and so on. I know each and every maid and warrior here will have a wonderful, unforgettable summer as a Heckawah."
>
> The children were spellbound. It wasn't what Uncle Billy said. It was how. The year before, a couple whose names were anathema made an indifferent job of directing and diverting the children. But with his first words, Uncle Billy breathed vitality back into Hector's Day Camp.
>
> The new chief went on. "Now, my loyal Heckawahs, we begin the division into . . . tell me, please, what is the blond squawlet with the pigtails hiding in that box?"
>
> Half a dozen voices volunteered, "A bunny." Toddy remained mute before the omnipotent chief of all Heckawahs. Aunt Lois approached

and asked in the softest voices, "May I see your bunny?" Toddy suffused in blushes, moved the cloth cover aside. Aunt Lois and Uncle Billy peeked reverently. Straightening, Uncle Billy thundered in magnificent tones, "Behold!" The nature hutch of the Heckawahs has its first official inhabitant!" Toddy could scarcely breathe!"[3]

The day was divided into five activity periods—two in the morning and three in the afternoon. The daily (hoped for) standard was two swims. Aside from flag raising and lowering and milk and ice cream breaks, these were the only camp-wide activities. Parents paid an additional weekday fee for refreshments. In day camps with the parents nearby, you could not run swims like sleep-away camps did (and do)—swims everyday and in all weather, except thunderstorms. We had to be more discrete, so we always had to plan alternate events in case the weather was not perfect for swimming. Counselors liked swim time because all the kids were within a fenced-in area and easy to control and they had the extra help of the lifeguard. All kids were given "buddies," and at least once during the swim the lifeguard or the camp director would blow their whistle and everyone had to find their buddy—another control device.

One of our few effective disciplinary measures was to "dock" the miscreant for a few minutes. Mothers of often-disciplined kids would occasionally protest, "I pay money for my kids to have a good time and do whatever they want." We also had to provide activities for kids with colds whose parents did not want them in swimming. Usually a knock-hockey board would do. If we had a number of sick kids a counselor would be assigned to stay with them in the camp house. Notes from a camp paper:

Cowboys—We all enjoy swimming. We have swimming instruction every Tuesday and during the week we practice what we have learned. Some of the boys, Ken Shapiro, Jeff Slyper, and Gary Gindick, have learned to swim. Others are learning the dead man's float.

Tenderfeet—Another thing that we enjoy is swimming. We go swimming in the morning if the weather permits and in the afternoon. When we come back from swimming, we have cookies and milk. Following that we play in the sandbox or in the swings. After a busy day like this we go home very tired.

—Rachel[4]

Regular athletic times were devoted to softball, punch ball, basketball, volleyball, playground, field games, and tennis, if the colony had tennis courts. Other regular features included quiet games, music and drama, arts and crafts, and nature hikes. More notes from the camp paper:

The Tophands—The Tophands are learning the meaning of cooperation on the softball and volleyball fields. They have been learning that it takes only one man to lose a game, but the whole team's cooperation is needed to win it.

The Cowboys—This week was strenuous for the Cowboys. Their activities were varied. On Tuesday we played a three inning punchball game versus the Cowgirls. It was a good game in which both teams showed good sportsmanship. The score was nineteen to one, favor of the Cowboys.[5]

Each Monday a schedule would be posted with the week's activities. "Field games" was really a free-for-all time. Kids would go to one of our field areas where they were allowed to do anything they liked, short of killing or maiming one another. "Quiet games" were played in and around the camp house and included Ping-Pong, knock hockey, board games, and cards. A schedule would include a mix of all the events. The payoff from the music and drama periods were shows put on for the parents. These shows were usually performed in the casino at seven o'clock on Fridays—so that most parents were in the country, but early enough so that the evening wasn't shot for more adult pursuits. Some camps did camp-wide shows. We, however, would do four group-specialized shows: Papoose, Tenderfeet, Cowboy and Cowgirl, and Rancher and Rancherette. Our nursery show was the standard fifteen minutes of "Twinkle, Twinkle, Little Star" and other songs the nursery teachers used. Of course, all these tots had to do was appear on stage and the audience would cheer enthusiastically.

CAMP SHOW BIG SUCCESS

Saturday, July 31, the Cowboys and Cowgirls put on a show in the Casino. The show was completely made up of western songs and dances. Some of these were: "Home on Furman's Range," "Virginia Reel," "Ragtime Cowboy Joe," and "I Wish I Was Single Again." The children did a magnificent job. Credit also goes to Sheila S., Sheila D., and Una

Ellman. Special credit goes to Una for her very fine work in putting the show over. All the parents, I am sure, are duly proud of their children.

—O. Garston and A. Nathanson.[6]

I preferred to use show music for groups. These performances lasted about thirty to forty minutes and featured music of Berlin, Porter, and Rogers and Hammerstein. I'll never forget the image of a vampy, very pretty, eleven-year-old Elyse Duberstein leaning against a lamppost singing, "Love for Sale." No one complained and she brought the house down.

The Ranchers and Rancherettes did a full-scale musical, which I usually chose based on the kids—since Kassack's group was fairly stable, I knew my stars. My last summer we did *My Fair Lady,* because I knew Steve Feigenbaum was a twelve-year-old Henry Higgins. Today he's a CPA practicing in New Jersey.

Arts and crafts was, and is, a camp staple. Projects varied with campers ages, but the ideal project was engrossing, took a long time to do, and didn't cost a lot of money. Lanyard making was as close to ideal as you could get, and every camp had spools of colored lanyard plastic bought at the camp supply stores in Monticello or Liberty—businesses that are long since vanished. At the beginning of every season, head counselor and arts-and-crafts counselor would go off to see what was new in the arts-and-crafts world. Novelty was very important because many kids were repeaters and we wanted to give them new projects to do, if possible.

Some old favorites could be done in different guises. One summer, lanyards could be made into key chains. The next summer, bracelets. If a kid didn't finish a project, the arts-and-crafts counselor was expected to complete it so the kid would have something to show for the summer. Camp Note:

> The Ranchers—Arts and crafts has become one of the most enjoyable of Rancher activities. We are now working on bookmarks, rings, and puppet heads. When our puppet heads are finished, we may add bodies and present a puppet show. Irwin, our arts-and-crafts counselor, is very good in this kind of work and we are very glad to have his assistance.
>
> —Arlene M.[7]

Most places tried to have one project each week for kids to take home. A few places wouldn't let the kids take their creations home until the end of camp, when a massive "crafts show" would be staged so that parents could see great masses of projects at one time. Craft shows were usually held the last day of camp so that parents could find the staff easily accessible for tipping.

Nursery kids did a lot with coloring, paper cutouts, and fingerpaint. Older kids made things from papier-mâché (puppet heads molded over balloons), slap sticks (jewelry boxes of glued-together sticks with lids ornamented with macaroni and gilded with gold paint), and plaster of paris (molded figures). We also did leather craft (prepared kits that were tooled and assembled), basket making (willow), glitter craft, copper enameling (jewelry, such as cufflinks, earrings, tie bars), and copper tooling. The copper-tooling craft, perhaps more than any other, demonstrated how crafts changed in relation to demand. In phase one, kids would be asked to trace a picture from a magazine, then, using carbon paper, trace the outline onto a piece of copper, and finally, tool it with a combination of outline and *repoussè*. This was an excellent long-range product that took hours to complete. The final product was mounted on a piece of scrap wood. The results were highly variable, but individual. By the time I retired from camp, there was demand for crafts that were more perfect looking. Copper tooling changed; now one bought a kit. Next, copper arrived bonded to a plastic mold. The camper tooled by pushing the copper into the mold. Once the project was finished, you removed the plastic mold and mounted the finished tooling on the provided wood-grained plastic plaque. Parents loved them. When I go through flea markets today, I often see these things for sale—and I smile.

Perhaps the least appealing aspect of being an arts-and-crafts counselor was that, after seeing that your work area had been straightened up, you had to finish off the projects that the kids didn't complete so that they had the requisite artifacts to take home. I still shudder at the thought of all the misshapen baskets I helped to bring into the world. Keeping camp houses clean varied from place to place. At Furman's I was expected to sweep up at the end of the crafts day— at Kassack's, as at most of the larger places, the handyman would clean up daily.

Most kids wanted to please—they worked very diligently and they bloomed with some praise. One learned about a few perils related to this trait. Dave Burcat, the future dentist, had great manual dexterity, but he had never before been an arts-and-crafts counselor. Learning the crafts was easy. "Dave," I said, "never ask the Rancherettes to gather around while you do a demonstration." He forgot my warning the next day, and I happened to be in the camp house when he made his mistake. "Come close so you can see this." I remember watching youthful, good-looking Dave turn red in the face, crowded all too closely by eager nymphets. I smiled, watching his embarrassment, and he never made that mistake again. It was a vivid experience he still remembers very well. We laughed about it at his granddaughter's *bat mitzvah* in 1996.

All day camps needed buildings and facilities. An ideal circumstance called for a minimum of two buildings so that the preschoolers with their more flexible schedules could be separated from the rest of the campers. You also wanted a piano in the preschool building (the nursery) and a counselor who could play. Like everything else at the bungalow colonies, the buildings tended to be minimal. Usually frame, they were often unfinished inside. Bare wood floors were usual; linoleum was considered deluxe.

The nursery house was typically rectangular and had a bathroom and a small changing room. There were built-in cubby holes called "cubbies" on one wall where swimming suits and dry clothing were kept. Campers were required to be toilet trained, and in the event of "an accident" the child's parent would be called over the loudspeaker: "Mrs. Ginzburg, please come to the day camp." Mothers knew for what! The nursery almost always opened onto a fenced-in play area with sand boxes and some shade. The interior was furnished with small chairs and low tables.

The older children's camp house was similar, but larger. Older kids also needed separate boy/girl dressing rooms. At Kassack's, our boys' dressing room doubled as the arts-and-crafts storage room, thanks to locked cabinets. The main room had the ubiquitous "cubbies" and built-in tables with long benches used for arts and crafts. You learned quickly that you wanted the least possible amount of portable furniture. When kids got rambunctious on rainy days, this was especially important. In the vicinity of the camp house, you had a playground with swings, with nonrigid seats. A "camper powered" merry-go-round was an especially favored piece of playground equipment—a load of kids got on and one kid ran around propelling it. A few very large colonies had a separate "activities" building for additional indoor use, but at most places the casino served this purpose.

The heart of any day camp program was sports (including swimming), which consumed the lion's share of the day. Central to sports were the games played against other colonies that were within a five mile radius. These "varsity" sports were boys softball and girls punch ball, played with a pink Spaulding rubber ball. Both were grouped by age: eight to ten, and eleven to thirteen. Our regular league included Meyer Furman's, Kassack's, Kare Free, Lansman's, Damoshack's Woodland Colony, and Jacoby's.

MIDGETS LOSE TO KASSACK'S

Monday, Aug. w, [*sic*] the Furman Midgets lost to Kassack's in a return game. Things looked good in the first inning when Chuck Berman doubled and Steve Pershan singled to drive in a run. But in the last of the second Kassack's Juniors scored four runs.

In the fifth Brian doubled and Chuck drove him in with a sacrifice. Kassack's retaliated with a run in the bottom half of the inning. The sixth inning saw Harvey D., Allan N., and Ronnie Mitninsky single for our last run. The final score was five to three. The lineup: A. Ellman, 2B, A. Lazarus, C., C. Berman, SS, Steve P., P., Bob H., 3B, Bob D., 1B, T. Schwartzwald, LF, H. Dareff, CF, A. Nathanson, RF, and R. Mitninsky, SGF.

Coaching were [Counselor] Bob Abrams, [CIT] Ron Pershan, and Sol Ellman. Harry Lazarus umpired. Thank you Harry, and better luck to the Midgets. Our next opponent will be Lansman's Bungalow Colony camp team in a home and home series.

—C. Berman[8]

Counselors loved the games, especially home games, because they occupied a whole morning without much hauling and often other groups wanted to watch. Frequently parents, particularly fathers on vacation, would come down to the field. Occasionally we had to deal with the circumstance, familiar to little league coaches, of athletic parents trying to push their athletically disinclined children. This often had nasty results, especially to the children—many of whom seemed to suffer from asthma. The larger the colony, the more kids to choose from, the stronger your team. You also had more bench warmers and more bruised egos to deal with.

Lansman's was the only team in our league that had "official" vehicles identified with their logo. For most of the travel in those innocent days, we would simply cram the kids and their counselor into one or two cars driven by the head counselor and the "farmer" or his wife. Occasionally parents would also drive over to watch their children play. In 1960, Leo Kassack, who was usually frugal, bought a Lincoln and fulfilled a lifelong dream. Leo was a "farmer" who earned money for his colony by running the local taxi service for many years. He appreciated a comfortable car. He sold the Lincoln the following year because it only got about five miles to the gallon, but that summer we traveled to games in style.

I always had a problem with these "varsity" sports because I was very naive about the craving for victory fostered by parents. Always the last-picked athlete myself, I insisted that every kid in a group play, and insisted that all eligibility rules of the league be scrupulously enforced (no small eleven year old, however talented, playing on the eight-to-ten teams, no fourteen-or fifteen-year-old CITs playing on the eleven-to-thirteen teams). These dishonest practices were routine, and I learned that they were actively encouraged by head counselors who were under pressure to win and by owners who liked to brag that their teams were number one. At first our teams consistently lost; the kids were dispirited and the parents angry. I would like to say that I remained Simon pure, but I can't. I perhaps took the most cynical way out: the executive disassociative tactic used by rulers to great effect—at least since Henry II proclaimed of Thomas à Becket, 'Who'll rid me of this papist priest?' I simply told my counselors to try to win some games, and I left the games once they were under way. Thanks to this system, over the years we had a few winning teams—nothing sensational, but a balance was maintained. I had one especially unscrupulous male counselor who was always good for a few victories, and a female counselor with so formidable a mouth that she scared off any would be cheaters. My summers at camp would leave me with a distaste for organized kids' sports.

Adding extra variety to the camp days were visits from outside experts. Once a week we had a dance instructor, Mr. Mack, come in—in one day he would instruct all of the groups. He led some in square dancing and others in social dancing. Every other week the skaters came—they would provide the kids with wooden-wheel roller skates so that they could skate in the casino. Some camps also regularly offered pony rides.

When we had a cool spell in August, we used the opportunity to send the campers on a hike. We had a very convenient loop of six miles, which led to the town of Hasbrouck, with its broad river beach, and back. This required day-ahead planning because the kids had to bring their lunches—and it was quite the organizational operation. It was naturally limited to older kids.

Parents were always asked, at the onset of summer, to put labels into their kids' clothes, but most didn't, and by the end of summer a huge box was full of moldy underwear, socks, and towels that hadn't made it back home after a swim. Occasionally a brave mother would come in to go through "lost and found," but that was rare.

The nightmare of every camp director was a rainy day, and, as a matter of fact, the last camp director I worked for solved the problem (for himself) by disappearing on rainy days. This was a more successful strategy when you had multiple buildings—everyone assumed you were in another structure. One rainy day was bad, two or three in a row were disasters. We would split up the kids (in changeable groups, nursery excepted) between the camp house and the casino.

CAMP HAS PING-PONG TOURNAMENT

Tuesday's dismal atmosphere was brightened by a Ping-Pong tournament among the Ranchers and Tophands. The semifinalists were: L. Rademan and C. Berman of the Ranchers and S. Dareff and B. Daniels of the Tophands. Chuck B. and S. Dareff were the winners. A championship game between these two pongers has not been as yet made.

—A. Mittleman[9]

Quiet games, arts and crafts, and even show rehearsals could only go so far. By the second day—after we had put on puppet shows and the staff had exhausted the repertoire of tournaments and other amusing pastimes, we would arrange to get a movie. Unfortunately, on those days every other camp wanted a movie, too, and the distributors just had so many. They had "rainy day" movies that were unbelievable turkeys. I remember one three-reeler where the projectionist started with reel two. He then showed three, followed by one. The movie was so bad that no one much noticed. At the end of a rainy day at camp, I would go home, lock myself in the living room, turn on soft music, and stare at the wall.

All camps had special events. We would have at least one trip each summer. The local trips took us to a "farm," which existed to serve camps. There we took hayrides, at first on horse-drawn wagons, later on tractor-pulled ones. In a more formal vein, there were trips to the summer theater in Forestburg, or the ultimate trip—a day at the Catskill Game Farm in Catskill, New York, about seventy-five miles away. Still in operation, it is a pioneer private zoo park. For these excursions, we always rented a school bus from Wilson Bus Service. The worst part of these trips was that it was difficult to convince the counselors that they weren't on vacation, too.

The counselors were drawn from three sources. They were children of tenants, local (usually Jewish) kids, or kids from other bungalow colonies. Typically, they were fifteen when they became counselors and they ended their careers when they reached eighteen. Several lingered on for a few more years. One of my most unforgettable counselors was Jay Goldin, who worked for me for three summers, starting when he was eighteen.[10] Jay's parents stayed at Lansman's, and he had his own car. He was crude, coarse, and virtually amoral—but also very efficient, smart, and strong as the proverbial ox. He could do twenty one-arm pushups in a row.

Jay was always responsible for the older boys, who mostly idolized him. Those who didn't, he terrorized. He ran a tight ship. Rumor had it that he had once given a kid "a ten-finger sharkie" (an incredible two-handed pinch on the upper thigh) that sent the kid through the roof. Fact or legend, Jay could control his group with mere glances from his heavily lidded eyes. He also had a very strong, and seldom concealed, attraction toward women. Once he bragged to me that he was having an affair with his best friend's mother. I still wonder that he didn't come after me when I responded by asking if his best friend was returning the favor.

Jay, at one time or another, went after most of the sixteen-year-old-and-up female staff. On his last summer he met Selma, a counselor, who was engaged to George, who worked in the city during the week but came up to the country on weekends.[11] After a few weeks of Jay's blandishments, Selma gave in, and she and Jay were a week-time item. Innocent George had the weekends. This arrangement suited Jay very well, because he had well-organized weekends spent cruising the various hotels. One weekend, George made the mistake of showing up early on Friday, shortly before flag lowering. He made the bigger mistake of identifying himself and asking one of the older girl campers where Selma was. She couldn't wait to spread the news, and soon a buzz went through the camp. Everyone, from nursery school up, knew about Jay and Selma. That afternoon at flag lowering time, as George looked on, the campers burst into a spontaneous chant, "Jay loves Selma," "Selma loves Jay." George, in fury, ran toward Jay, who quickly and viciously decked him. Later George tried to run over Jay in the parking lot. It was the most memorable of flag lowering ceremonies. I've lost track of the three, but Jay and Selma did not stay together and, when I last heard, Jay was a very successful lawyer.

Why did the youngsters work? It was something to do. The pay was not very good, but these kids didn't need money to the extent that they would later. In New York City you couldn't drive until you were nineteen, so car expenses were not an issue.[12] Hotel jobs were much more lucrative, but they were harder work and more demanding of your time. The other available summer jobs were working in local stores or restaurants. The junk-food era had not yet reached the mountains, and there was no McDonald's.

Early in the season, one had no trouble finding new counselors, but it was more difficult once the season got underway. Occasionally you had to fire a counselor. It was especially difficult to get rid of tenants' kids, but if they were careless or dangerous firing was possible. Beyond staff incompetency, your major personnel problem was two or more competent counselors who hated each other, and you had to keep them separate. Here again Jay was a problem. One year he and Jean,[13] the counselor of the oldest girls' group, took an instant dislike to one another. You dared not leave them alone together—anywhere, anytime. This was all the more strange, because Jean had had or was engaging in sexual relationships with almost every other male staff member that summer, excluding our only gay counselor. No matter how discrete we thought we were, the campers knew what everyone was up to.

DIS AND DAT

Rest seems to be a very popular place . . . especially after camp hours. What makes the Neversink River so interesting at night?[14]

It was absolutely forbidden for counselors to hit kids, but the counselors were kids themselves. One knew that counselors hit campers, although I never witnessed an incident. Jay was caught in the midst of one of the most bizarre instances I dealt with when the son of a local merchant, one of our campers whose mother regularly beat him, told her that Jay had strangled him. The mother became a fierce lioness defending her young. When confronted, Jay characteristically told the mother to "go to hell," and he assured me that he hadn't strangled the kid. I believed him. If Jay had, there would at least have been finger marks—if the kid were still alive. Besides, strangling wasn't Jay's style.

Minor injuries were more common. I was lucky that no camper broke a major bone during my camp director days, but there was the nose-to-stage incident I described earlier. Emergency first-aid was expected of head counselors and nursery teachers. Sol Ellman had taught me the secret of getting a cinder out of a kid's eye. Have the child pull down the eyelid, hold the nostril on the affected eye's side, and have the kid blow his or her nose hard. It almost always worked. I was squeamish about blood when I started as a counselor, but I got more comfortable after the first bloody nose or two. "Lay down with your head back and keep these wet paper towels on the bridge of your nose." I handed out or applied hundreds of Band-Aids and daubed many a bee sting with ammonia and rashes with calamine lotion—all items in our regular first-aid kit. On a few occasions, kids got cuts requiring stitches. At Kassack's, the owners had a regular arrangement with the local doctor—just get them there quickly. Sometimes at the end of the day I'd look like a butcher—but that was, fortunately, rare.

The campers were middle-class Jewish kids (we did have two Italian boys once), and they were mostly guided by middle-class mores. Occasionally we would have a child with emotional problems forced on us. Since we had no expertise in dealing with these problems, some of these kids had to be removed from camp. Usually these children had parents who were in deep denial. One little boy I will always remember. He was a four-year-old, and one day he started to strangle a three-year-old. "Hi jinks," we said. The next day he tried to hit another kid's head against a cement pier. We became very suspicious. The third day this four-year-old smuggled a nail-studded stick into his play group and attacked the counselor who, fortunately, was only mildly injured. His mother denied that the kid had ever been in trouble. "It was all your fault. You're unfair. I demand you let him back in camp!" Later, a neighbor told us that the kid had been kicked out of several nursery schools as well as two day camps the previous summer.

The campfire was an important part of every camp. At day camps no one cooked a meal, nor were campfires held at night. Traditionally, they were on Friday afternoon when parents could attend, and such was the case at Hector's Pond:

> Some of the men of Hector's took Fridays off. They converted ten days of vacation time into three-day weekends. Between these, and others who made it a point to arrive early for the occasion, Campfire had a big turnout. Old-timers girdled the flagpole with folding chairs. The rest squatted in the grass or stood around. Fathers prowled about with eight-millimeter cameras, making movies of everything.[15]

What made the event so attractive at Hector's was that dozens of camp awards were given out at the campfire each week. "Best Anything" and "Most Improved" awards were given away by the bale. Other places had less hectic events.

CAMPFIRE COOKING

Last Friday when the time for our campfire rolled around, we were more excited than usual. Instead of having our fire at rest, we had it by the Neversink River. The fire was a success mainly because the starving campers had marshmallows. A large part of the enjoyment came from the entertainment; Sonia sang the national anthem of Colombia, S[outh] America, Sheila D. sang, and so did "Sound-Off" Ronnie Pershan. The campers learned a new camp song. The resonant voices of Bob Abrams and Sol Ellman led the sing. We had a good time.

—L. Rademan[16]

I was always very conservative about the number of awards, giving them at the campfire or at flag lowering on Friday. Each counselor could select the camper of the week. On the last day of camp we usually had a party after swim time and gave two all-summer awards as well, boy and girl "campers of the season," which were highly coveted.

A bizarre aspect of the 1950s was that the decade marked the beginnings of the unwitting precocious sexualization of children. Parents were depression babies who grew up with the movies and had seen all too many Shirley Temple and Andy Hardy movies. They wanted their children to be happy and popular—and to socialize at dances as early as the age of eight. When I started to work at Kassack's, I was asked to run weekly Thursday night dances for the campers. I learned that these were common elsewhere. The concept that these dances were to be dating events floored me. They were, at best, painful occasions to watch. And I actually knew of cases where parents and grandparents paid boys to take their little girls to the dances. After a few of these evenings, I absolutely refused to continue them—although some parents continued to run the dances themselves, on occasion. In this matter I was as "Simon pure" as a Jewish boy could be.

For kids the high point of the camp season came during "Color War." Color War is a camping tradition in which the entire camp is divided into two color-coded teams; a red and a blue, or a red and a green, at the places where I worked. The teams were each assigned a general, and they engaged each other in all the camp activities. The teams were even given demerits for unruly behavior—it was a camp director's dream. Everyone wanted their team to win and even the most uncooperative kids shaped up, either out of pride or in fear of what the older kids would do to them. Color War could last from three to five days and it always took place in August, toward the end of camp. Only league games were played as regular camp activities during Color War. For any non-league games you were either "Red" or "Blue." Just when Color War was to begin was always a secret between the camp director and the owner, and ideally you wanted to begin with a surprise. One day, a cowboy on horseback showed up right before lunch and tossed out a red and blue banner. Another time, the fire engine showed up with bells and sirens. In my best and most inspired kickoff event, a policeman showed up at flag raising to arrest Jay for statutory rape. Jay, who wasn't a morning person and was no doubt guilty, was really shaken. Future lawyer that he was, he asked to see the arrest warrant. It was red and blue, naturally!

The messenger starting the war always carried two scrolls naming the generals and the teams (compiled by the director.) The traditional end of the Color War was a grand scavenger hunt, which could range colony wide; this was the only time that kids were allowed to roam the whole colony during camp hours. Their quest was for items ranging from the natural history specimens that they had learned about on nature walks, to various counselors' personal and intimate attire.

TREASURE HUNT A SUCCESS

Have you seen something which resembles a squadron of jet planes pass your bungalow? Don't be alarmed. It was not an invasion from outer space. It was just the Ranchers and Tophands on a treasure hunt. The campers left no stone unturned in their search for clues. They were divided into two teams, called the Red and the Green. The Ranchers were the first to go on the hunt. At first it looked bad for the red, but the hunt ended in a tie. The Tophands green team won their hunt. The leaders, Ronnie, Bobby, and Irwin, are still recuperating.

—Arlene M.[17]

Camp took on a calm feeling as we approached the end of the season. The last day or two, parents dropped by to see the individual counselors—with envelopes in hand. Counselors usually got five or ten dollars as a tip, per child, big tippers gave twenty dollars. Some people gave as little as three dollars. Arts-and-crafts counselors and head counselors were also to be tipped—and here your greatest dread was if someone decided to "take up a pool" (give a collective gift). This was unfortunate for the counselor or director because people could give much smaller amounts of money in a pool than they would individually. The expected tip for an arts-and-crafts counselor was three to five dollars. The head counselor was usually tipped five to ten dollars. My first year as arts-and-crafts counselor at Furman's, the parents took up a pool and I was given a leather suitcase—somebody was in the luggage business. That was when Grandpa brought me the money in the grapes.

At fictional Hector's, Ann wondered how much to tip, but found that no two women agreed on what the tip should be. Eventually, "She followed Lonnie Miller's advice. The usual is ten dollars to the head counselor and give to each counselor the child is under."[18]

At some places the counselors gave the camp director a gift. In 1961, the year I retired, the counselors gave me a gold Witenaur watch—engraved, "The Counselors, 1961." I retired at age twenty-four. Fortunately, Anthony Cino, Kassack's only Italian tenant, was in the jewelry business and he got the watch for the counselors—wholesale, of course.

Campers took home their memories and their camp picture. Every year near the middle of the season, a photographer came to take individual and group pictures. Each group picture had the campers, their counselor, and, often, the camp director in it. Parents paid for the pictures they wanted and the owners got a kickback.

After 1961, I never spent a full summer in the mountains. From 1962 to 1972, however, I spent virtually every weekend there from May through October, and over the years following I have always spent some time in Sullivan County. I have watched the industry change. I saw it almost die, and I have seen it be reborn. And I have seen the function of the day camp change radically to serve the needs of the ultraorthodox Jews who now dominate the bungalow industry. But a recent advertisement tells me that the old ways still linger:

LANSMAN'S DAY CAMP
Woodbourne, N.Y.
[is]
LOOKING FORWARD TO SPENDING
SUMMER 1996 WITH YOU[19]

Few men had sports clothes in the 1930s. Their time in the country was very brief because most men didn't yet have their whole weekend free. Taken at Reddish's *kuchalein* in 1935, the picture also speaks volumes about the sparsity of lawn furniture. Irwin remembers seeing people lounge on tables. Visible across the road is the Hamilton house, the home of a prison guard. (Photo: Unknown)

Bertha in shorts and a halter and a stylishly dressed friend at Reddish's *kuchalein* in 1935 provide a contrast in city and country garb. (Photo: Unknown)

The year was 1945, and the Conga, a line dance, was all the rage. They sang, "One, two, three, La Conga," and kicked off to the side. This is the quintessential Catskill picture of the 1940s. I've seen variants taken at many colonies and hotels. Bertha is third from the left. Irwin also has a photo of a kid Conga line, but it is too blurry to print—kids are often in motion. Note the light fixture attached to the tree that appears over the head of the central figure. You can see a wonderful impromptu Conga line re-created in the film *Radio Days*. (Photo: Unknown)

The Sunshine Colony near Greenfield Park in 1993. It was owned by the Levinsons, the same family that owned the nearby hotel, The Tamarack Lodge. At the Sunshine you got 'full hotel privileges' with your rental, which meant you could use their athletic facilities and the card room, and go to shows.

(below) The backsides of Catskill bungalows were always less appealing than the front. Maintenance was often more haphazard. This 1993 rear view at the Sunshine Colony shows the sheds housing propane tanks.

(above) Bertha's friends Sid and Fran rented this bungalow at the Sunshine Colony from the 1980s to the early 1990s. Note the 1993 presence of the commercial picnic table and bench, the aluminum and nylon web chair, and the gas grill. The string of lights strung between the two units have owl-shaped shades.

Miriam Damico and "her ladies" at the Monticello Raceway Flea Market in 1993. As Bertha Richman did, Miriam provides transportation for her tenants on shopping expeditions.

A typical day camp photograph. The camp director poses with the counselor and her group on the baseball field at Kassack's in Woodbourne. (Photo: Unknown)

The day camp buildings at Lansman's in Woodbourne. A co-op in 1993, the buildings are essentially unchanged from the bungalow colony days. The fenced-in play area for little kids was and is typical.

A shop window in Woodbourne, photographed in 1991, with a reward poster for the Papier murders. B'er Main soda is *glatt kosher*.

Crime and Punishment

ominating Woodbourne was its other, its most enduring industry—the Woodbourne Prison—which loomed on the skyline for many years. Established in 1934, the red brick pile has been expanded over the years, but its great smokestack was torn down a few years ago.[1] The prison is a distinctive element setting Woodbourne apart from the other Sullivan County hamlets. The prison guards and their families were, and largely remain, a distinctive social group. As goyim, they interacted very little with the summer people, but you often recognized them in town by their uniforms: light blue shirts, dark blue ties, and trousers. Grandpa knew some guards because he knew their parents, and our next door neighbor, Mr. Armstrong, was a guard before he and his family sold their place to summer people: the Yustmans and the Puttermans. The guards were usually drawn from local farming families and most had neatly kept small houses characterized by large vegetable gardens and large chained dogs.

After the 1960s, while old-fashioned guards continued in evidence, new categories of prison employees were added. The vo-tech teachers became increasingly important in the county, moonlighting during the summer season as electricians, carpenters, and the like. They filled in for the older craftsmen, especially the Jewish ones, whose children generally didn't choose to stay on in the area.

Our plumber in 1950 was Jewish; our plumber in 1990 was a Christian, moonlighting prison instructor.

From the 1950s on, there have been a small number of Jewish guards. These were generally people who liked living in the region, lacked specific skills, and wanted a year-round paycheck and job security. Typical of these is a man named Frank Fabian. The local Jews called him "the Vet," referring to his role in World War II. Why he was singled out for this distinction, I don't know, but he was. Frank owned a small grocery, worked as a guard, and dealt in almost any other kind of merchandise he could get his hands on. A few years after he retired from the prison, he moved from Woodbourne to a nearby town. At this time, he and his wife divide their time between Sullivan County and their home in Florida.[2] Since the 1970s, guards who are people of color have been added to the local mix, but few live in Woodbourne.

The prison lent a certain sense of danger and adventure. When you drove into Woodbourne on Route 42, you saw gangs of prisoners working on the prison farm, which today grows mostly corn. You also saw open trucks filled with prisoners pass the colony once in a while—a work detail on their way to a job site. Another common Woodbourne sight was to see a guard waiting for the bus with several, uncomfortable, suit-clad young men who had just been released from prison. Most were white.

In an age of innocence and openness, the prison was fascinating as a place "you couldn't go." As kids, we wanted to walk down the back road we commonly called the prison road to see the Do Not Enter signs, and we would hope to get glimpses of patrolling armed guards. One day, when I was twelve, I was walking down the prison road when I heard someone call out, "Hey kid." I turned and saw two black Cadillac limousines, a rare sight in Woodbourne, except for funerals. "Is this the way to the prison?" "Yup," I answered, as I looked at the cars, both filled with swarthy hoods. They had what, years later, would be called "the Godfather Look." The hood look was not unfamiliar to me. I grew up in a section of Brooklyn similar to the one depicted in the film *Goodfellas*.[3]

The prison also made more noise than anything else we knew of in the mountains. Loud clangs and whistles were common, and we especially listened for long, wailing sirens—and the delicious horror of a prison break—or the imagination of one. One July day in 1950 there really was a prison break. We were living in one of the bungalows at the time. I was sleeping in the kitchen (my folks were in the bedroom), when there was the noise of someone trying to get into the bungalow. Someone was pulling on our screen door—and it was about two in the morning. Then there was knocking. I was terrified. Now my parents woke up. We peered through the curtain—nobody in prison garb, just a haggard-looking middle-aged Jew. It was the butcher, making a delivery to our next door neighbor, the other half of our duplex bungalow. The city butcher, who was staying in Woodridge, had been stuck in one of the notorious traffic jams on the Wurtsboro hills and his car had overheated. Like many small merchants in New York City, he would bring orders up to his customers in the country—"after all, I'm going up there anyhow." Next day everybody laughed about the two o'-clock meat delivery, including double entendre jokes about "meat," or *"fleisch"*—the butcher bringing his "meat" to the lady of the bungalow whose husband didn't have enough "meat." The incident entered our folklore.

The sight of official uniforms was rare at the bungalow colonies, except for the day in August when the local volunteer firemen came around to sell tickets to their annual Firemen's Show and Ball, held each summer at the Tamarack Lodge. Borscht Belt entertainers and musicians donated their talents, and huge crowds attended. (A third grade joke: "Why do firemen have bigger balls than policemen? Because they sell more tickets.")

The appearance of a policeman was ominous. There was my early run-in with Elmer-the-cop when one of us broke the car window, and then there was the story of Mrs. Fabricant,[4] which my mother just told me in the summer of 1996. Florence Fabricant was a well-remembered part of my childhood. A tenant in the house during the early 1940s, she owned a feisty, ugly Pekinese dog she called *Scheine Punum* (Beautiful Face). It was wartime and meat was rationed. Florence fed highly coveted minute steak to *Scheine Punum* and hamburger or chicken to her husband, who often lamented in Yiddish that 'he only wished that he had as good a mistress as that dog did.' Florence Fabricant was also a kleptomaniac who shoplifted. One night, after I was asleep, the local police came to arrest her on the complaints of several local shopkeepers. It was only Grandpa's influence and persuasive powers that saved her. He convinced the merchants to drop the charges, the police to "forget it"—and Mr. Fabricant, as always, paid the bills. While this event was big news at the colony, nobody spoke of it in front of the children.

Sullivan County also had its share of crime, and well-known criminals were part of the human scenery. This history, like much else, is very well handled in *A Summer World*. Author Stefan Kanfer notes that Seymour Rexsite, a Yiddish performer in the Catskills, had been tipped an unbelievable fifty dollars by the notorious Louie Lepke to sing, *"Mein Yiddishe Momme."*[5]

Sullivan County historian John Conway has a book in press, *Gangsters of the Catskills,* and according to it local legend holds that there are bodies still at the bottom of Loch Sheldrake Lake from the gangster days. While none of us knowingly saw any gangsters, we talked about gangsters a lot. Kids shared stories they heard about one or another of our nice, deep, local lakes. There were rumors that Lake Louise Marie was owned by Alfonse Capone, who incidentally ran errands for my grandfather when the once-and-future mobster was a kid. "He was a bum then," my grandfather recalled, "I used to give him a nickel to get his uncle for me; his uncle worked for me." In *Summer on a Mountain of Spices,* Harry Craft mentions the Capone story as he passes Lake Louise Marie.[6]

Sullivan County still has something of a reputation as a dumping ground for mob hits, and there's seldom a spring where a dumped body or two isn't discovered along an isolated roadside. Some things never change: My kids were also excited to be driven along the local dumping roads. In the summer of 1990 we hosted an exchange student from Germany, and when we visited Sullivan County the kids insisted on showing Nicholas the stretch near Woodbourne with a history of body dumping.

Crime, to us, was always a delicious titillation—perhaps tinged with a sleazy glamor. This was the cinematic world of Jack "Leggs" Diamond, Louie Lepke, and Al Capone. For the most part, as far as summer visitors are concerned, the mountains are safe. When my mother is in Brooklyn, she lives in a fortress. However, she feels safe living alone in her big house in Woodbourne, although, for the first time in fifty-eight years, the house was broken into over the winter of 1995. Go shopping in area supermarkets or go to the bargain movies at night, and you will see bungalow people, many elderly, wearing the gold chains and diamond rings they don't dare wear on the street in New York City. The fact that they are out at night is itself a testimony to a sense of security. This said, one should not infer that violent crime does not exist in the county. It does, but it rarely touches the summer people. If you read the *The Middletown (N.Y.) Record,* the local newspaper of authority, you know that there is crime. Fortunately, most summer people read the New York City papers, which are, except for the *New York Times,* much more lurid than *The Record* and seem to feature "the New York City crime of the day." Most local crime is centered in the large minority communities of Monticello and Liberty and among the transient workers employed by the hotel industry. The day has long since passed when most hotel employees were college students on summer break. As hotels became year-round operations, they needed increasing numbers of minimum-wage workers, and crime followed. In the staff quarters of the Catskill's most posh hotel, The Concord, there was a fatal stabbing in May 1991, and also "an attempted murder . . . and a double murder in March 1990, when two employees died in a fire set by another employee." The police report that other big resorts have been similarly affected, "but hotel guests have never been threatened."[7]

On the night of 8 July 1991, the quiet, dirty secret of the hotel industry spilled over horribly into the bungalow world when an elderly Jewish couple, Lazar Papier, seventy-five, and his wife, Miriam, sixty-seven, both Holocaust survivors, were brutally bludgeoned to death in their bungalow at the Ryke Inn bungalow colony, on the shore of Kiamesha Lake, near The Concord.[8] A hammer was found near their bodies in the bedroom of their bungalow, "which was at the back of the grounds of some thirty bungalows, near the woods, where transient summer hotel workers often camped out." It was believed by neighbors that this "bad element" had killed the couple, who were Hasidim from the Borough Park section of Brooklyn, and who had summered in "their faded Catskill Haven" for years. Missing from the small bungalow were several pieces of jewelry, some money, and a *tallit* (prayer shawl). State Police Captain Michael F. Cahill theorized that "the killer or killers were burglars who believed . . . the shawl . . . was of value and perhaps used it to carry the jewelry."[9]

Around the colony, people tried to return to their normal lives, as many Hasidim "visited the nearby Hillcrest bungalow colony where the Papiers's three sons and two daughters were sitting shivah." The Hasidim "came from scores of bungalow communities that were now protected by private guards." A ten thousand dollar reward was offered for information leading to the arrest of the killers.[10]

In my years of going to the Catskills, I never before witnessed any local trauma that affected the area like this. Everyone talked about it, and everywhere you went you saw posters in English and Yiddish offering the reward for information. Holocaust survivors were especially shaken by the atrocious crime, which reminded them of what they had lived through. A special thirty-member task force was set up, but evidence was sparse. Several tenants, however, remembered hearing a motorcycle leaving the area about the time of the crime, and this led to the arrest on 16 August 1991 of Anthony Valentino Burton for the murder. The police had traced the ownership of all motorcycles in the country, questioning owners. Suspicious of Burton, they found that his fingerprints matched those found in the Papier bungalow.[11]

Burton, who had a criminal record, was an African American Marylander who had been working as a "baker's porter" at Kutsher's Hotel, about three miles from The Ryke Inn Colony, since December 1990. The hotel's vice president, Mark Kutsher, said, "He's not been a problem here at the hotel. . . . He was a quiet worker, not the type anyone would really notice."[12] In the wake of the arrest, a chorus of protest was raised against hotel owners who continued to hire transient help, but Sullivan County District Attorney Stephen F. Lungen defended them: "The hotels take a significant knock because of the people they hire for minimum wage, but this is a tourist county and we need them. . . . Without them we could not run the county."[13]

Newspaper reporters interviewed people about the capture and their reaction to the Catskills. The responses were predictable—relief—but the overall reaction of many who summer in the bungalow colonies, Hasidim and others, was voiced by one woman who observed, "It was the one place that you can go away to."

In November 1992, Burton "was convicted of twenty of twenty-two charges against him, including second-degree murder, rape, and burglary." After being sentenced to "at least seventy-five years in prison" by Sullivan County Judge Anthony Kane, Burton protested his innocence. "I wasn't found guilty by law. . . . I was found guilty by prejudice. You needed someone to put this on—that's why I was found guilty."[14] Friends of the victims raised a seventy-five-thousand-dollar memorial fund to honor them. When Leah Cohn, the Papiers' daughter, learned of Burton's sentence, she was pleased that justice was done. "But what can we say? We lost our two parents."[15]

In the summer of 1991 an innocence was lost.

14

An Age of Change

I n 1961, the Kassacks were very upset because a number of their best, long-time tenants had bought summer homes at Emerald Green, at Lake Louise Marie near Wurtsboro. Emerald Green was the first successful post–World War II summer home development in Sullivan County, and it was a portent of doom for major bungalow colonies. Those former tenants who could afford it would now enjoy the communal life of a colony, completely on their own terms. Many of the houses were quite luxurious, by middle-class standards, and at least two of Kassack's tenants opted for Lake Front homes—the development's most expensive units. The site (allegedly once owned and used as a dumping ground by Al Capone) was attractive, very close to the Route 17 Quickway, and "Emerald Green at Lake Louise Marie" didn't smack of the "Borscht Belt."[1] Most of the successful home communities to follow immediately were located at White Lake and Smallwood—both have a certain elite ring. In subsequent years, communities have been built throughout the area, many of them destined ultimately to be retirement homes for a population that has given up metropolitan New York and prefers to winter in Florida. Reflective of a new clientele (the many-childrened New Orthodox), the Regency Country Club in Woodridge, New York, offers seven-bedroom summer homes.[2]

While summer home developments skimmed the cream of the bungalow clientele, the rise of suburbia also greatly reduced the tenant base. One of the principal reasons for going to the country was eliminated when New York City's Jews left the crowded Brooklyn and Bronx and the older, cramped, settled areas of Queens for the new open communities on Long Island, Westchester County, and northern New Jersey. Not only did most now have lawns and trees in suburbia, but they also had access to swimming pools, either at their country club or their Jewish community center—or even in their own backyard. Residential air-conditioning was also devastating to the mountains—one of whose prime attraction was that it cooled at night. Now with a press of a button you, too, could have it cool at night—reliably.[3] The Hitchcock classic *Rear Window* shows a New York summer in a well-to-do neighborhood of 1954.[4] A few years later the story would be impossible to do credibly, because all the action James Stewart's character observed would be carried out behind air-conditioning units and drawn curtains. One unpleasant little secret is that sometimes, when hot humid air blankets the Northeast, even the mountains do not cool off enough at night. The summer of 1993 was so hot and humid that my mother seldom slept upstairs because it never cooled down. Fortunately for tenants, most bungalows are now air-conditioned.

Another factor reducing the client base for the Catskills, its hotels and its colonies, was the decline in legal discrimination. In many ways the Catskills flourished because it was one of very few places Jews could comfortably and safely go in the summer. Civil rights legislation in the 1960s and 1970s removed the barriers at many "Christian-only" resorts. The jet age also had its effect and opened up new areas for Jewish vacationers. Trips to Europe and Israel became commonplace.

Ethnic *chic* had not yet become important in the 1960s and early 1970s, and the mountains simply were too Jewish, too immigrant-oriented, for the younger, upward-bound Jews. The rise of the women's movement and the frequency of two-income families provided the *coup de grâce* to an industry in decline. With both mother and father working, there was no possibility for a bungalow summer. City and suburban day camps boomed, as did sleep-away camps. Family vacations would be compressed to fit mother and father's time off, and the vacation weekend would become popular.

It was the young marrieds of the late 1950s and early 1960s who were the most likely to suburbanize, and it was this generation that increasingly turned its back on the Catskills and the bungalows.[5] Rentals remained decent for many owners through the 1960s, but the bungalow crowd grew older. The immigrant generation who came to America before 1924 and many of their native-born children remained faithful to the Catskills. Those people who began renting bungalows in the 1930s, 1940s, and 1950s often continued to do so. Their children did not. If their children and grandchildren liked "the country," they tended to buy houses at Emerald Green and its successors, or in the new co-op colonies. Many were weekenders. The renter generation was aging and dying off. The hyper-inflation of the Ford and Carter years saw a lot of small- and medium-size colonies go under as expenses increased, as the market shrank, and as retirees, hurt by inflation, stayed home.

Jennie Richman (no relation, but the other Richman in the local telephone directory), who operated "a thirty-seven-unit bungalow colony in the once thriving hotel district of South Fallsburg," lamented in 1971 that she'd recently lost all of her neighbors; all were small hotels. She observed, "the mountains are doing very badly." Mounting costs are the problem. "We work very hard, and I have not seen in four years a nickel for myself." And "with $1,500 in insurance, $2,700 in taxes, utilities, and repairs, for a little guy, he's got to close. . . . This is a disaster area." How does she keep going? By investing money she earns as a waitress in New York City. Notes the forty-six-year-old woman, "If I had to make a living from it, I'd have to close, too."[6] With slight variations, this theme resonated throughout the mountains.

At Richman's, we saw our net income decline and, more dramatically, we can date the beginning of our end to the day in 1977 when Louie Resnick died during his card game. After 1980, when she stopped renting, Mother kept in touch with many of her long-time tenants. Most simply stopped going away in the summer, feeling that they were too old to find a place where they'd feel comfortable. Several were in retirement communities or nursing homes within a year or two. Sadie Margolis and Bessie Resnick rented at a colony near South Fallsburg. The owner had bought the thirty-plus-unit colony in the mid 1970s for under thirty thousand dollars and did most of the work herself. Her husband worked in the city. The now immaculately kept colony, which had a pool and a main house and bungalows, soon gathered in a following of older people who moved from dying and closing colonies. Most of these were "snowbirds," or Floridians: people who made their principal residence in Florida and came up to New York for the summer. Willie Weinberg, age seventy-nine and a resident of nearby Monticello, likens the snowbirds to salmon: "They grow up in the river, and then they're going to the sea, and [then] . . . they're coming back."[7]

Bessie Resnick met a widower at the colony and remarried. Both these women continued to maintain their apartments in New York City (Sadie in Brooklyn, Bessie in Manhattan) and go to Florida in winter and the country in summer. In the 1990s, with both of these women approaching ninety, they gave up the summer colonies. Mary and Morris Ossip remained true to Woodbourne and Brooklyn; they took a summer apartment in a lesser place, recently purchased at a bargain price. The clientele here was less affluent than at the colony where Sadie and Bessie went, and most of the people were religiously observant. For their tiny apartment, up a long flight of stairs, they paid $825 the first season. In the autumn of 1991, the rent was now $975 and Mary told my mother that she was afraid the colony wouldn't open again. The colony, though, ever more shabby, still limps along.

The younger generation of American-born snowbirds are now in their sixties, seventies, and eighties. They are more comfort-minded and convenience-oriented than their elders, and willing and able to pay more for their summer pleasure. They want entertainment as well as comfort. A few surviving small hotels have added bungalow colonies designed to cater to "Floridians." The Aladdin Hotel across the river from our place is one of these hybrid resorts, and we sold them our bungalows for $5,000, with the condition that all debris be removed and the ground restored to pristine condition. It cost about $28,000 to move the eight units across the river. Mother cried as she watched them leave. At the Aladdin site, they joined a band of other bungalows assembled from nearby colonies—jumbled very unattractively on a crowded site. All of these bungalows now have wall-to-wall carpeting, remodeled kitchens and baths, finished walls, heat and air-conditioning units, and cable television. Carrie Komito at eighty-eight (in 1993) recalled that she had "saved The Aladdin by buying the bungalows."[8] Tenants have full access to the hotel facilities, including the indoor pool, the daily entertainment provided by the resident *tummler*, the dance instructors, and the shows and movies presented nightly in the Ali Baba Room nightclub.

Murray Waxman, the long-time M.C. at The Aladdin, has been a Catskill M.C., or *tummler*, for sixty-two years.[9] Pencil-mustached Waxman "may be the last of his kind" at this hotel bungalow colony, which "is a temple of American history, a museum of American history, a museum of memories, a Kiddish of Catskill Kitsch."[10]

Saturday night is still the big show night at The Aladdin. "Green lights illuminate the Ali Baba Room sign. . . . Red lights glow from a neon Rheingold sign at the always-empty bar at Rafael's Coffee Shop." When you go inside, you are in an old casino that has been tricked up with Formica tables and red-and-green vinyl chairs. On the walls are glossy photographs of acts that have played here: Allen and Rossi, Jan Murray, Van Harris, and Jeannie Reynolds. There's a band, Stan Pole and his trio, playing familiar music of the 1940s and 1950s: "I Love Paris" and the like. You'll see the regular staff. Nattily attired Murray Waxman usually warms up the audience for the show, but not tonight. His cosmetologist wife, Ruby, is there "in a tight sweater dress with orange, green, and blue glass stones, her shocking pink tights complementing her pink lipstick." General manager "Sylvia—I'm seventy-one with two facelifts not one but two—Berger . . . [is] wearing gold lamé shoes, gold lamé pants, and a red sweater with gold lamé swirls, which highlight the gold highlighted in her coifed hair."[11]

The elderly crowd shuffles in, some from the hotel but most from the bungalows. The dances played are rumbas, fox trots, waltzes, cha-chas, with an occasional samba or a slow lindy. One couple dances; a few women dance with women. After about an hour, everyone settles down for showtime. Tonight Murray has bronchitis, so with a drum role Stan Pole announces, "He's worked at Atlantic City, opened for all the big names, done the cruise ships extensively. He likes to be called the singing impressionist. Let's welcome Johnny Timpanelli!" Tuxedo-clad, the twenty-eight-year-old man comes on stage singing, "The world's still the same—don't you change it." He does forty minutes. In a blond wig he's Carol Channing. In a gray beard he sings, "If I Were a Rich Man." He asks his audience to "close your eyes and picture yourself sitting in the Copa Cabana and welcome Mr. Romance . . . Johnny Mathis." He croons "Chances Are" and closes on an Anthony Newly song. Vigorous applause follows.[12]

The trio plays "When You're Smiling" as the guests and staff amble out of the nightclub. "It's a good way of life here, and we hope it will continue for a long time," said guest Jeanne Myers, "but we know that the end of this generation will be the end of this way of life. So we have to enjoy these blessed years while they're blessed."[13]

In nearby Greenfield Park, the Sunshine Colony, owned by the Levinson's who owned the Tamarack Lodge for many years, was also caught in a time warp. After the Levinson family sold their resort, the new owners faced financial troubles and they never opened for the 1994 season, keeping the deposit money of dozens of elderly Jews who were paying between five and six thousand dollars for their bungalows with complete access to hotel facilities. One of my mother's friends was a victim who lost a thousand dollar deposit.

At least since the late 1940s, there had been what were in effect private bungalow colonies owned by a family or a group of friends and not rented to the general public. One such place in Woodbourne was SIG's Country Club, named for Sarah and Isadore Goldstein who were the common parents, in-laws, or grandparents of all the occupants. Beginning in New York City in the 1970s, many rental properties were turned into condominiums and cooperatives. The trend reached the Catskills as the traditional industry was in decline. Groups of former tenants converted old colonies into co-ops where they, and their self-selected kind, could also recapture the past. They spruced up the bungalows and refurbished the casino. "In the late eighties visitors could hear the familiar click of mah-jongg tiles and the shuffle of pinochle cards."[14] These people, like the Komito crew, re-created an environment very different from that of their children or grandchildren. Their world is the late 1940s and early 1950s, and they now own it.

Paula Yeager, a Liberty real estate agent who had spent her summers in bungalow colonies, notes that most buyers felt "a sentimental value besides the land values. They all seem to feel like they're coming back home."[15] Green Acres Colony, between Loch Sheldrake and Liberty, is a case in point. Similar to other nearby colonies—Breezy Corners and Sunshine Colony—Green Acres became a co-op when one man, in this case, Henry Dyzenhaus, persuaded eighteen of his friends to buy the colony in 1981 as a home for July and August. "We used to come to the Catskills with our children," Dyzenhaus recalled. "We rented a bungalow. Then we went to The Raleigh and Grossinger's and Brown's. Then we decided to come here for a little longer—the whole summer."[16]

Green Acres is maintained by a five-member committee that oversees the colony and sets an annual maintenance fee, usually at less than five hundred dollars. Like most bungalow colonies occupied by the elderly, the swimming pool is meticulously maintained—but almost never used. The common thread at Green Acres is that the majority of investors are Polish survivors of the Holocaust. Israel Korman, a co-op member, felt that "the Germans had taken their relations, so this became a family."[17]

Even when the normative bungalow colonies were in full-swing, Holocaust survivors would often segregate themselves. Author David Gold recalls that at Cutler's Cottages the Holocaust survivors rented close together in one area of that sprawling complex.[18] About a 120 Holocaust survivors are expected to be interviewed by field researchers for the Shoah Visual Historical Foundation, the organization founded by Steven Spielberg and made possible by profits from the movie *Shindler's List*. Jane Beallor, one of the Sullivan County interviewers, recalled in 1996, "one of the first things we did say, 'We've got to cover the bungalow colonies. . . . We really felt it was important in the summer. It's a great opportunity to reach a great number of survivors.'"[19]

At Green Acres, the new owners renovate their own units, and while most people keep their knotty-pine walls, many have remodeled the kitchens and baths and "added mirrored closets." Co-ops often bloom with flowers, which are usually sparse at rental bungalows. Before I knew its story, I had noticed many times the white-painted rowboat that Mr. Dyzenhaus uses as a planter near his front door. He keeps it filled with marigolds and petunias.

Reflective of its current cooperative owners' ages, the former Gold and Rados Bungalow Colony in Kiamesha is now named Silvergate. A younger co-op community of Catskill-goers can be found at Lansman's in Woodbourne, where most families actually have young kids and live a very up-to-date life. Another co-op trend is bringing an entirely new clientele into the Catskills. These are young people, often residents of Soho or other trendy places in New York City, who want "an inexpensive way to have a summer place." Gerry Laybourne, whose "grandmother was from a farm in North Dakota" and who worked for Nickelodeon, wanted a summer place: "But given our financial situation, . . . we couldn't find anything we could afford until we joined five other couples, with a total of ten kids," and bought at a colony.[20] The Laybournes have taken down the ceilings, removed the partition walls of their formerly two-unit bungalows, and were planning the installation of sky-lights. In the 1980s, a double bungalow with two to four bedrooms, two kitchens, and two baths typically sold for ten to twenty thousand dollars, with maintenance fees in the $700 to $1,800 range. Other co-ops have also attracted young artists. Like those colonies which appealed to fussy renters before them, successful co-ops are based at the minority of colonies that were well-built, well-sited, and had good facilities.[21]

It is the people from places like The Aladdin and The Silvergate—the second-home owners—and the New Orthodox bungalow tenants who crowd the bargain movies in South Fallsburg and Loch Sheldrake on a summer evening. When I was a kid, the sight of a Hasidic Jew was a rare novelty. Every year in August, a Hasid, *pishke* in hand,[22] would come by to raise money for Israel, but that was the extent of it. Change became evident in the late 1950s as sightings of Hasidim became more frequent. While we had always had a religious tenant or two, they blended into the dominant culture. In 1959, a man approached Grandpa about renting the whole place, our living quarters in-cluded, for a group of religious Jews. He also discussed it with my father, but they refused.

In 1978, we had our first ultraorthodox tenants since the 1940s. They were two couples in their early sixties who rented both sides of a new bungalow, and they even put up an *eruv,* which was my first indication of how different these "New Orthodox" people were. An *eruv* is an enclosure within which you can do ordinary chores, like picking up a child, on the Sabbath. It is a symbolic ex-tension of your house and yard. Their *eruv,* physically, was simply a heavy cord strung between trees. In subsequent years, I learned that there are community *eruvim* erected around orthodox communities across the United States. In most communities, there is an "*eruv* [phone] line" that the observant can call as the Sabbath approaches to make sure the *eruv* is intact.[23]

In the film *Sweet Lorraine,* the hotel owner talks about her annual offer from the Hasidim for her place, but she won't sell. By the mid 1960s, it seemed that everyone was selling to the ultraorthodox or the Hasidim—and they would transform the heart of the old Borscht Belt. Indeed, one might agree with au-thor George Kranzler that "one of the by-products of the Hasidic revival . . . [is that] they have saved the 'Jewish Mountains from total ruin.'" While there are many ruined resorts around, "the better ones have been taken over by Ha-sidic *yeshivot* [schools] for their boys and girls. Others have become centers of bungalow colonies."[24]

The 1960s saw the rebirth of a young modern orthodoxy whose members are very traditional. Their women wear modest clothing, never appearing with bare leg or limb; the men seldom appear in shorts, but they do wear sports clothes. The men all cover their heads with yarmulkes and wear *tzitzit,* or fringed prayer garments, under their clothes. The local goyim started referring to such Jews as "yammies," a reference to their head coverings.

Religious observations aside, most New Orthodox colonies operate like old-line colonies. They have active day camps and entertainment in the casinos, which starts very late on Saturday night. Frequent discussions concern whether a couple is "FFB" (*fromme* [religious] from birth) or "BT" (*Baal Teshuvah,* for-merly nonreligious persons who have returned to the fold).[25] The recessionary early 1990s had a baleful effect on many New Orthodox, as on society in gen-eral. Summer rentals declined, as did most local business. These trends, and per-petual tenant complaints (with religious variants), are highlighted in the whin-ing and bitter essay "Catskills on Self Destruct,"[26] which appeared in an orthodox newspaper. This is worth careful study because it reflects both the eternal trends in the Catskills and the lifestyle and concerns of the New Orthodox.

The essay's anonymous author recalls a ten-year period of summers spent in "a modern orthodox bungalow colony," where "the bungalow is small, but the facilities are very adequate and the grounds are clean." Problems for the author began when she and her friends went to rent their bungalows and were told by the owner that only husbands could sign the rental contracts. This woman was probably a BT, while the owner was an FFB. When her husband, who had to make an extra trip to the mountains, read the contract, he learned about the extras: entertainment, day camp, and "five dollars per day for each guest that sleeps over." And the rental is subject to an occupancy tax. He also learned that the colony owner (like my mother) appreciated *"Tish A' Bov,"* because in the contract the owner states that the pool will be closed for the nine-day observance "even to the day campers for instructional swimming." Among the New Orthodox world, pleasure swimming during the holiday is forbidden. Educational use of the pool is not. This owner was making his own rules. To the owner, there was money to be saved in keeping the pool closed to all.

Once the season started, she noticed that her owner was not a very trustworthy person, but a tightwad, out to get extra money from tenants at every turn, starting with a four dollar key deposit. The owner won't let the tenants install their own air-conditioners; tenants must rent one from him—and only one air-conditioner per unit is allowed. While the author believes this unreasonable, I imagine that the limit on the number has to do with the electric wiring, otherwise, renting of multiple units would be financially desirable. Other of the owner's decisions seem more capricious. He locks the laundry facilities at 8:00 P.M. and he won't allow tenants to play tennis with their guests. Only tenant to tenant play is allowed. The owner, understandably, collects bicycles left overnight on the sidewalks. But, the next day he "was too busy . . . to return them."

The owner is not even cooperative about use of the colony's *shul.* He won't allow the use of the *shul* for an *oneg* (postmeal celebration) on Friday night, and, while the *shul* is air-conditioned, on Saturday worshipers discover that the units are set on low and "controls are removed and sealed up." The owner also will not allow a *kiddush* to be served in the *shul* after services. Here he was probably concerned with cleaning costs. On the Sabbath, the owner "is nowhere to be found. In fact, he never leaves his home at all on *Shabbat*. In fact, he and his family never come to *shul* to *daven* (pray). Never!" Obviously, from an outside observer's perspective, the owner was taking the "day of rest" concept very seriously; he considered mingling with his tenants "work." The owner was also mysterious. He assured tenants that the *eruv* was intact, but he wouldn't show the local *eruv* committees its boundaries. After-the-Sabbath conditions were no better, "Saturday night entertainment is an insult to your intelligence. Outside guests are allowed in for a ten dollar entrance fee, and after a while you learn not to attend yourself." If you want to form an entertainment committee for next year, "the owner says go someplace else if you don't like it." The alternative to the casino is the movies and then a place to eat. This, too, has its shortcomings. "The few kosher places [all run seasonally by New Yorkers] are crowded, dirty, and not well-managed." However, the author realizes that "the locals want your summer trade, and the local authorities do their best to maintain order with their limited summer staff." Making matters worse for tenants: "You return home to find the tennis courts well-lit, ready for play, and . . . locked. The owner is asleep."

The first Sunday of the season was a disaster. Even though the baseball league was in full swing, the owner would not allow a game to be played on his field because it rained the night before and he was afraid someone would get hurt. "The knish man is here. The bread man is here. The sock man is in the parking lot. All have paid their *vigorish* [kickback] to the owner to hawk their wares." Still, tenants could go swimming: "The pool is open to all, but the water is ice cold. The owner filled it [at] the last minute as the lifeguards weren't hired to arrive early [actually lifeguards are not needed for a locked pool. The owner was saving money on electricity and chemicals]. No floats or tubes allowed. The seventeen-year-old lifeguard will save your children. Pool is locked at 6:00 P.M. No time for a late swim." Sundays were barbecue days. After cooking and serving your guests, it's clean-up time. But there is "no outside water spigot. The owner refuses." He is obviously very frugal.

Since everyone basically sacrifices for their children's sake, one would think that conditions for children would be of prime concern. "Children need summer *shiurim* [religious study and lessons] and the parents decide to hire a *rebbe*," but the owner refuses to let them use an empty room as a *cheder* (school). "Learn on the grass" was the landlord's attitude. Day camp was a disaster. "Children wandered all over the place. Counselors are no better or older than babysitters." When inventory runs out after the first week, parents had to buy additional supplies! Then there are the owner's children who "attend camp and wreak havoc in their own groups. They usurp authority and threaten the campers with insults backed by their parents' supremacy." There was no help from the head counselor, "a local in need of a position." The camp lacked everything, "no direction, no supplies, no sing [*sic*], no color wars." Eventually, "parents decided to pay the day camp across the road and sent their children there." In the fall of 1990, when tenants had to decide about the next year, rates were due to go up and "there are new restrictive clauses in the rental contract. If you sue the owner it must be done locally." And worst of all, "the owner is considering renting to *Goyim* or non-*Shomrei Shabbat*."

Came the summer of 1991, and your old colony has over forty empties of the ninety units. "There is only one struggling Sunday morning baseball team. The *shul* has only one *minyan*. . . . Neither the owner nor his now grown children attend services. They are driving people away with their ever-rising rates." The owner will never learn. "He will be the *Rebbe*, the *Mashgiach* [religious arbiter], the Laundromat and supplier to all that have no other alternatives for a summer away from the hot city." But the disgruntled writer feels she does not need the greedy landlord's place. There are other alternatives: "Yeshiva day camps and summer sleep-away camps. Weekends away with family." All of these would cost less. "This bungalow owner is on his own mission. No, he will never learn, the Catskills are on self-destruct."[27]

Humorless, and even grim, the author's 1990s laments are basically the same as Joey Adams's more humorous accounts of the late 1920s and 1930s. Good tenants versus bad landlords. The sweet, reasonable tenant is always working for the common good. The landlord always wants the last bit of profit, and he even expects to sleep at night. While "The Catskills on Self Destruct" revolves around nasty tales, happier landlord-tenant relationships are, no doubt, more common; but then, nobody writes odes to landlords.

There is a brighter side. Fialkoff's, in Monticello, is an example of a well-run and friendly colony that successfully caters to an orthodox crowd. It has 110 bungalows and a real Olympic-sized pool. Perhaps the most deluxe modern-orthodox variant on the bungalow colony is Vacation Village in Loch Sheldrake (on the grounds of the former Hotel Evans), where the accommodations (down to the tasteful brown-colored siding) look more like suburban accommodations than they do bungalows, and "where the families of accountants and diamond merchants languidly push baby carriages along the lake."[28] In 1995, author Robert Eisenberg observed, "Ten weeks in the Catskills isn't cheap. . . . A simple bungalow in just a run-of-the-mill colony costs about $2,000 to $3,000, not including food or transportation."[29]

Many Hasidim avoid clashes with their landlords, because most Hasidim go to bungalow colonies owned by their groups or congregations. The remnants of Europe's Hasidic movement made their way to America by 1950, and they settled mostly in neighborhoods in Brooklyn and did their best to re-create their old world. Like the New Orthodox, the Hasidim have large families and do not ride on the Sabbath, but unlike the New Orthodox, they must be near their *rebbe,* or leader. Here then, in these orthodox groups, you have a large group of Jews voluntarily bound by many of the previously externally applied bonds—bonds rejected by an earlier generation of secular Jews. These groups also turn their backs on America's changing mores and values: Those which most Jewry have so triumphantly embraced. The wives usually do not work outside the home; they observe the *mitzvot* of women, which is to be home-bound. They have large families. Families of five to seven children are routine. Ten or twelve children is not unusual. Most Hasidim live in crowded urban neighborhoods, such as Williamsburg, Borough Park, and Crown Heights in Brooklyn, where there is little green space or places to play, other than the streets. In most of their neighborhoods, they live in an uneasy state of truce with their Black and Hispanic neighbors. It is very difficult for many to have adequate room to house their large families because of the geographic constraints of the neighborhoods. If they leave their reconstituted *shtetlen* (small towns), they need the support of a community, a *shul* that's exactly right, a source of *glatt* kosher food,[30] and even of kosher socks.[31] The Hasidim even have

a center where teams of expert *dayanim,* judges, and *poskim,* rabbinical ritual authorities, meet regularly as announced in advance in the weekly *Der Yid. Hatzolah,* the superb medical emergency volunteer corps, has a number of stations in the Catskill mountains whose teams are available at all times and work closely with the local police, physicians, and hospitals. A large number of vans, cars, and buses commute daily from the city to the mountains and back, in addition to regular bus service.[32]

The Catskills is a perfect place for them. From the 1960s to 1980s, they bought numbers of properties increasing in geometric progression. The transformation was not happy for everyone. "When the religious people came along," recalls seventy-six year-old Morris Franzel of Brooklyn, "they kicked us out in a manner of speaking. They told us they were religious and if we could abide by their rules we could stay, but we're in the Reform movement." Franzel and his wife left. "So we looked around until we found this home of the aged," he said, talking of Kaufman's Bungalow Colony.[33] The Hasidim and the New Orthodox are not always kindly to their less-religious brethren. One day I saw several husky women try to push their way ahead of my frail, but still very vocal, mother in a bakery line. "I didn't let them get away with it," Mother said proudly.

The most visible sign of the transformation of a bungalow colony into a New Orthodox or Hasidic, hermetically sealed world is the swimming pool. The pool, usually surrounded by a chain-link fence but visible to all, must now be rendered opaque. This fence must be converted into a *mechitza*.[34] The favored way is to attach eight-foot fiberglass awning sheets to the chain link. The orthodox do not permit mixed-sex swimming, and so there are men's hours and women's hours for the pool. Much more subtle, of course, is that each place is surrounded by an *eruv*. At most Hasidic colonies, the casino and day camp buildings are turned into a *shul* and houses of study. At the Hasidic colony Camp Tiferes, Rabbi Mordechai Perl drills "seventeen children in the lessons of the Talmud" for four hours a day under uncomfortable conditions. "Life in the bungalow is hard," he observed, thinking about his first-rate Brooklyn classroom. "We do it for the kids."[35]

Most Hasidic colonies are owned by their tenants' religious organizations, and since colonies have religious facilities, the organizations invariably ask for and receive tax exemptions. As a result, an incredible percentage of the real estate in the town of Fallsburg has been removed from the rolls—and tax rates for the remaining property owners are among the highest in the state. This has created great tension between older residents, Jewish and gentile, and the Hasidim, who show up everywhere in the region except on the tax rolls.

In Brooklyn, an Hasidic family might have a five- or six-room apartment; in the mountains, that shrinks to two or three, but they gain the outdoors. Kanfer quotes Terry Fuchs—whom he calls "the eternal Catskill wife" and who is the mother of five young—regarding Hasidic wives: "The husbands of most of them don't like it here. . . . For the wives it's an easier life. There's less housekeeping, and when you don't have your husband here you don't cook as much."[36] The Hasidic communities in Williamsburg do their best to help the husbands get through the summer. A special summer cafeteria has been established in the neighborhood center, "which serves ample and nourishing food to husbands . . .[who] would otherwise have been forced to subsist all week long on their own makeshift provisions or the rather expensive restaurant meals, instead of the nominal fee charged by the communal cafeteria."[37]

Religious observances aside, some aspects of life at the orthodox and Hasidic colonies are familiar. Clothing and food peddlers visit regularly. At one colony, Kanfer notes the weekly arrival of a sneaker salesman—whose van bears the license plate "King Shoe"—followed a few minutes later by 'Dave the Pickle Man.' The Hasidic bookmobile, featuring orthodox children's books, also visits.[38]

Always looking for 'kosher' experiences, the orthodox camps and family groups visit Taivail Farm in Woodbourne, which advertises itself as "An Authentic *Shomrei Shabbat* Farm in the Catskills," where visitors can take hayrides; buy goat's milk, eggs, and organic vegetables; "Pet and Feed" the animals; and purchase "Judaica Art by Kalman." Run by artist Kalman Freidus, his wife Gittel, and their nine children, Taivail Farm is part stage-set from *Fiddler on the Roof* and part Knotts Berry Farm. All the human males wear *tzitzit*.[39]

The New Orthodox and the Hasidim are in many places—in the supermarkets and at phone booths. You don't see the Hasidim at the movies, which they avoid as too worldly. Hasidim have to be among America's worst drivers—being urban dwellers does little to help. Their vehicles, of whatever age and grandeur, usually have an overabundance of road wounds. Hasidim are rarely seen driving well-polished automobiles.

Baseball has a special place in male orthodox life. The opening sequence of the film *The Chosen* revolves around a game between orthodox and Hasidic boys in Williamsburg.[40] Sports are an acceptable outlet for *yeshiva* students who go to school from 8:00 A.M. to 6:00 P.M. Pick-up games of stickball and punch ball are also good ways to let off steam.[41] Rare organized sports activity favors baseball. Baseball is not only a very American sport, but it is one you can play wearing traditional clothing. Leave off your jacket and your hat, put on a pair of sneakers, affix your yarmulke with several bobby pins, and you are ready to play.

In the Catskills, the Hasidim organized the OBBL (Orthodox Bungalow Baseball League), which really plays softball. The league has grown from five teams in the 1970s to four divisions of thirty-two teams (four hundred members) in the 1990s. Teams are invariably named after their colony. Players from the Clearview Country Club compete as the Clearview Crowns. They play the Beverly Hillbillies, Green Tree Niners, Beaver Lake Gentry, and others, in an eight-week season beginning July Fourth weekend. This is a world where the New Orthodox and Hasidim can compete. Indeed, this is viewed as the only event that can "bring together various Jewish communities in the area."[42] Their games are played on Sunday morning and reflect a wide spectrum who regularly take a three-day weekend. Many Hasidim are self-employed or work for other Hasidim in discount merchandise. They dominate the New York City discount electronics field, and are very active in the jewelry field as well. Many come to the mountains Thursday night and leave on Sunday. Smaller numbers work a half-day on Friday. They absolutely cannot ride on *Shabbat* so that if there were to be a traffic delay or a breakdown on Friday and they could not reach their destination by sundown, they would be stranded until Saturday night.

The very roads to the Catskills have been changed by the orthodox. Billboards announcing "Moshiach Is on the Way" were placed along Route 17 by the Lubavitcher Hasidim who believed that their aged *rebbe,* Menochem Schneerson, was the Messiah. Now the movement is split into factions over whether or not the now-deceased rabbi is indeed the Messiah. Billboards, newspaper ads, and Web sites try to provide answers.[43] To thirty-four year-old Solomon Weber, an orthodox customs broker, "if the Messiah is going to come, it is going to be right here on the Thruway. Here all the Jews can get together."[44]

Only at the Sloatsburg rest stop on the Governor Thomas E. Dewey Thruway will you find a "*Mincha* Area." *Mincha* is the prayer devout Jewish men recite each day, in groups of ten or more, between midday and sunset, while facing east. The reason *mincha* is recited on a small patch of state land is reflective of the new, and perhaps more aggressive, complexion of Sullivan County's summer Jewry.

The story begins in the summer of 1989, when a thruway official sent a memo to highway police about "a very dangerous situation" that existed outside of the Harriman Toll Plaza, "the gateway to the Borscht Belt."[45] Every summer hundreds of thousands of orthodox Jews pass here "on their way to summer communities, homes, and bungalows in the Catskills." The most dangerous night of the week was Thursday at about six o'clock, when thousands of men leave Brooklyn after work. Fearing they wouldn't get to their destinations in time, orthodox men would pay their toll and then pull their cars over on the shoulder and "begin to wave down others until they had the quorum of ten required for prayer." As the men prayed, any children they might have with them "played at the rim of the thruway, and the traffic slowed." State police spokespersons described the practice as "a situation meant for disaster." Alarmed, police and highway officials worked with the governor's office to find a safe place for worshipers to pray, away from the traffic flow. Temporary *mincha* areas were established off the highway, and in 1993 when the Sloatsburg rest stop was opened, it had a permanent, dedicated spot. Rabbi Edgar Gluck, special assistant for community affairs for the state police, is very proud of the new facility that is probably unique in the world. "The sign says 'Service Area,'" he said, "and we take it literally. We hold services." The *mincha* area serves the whole spectrum of Jewish orthodoxy from the casually dressed New Orthodox in their polo shirts and knit yarmulkes to the Hasidic groups. "In addition to the better-known groups like the Lubavitch and Satmar, there were also the Popa, the Spinka, the Munkatcha, the Signet, the Kasho, and the Nicholsburg." Only an expert can tell them all apart. The American Civil Liberties Union questioned the propriety of setting aside a "*Mincha* Area" on public property. They suggested a more neutral designation, "Meeting Area."[46]

Woodbourne, my summer hometown, is reflective of the changes within the bungalow world of the Catskills. Hotel people were a moderate presence in town. Woodbourne had no major hotel, and hotels generally made a terrific attempt to keep their guests on their grounds. Previously, I have described the Woodbourne of the normative, Jewish, middle-class years. When I went to town during the 1940s to early 1960s, I knew all the shopkeepers and many of the other people on the street. By the end of the 1960s, many of the older merchants had died, their stores closed, and Woodbourne was abandoned at night. Stores that had closed at midnight, or later, now closed at nine o'clock. Then came the surge of the New Orthodox and the Hasidim, and by the mid 1970s the main street of Woodbourne hummed once again, but with an altogether different street persona. An evolution was underway that would transform Woodbourne's business street from a year-round operation to summer-only.

When I go into the village now, I feel like a stranger in a strange world, and my mother has largely stopped going into any store in Woodbourne besides the bakery and the drugstore. Woodbourne's luncheonettes now have names like "The Glatt Spot," and the teenage favorite, "The Kosher Inn," which adjoins a game arcade and sells soft ice cream, *glatt* kosher, of course. There's a kosher pizzeria and a changing group of other establishments with an orthodox emphasis. For a few years there was the *Aliya* Center, for recruiting immigrants for Israel. There are clothing shops that sell the long-skirted, high-necked, and long-sleeved fashions required by orthodox women. They also sell the scarf-like head covering women wear, especially when not wearing their *sheitelen,* or wigs.[47] Most orthodox women no longer shave their heads after marriage, but rather keep their hair closely cropped. During the day the street is alive with long-skirted women and their young. The little girls are in bright colors, but always wearing tights. The boys are already in white and black, and they sport side curls. They buy fruit from a street vendor, and on Thursday and Friday a flower vendor sets up on the street in front of the small supermarket, Semel's, which is the branch of a store in Borough Park in Brooklyn. "Stranded in the Bungalow Colony?" an ad for Semel's asks, "Use the SEMEL'S SHUTTLE to get you out of your dilemma and into a Woodbourne Shopping Frenzy." In addition to shopping at Semel's, you can go to the bakery, the drugstore, the post office, the bookstore. Buy pizzas, ice cream, and take-out food, "and enjoy lunch at our many restaurants." The Semel Shuttle is free with a fifty dollar grocery order. "When you are finished shopping in Woodbourne, the SEMEL'S SHUTTLE will take you back to your colony." Demarking the town further is a bookstore, Hakol B'sefer Judaica, that sells commentaries on the Talmud (and copies of the Talmud, itself), stylish yarmulkes, and Yiddish and Hebrew music, samples of which blare all day. There is also a South Fallsburg branch. Both offer "Fax and Photocopy Service."[48]

While the Orthodox women may look quaint to passersby, they are not the Yiddish *mommen* (mothers) of yore. Many don't cook from scratch, especially during the week when the husbands are away. A number of food stores offer strictly kosher take-out—BBQ chicken and other variants on normative, multi-ethnic, and convenience foods. (A sixth grade joke: A man walks into a Chinese restaurant. After being seated, he asks the waiter, "What is your specialty?" "Pizza," replies the waiter. "Pizza in a Chinese Restaurant?" he asks in wonder. The waiter responds, "This is a Jewish neighborhood!")

Yum-Yum Glatt Kosher Gourmet in Woodbourne offers "Fast Food Take-out." Kosher Cholov Yisroel of South Fallsburg asserts, "We have the cleanest kitchen in the mountains! Our kitchen is always open for your inspection—for *Kashrus* and cleanliness! (No tricks, no jokes.)" They offer knishes, New York style pizza, and baked ziti. Weiss *Heimishe* Kitchen of South Fallsburg, which specializes "in *Brissim* and *Kiddushim—milchigs, Pareve, Fleishigs*," also delivers "Suppers to All Bungalow Colonies."[49] Hunan Village posits, "I'm on vacation, why should I cook?" The restaurant can provide "a full selection of delicious traditional *Shabbat* foods made on our premises," with free delivery provided, naturally.[50] They also feature kosher Chinese food.

All orthodox communities need a *mikvah,* or ritual bath. Women, for example, must go to the *mikvah* after each menstrual cycle to purify themselves before resuming sexual relations with their husbands. Once a rarity, *mikvahs* are found all over the Catskills today. Woodbourne's is located at Camp Shearith, which was the Woodland Bungalow Colony. "A special side entrance with parking area has been provided for your convenience."[51] It was with good cause that Catskill comic Mal A. Laurence quipped, "You can't miss Woodbourne. There's a giant crocheted yarmulke hovering over it with a giant bobby pin in the back. You get great reception on your Walkman."[52]

The year-round business community of Woodbourne has almost disappeared. In 1995, even the post office left the center of town. Today there is a bar (a goyish hangout), a Laundromat, a pizzeria, and a few service businesses. The last old-line store, Lebed's Drugstore, became an odd lots store run by the owner of Hakol B'sefer Judaica. In 1996, it became a restaurant, Pita Mountain. Meyer Lebed was a Woodbourne institution, as well as owner of the last main-stream Jewish business in town. Meyer's parents owned a luncheonette and candy store on Main Street. In the 1950s, Meyer, already married and a father, decided to go to pharmacy school. He transformed Lebed's into a drugstore, going into direct competition with Godlin's Pharmacy across the street, run since the 1930s by Abe Godlin, the son of Woodbourne's first rabbi and one of Woodbourne's Jewish pioneers. Abe was a very successful businessman who had a bungalow colony, behind his drugstore, and other real estate. He owned the largest part of downtown Woodbourne, later owned by his nephew. The 1950s were boom years for Woodbourne, which could easily support two drugstores. The disastrous fire that destroyed most of Woodbourne in 1964 spared Godlin's but burned Lebed's to the ground. Lebed rebuilt a large, modern drugstore that, reflective of its time, was one-third drugstore and two-thirds variety store. The soda fountain was not replaced. Shortly afterwards, Godlin's remodeled and did away with their soda fountain as well. Abe Godlin died in the early 1980s, and Godlin's store today houses You Name It, a summertime toy and tee-shirt emporium where you can buy tee-shirts emblazoned with slogans: Torah's Terrific; Kosher; Enjoy Torah, It's the Real Thing; America, Don't Worry, Israel Is Behind You; and, I Got Stoned in Mea Shearim. This last one features an obviously pirated lethargic Snoopy. "We carry all you need for your bungalow, our kids, and all fun stuff we're famous for!"[53] They also have an odd selection of houseware, hardware, and greeting cards.

Lebed's was the Shortline bus terminal when Woodbourne was served by two bus lines; Godlin's was the Inter-City terminal. When New York got a lottery, Meyer became the local agent. "Meyer's," as the locals called it, was the place to buy the daily and Sunday papers, and huge stacks of *The News, The Mirror, New York Times, The Forward,* and, later, *The Middletown Record* stood on a bench on the sidewalk outside the store. On Rosh Hashona, free-thinker Meyer always closed and went on vacation. In those days, until the early 1980s, the papers were left outside in front of the store. You helped yourself and paid after the holidays.

When the Hasidim and the New Orthodox came, Meyer flourished anew, but in 1989 he said, "enough," and sold to an Indian-born pharmacist, whose business dropped off precipitously because the ultraorthodox prefer to deal with other Jews, even nonobservant ones like Meyer. In that same year, one of our local gas stations was also acquired by Indians, in line with a trend in New York City where Third World immigrants have taken over many of the Mom-and-Pop businesses traditionally run by Jews and Italians. As the ultraorthodox became normative on the summer street, the older Jewish residents often avoided the stores. "There's nothing to buy" or "They're filthy," they would complain.

Most Hasidim I've seen have looked very clean, but, as mentioned before, they do not take great pride in the appearance of their cars, nor in their bungalow colonies. Most colonies have a very ragged appearance. This is not as true of the New Orthodox. The summer stores that both groups run, however, are shabby—repairs and improvements are minimal and cheaply made. If their establishments are not exactly unclean, in their shabbiness they do not appear to be clean. The new groups also litter very heavily. Woodbourne in summer, despite having far more trash barrels than ever, has more litter on the streets than it did earlier.

Many of the goyim and a lot of Jews simply will not go into the center of Woodbourne any day except Saturday, when most of it has closed. Their casual business goes mostly to the Stop and Save convenience store at one end of Woodbourne, now owned by Indians. The Stop and Save is a place where locals meet to get a bagel with *schmier* (cream cheese) and buy the paper. They also meet in the post office, on Saturday, and in the bank, which, like the post office, is across the Neversink, apart from most of downtown. While the summer bungalow population has declined over the years, the year-round population of the town of Fallsburg (of which Woodbourne is a hamlet) has grown from 6,321 in 1950, to 7,959 in 1970, and 11,445 in 1990.[54] Many of these new residents are retirees who have left New York City. Additionally, Woodbourne's contingent of prison employees has grown phenomenally, as the prison, in line with a deplorable national trend, has expanded.

If you want to see the new Woodbourne at its most dramatic, visit it over a summer weekend. Friday afternoon it bustles with activity. *Challah* is to be bought at the bakery. Flowers and fruit and dairy are purchased for *Shabbat*. As the afternoon draws on, activity slows; by six o'clock everything is shut, except the bar, and Woodbourne is as quiet as prior to the season. Parking spaces are everywhere; no one double-parks. On Saturday, only the post office, the convenience store, the bar, and the bank are open. The center of town is almost deserted. The only people you see in the morning are locals, coming for the papers or going to the post office, a few prison visitors waiting for a bus, and an occasional orthodox man hurrying to *shul* wearing a *tallit*. In the afternoon, you see a few families out for a stroll—father wearing a *streimel* and his best *caftan;* mother in a long, shapeless, very colorful garment, which looks like a housecoat; and a group of children with heights organized like steps. There are never infants being carried or pushed in strollers, because it is considered "work" to pick up or carry a baby outside of the *eruv*.

As night falls, the town is again very quiet. By ten o'clock the town begins to come alive. The stores open and the orthodox emerge. On Saturday night, the orthodox do not have their evening meal until after prayers, which are not completed until after sundown. After the meal is the *havdalah* ceremony. When the Sabbath is over they celebrate. The crowd grows and is at its height at about midnight, and Main Street is crowded until two or three. It's a polyglot crowd; bunches of New Orthodox boys who look like normative young teens, some of whom are hip-hop clones, except for the *tzitzit* tassels that stick out of their pants and the tiny yarmulkes that perch on the back of their heads with help from a bobby pin. New Orthodox girls look curiously like 1950s high schoolers, except that they wear tights under their long skirts. Some girls wear short sleeves. Many of their parents come, too. The more modern fathers wear normative sports clothes, with long pants of course, but many of the men are in dark pants and a white shirt, if informal, or a dark suit and white shirt and a tie. A few have beards. All wear the requisite head covering, a yarmulke, usually black, or a hat. The wives are as fashionable as possible, given their constraints. The women were very happy when long skirts were fashionable. The new near-nudity of contemporary attire makes them feel as outsiders. These ladies wear fashionable wigs that look like their own hair.

Then there are the Hasidim, those with side curls, or *payess*.[55] Their teenage boys are in white shirts and dark pants, wear bigger yarmulkes, and have more obvious *tzitzits*. Their girls wear longer skirts and longer sleeves than the New Orthodox, and the girls and boys don't banter back and forth—let along engage in one-on-one boy-girl talk like some of the New Orthodox. Their fathers always have beards and long *payess*. Some wear suits without ties and black hats, others wear ties. Some wear *caftans* and a few wear *streimlen*.[56] The women are often in their characteristic, long, shapeless, but highly colored dresses. They wear wigs, some of which are very far removed from the old *shtetl sheitelen*. Women wear jewelry, and diamonds glitter from fingers and ears.

Main Street becomes a rialto. People meet. People from different colonies see one another. They visit, they talk. They eat. They play arcade games and they shop. There are toys, clothes, including 'kosher' socks, gold jewelry, slogan emblazoned tee-shirts, and Judaica to be purchased. *Klezmer* music blares. The traffic during the 1980s was phenomenal; four to seven police tried to keep the traffic moving and the would-be double-parkers away.

In the 1990s the crowds thinned, as other attractions opened to compete for the Saturday night crowd. Loch Sheldrake's Hunan Vacation Village touts "elegant dining in the Catskills, featuring superb kosher Chinese Cuisine plus a special American Menu (OU [Orthodox Union] supervision)" and a "Cabaret Comedy Night," which includes two comedy acts and a light midnight supper from 11:30 P.M. to 2:00 A.M. "Graduate from the Woodbourne mob scene. It's about time."[57] Catskill Funland—featuring Go Carts, a video arcade, and miniature golf, along with refreshments from Mendlesohn's Cholov Yisroel—offered *"Motzai Shabbot"* (post-Sabbath) fun from 10:00 P.M. to 2:00 A.M. [58]

Once or twice every summer, my kids, my wife, my mother, and I stop at the Kosher Inn (which started life as The Lucky Dip in the 1970s) for a late Saturday night cone *cum* people-watch. Once my mother said to me, "Don't you think you should wear a yarmulke when you come here?" "Why?" "To show respect." "Hell no. I was here first." Anyhow most people avoid us, politely. In July 1991, Mother, Susan (my wife), and I were having our frozen custard when a bearded gentleman approached us. He gave my mother a religious tract, and then he looked at my dark-haired, but blue eyed, wife—and his radar went off. "You're not Jewish?" he asked. She shook her head, and he left quickly. There is really very little interaction between the orthodox and the remnants of the earlier Jewish culture. The only time anyone voluntarily spoke to me on the street in recent years, was when the Lubavitcher *"Tfillin*-mobile" was in town and these proselytizers tried to bring me back into the fold.

"The trouble with the Hasids is that there's no way of knowing who they really are," relates Walter Klein, a baker at the now-closed, Liberty-landmark Katz's Bakery. One of his colleagues observed, "To them, we're the outsiders. We resent them and they resent us."[59] The Hasidim are like water and oil to other Jews, as well as to the gentile world. The gentiles did not welcome the earlier Jews to their towns, even though the Jews mostly cared about fitting in and being neighbors. Grandpa always urged us to behave in front of the goyim; and in the book *He Had It Made,* the hotel owner sends food to her sick, gentile neighbor. But the Hasidim don't want to be part of the community. When the Jewish settlements started in the Catskills, the gentiles looked down on the Jews. Then the Jewish farmers looked down on the summer people. What's new about this Catskill group is that the Hasidim look down on the earlier groups.[60]

One 1996 event upset many. At about one in the morning on Sunday, 7 July 1996, we were driving through Woodbourne on our way home after seeing a play at the Forestburg Playhouse. Woodbourne was alive with people, and we all remarked that the street was the busiest we'd seen it in years. Forty-five minutes later, an incident erupted between two Christian locals, ages nineteen and twenty-one, and several orthodox young men near the pool table in a local arcade. Once outside, the locals and an orthodox boy fought. Police were called. While the police were questioning bystanders, the twenty-one year old hit a police officer and started to run. The crowd ran after the local, but luckily the police got to him first. The New Orthodox and the Hasidim would not disperse, so the police sprayed pepper mace into the air to break up the crowd. "Bystanders said it was the first violent confrontation in recent memory between year-round residents and the many orthodox and ultraorthodox Hasidic Jews who spend the summer in communities in the surrounding countryside." The twenty-one year old was charged with, among other offenses, "aggravated harassment as a bias crime."[61] Was the event a fluke or part of a national trend of hatred?

On a quieter note, it is obvious that many local residents don't like the image Woodbourne has. On 15 July 1996, the *Times Herald Record* headline read, "Kosher Comes to Woodbourne." The inside story, "Woodbourne Gets Religion," describes the Woodbourne summer experience.[62] It elicited a number of responses from irate readers. Nancy Greene, "a year-round resident of Woodbourne," found the article "extremely disquieting." Greene responds, "We have twelve months of religion in Woodbourne, not just two out of the twelve. Our churches and synagogues do not close up." After listing the stores and services that stay open (auto repair, antique shop, and so on), she ends, "Our town does not dry up for ten months, it simply quiets down."[63]

Sunday mornings have a very different feeling now in downtown Woodbourne than they did in the preorthodox days. Town then was filled with people in the dairy store buying smoked fish and bagels. Papers sold vigorously. Since the Orthodox party so late on Saturday, they don't become much of a presence in town until about noon. You can always find a place to park before noon. By afternoon, though, the town is full, and in the late afternoon and early evenings you see cars full of orthodox men on their way back to the city—just as we saw in earlier generations.[64]

Another group of Jews, new to the Catskills, are the Russians. Ever since Gorbachev's USSR began to allow Russia's Jews to emigrate fairly freely, Russians, both Jewish and Christian, have transformed Brooklyn's Brighton Beach neighborhood into "New Odessa." Like earlier Russian, Polish, and Lithuanian Jewry, the Russians are finding their way to the Catskills, which reminds them of "the old country." Unlike earlier immigrants, however, these new arrivals don't speak Yiddish. Visually, they are very unobtrusive, looking like normative (often) lower-middle-class New York Jews, but they speak in Russian. Russian is familiarly heard in the supermarket, the movie theaters, and at the giant flea market open during the season at the Monticello Raceway. Some of the few remaining nonorthodox colonies, such as Ann Macin's in Greenfield Park, rent mostly to recent Russian Jewish immigrants.[65] My mother often uses car service in New York City to get around. One of her favorite drivers is Alex, a Russian, "who has a place in Monticello." An older cycle continues, quietly.

In Swan Lake, Leah Borodova, a seventy-one-year-old grandmother, spends two weeks at Willow Acres Colony with her two grandchildren, a boy and a girl, and her daughter-in-law. The girl's parents, computer programmers, are expected up for the weekend. They'll squeeze "their own cots into the two-room bungalow in the manner of bungalow dwellers past."[66] They pay four hundred dollars rent for their two week stay. Like many of the new Russian immigrants, they were not raised in the Jewish tradition. They don't cook traditional Jewish food, but Russian food. The grandmother has already made "a syrupy juice out of green apples she had picked," and soon she would "hunt for ripe mushrooms in the woods behind the colony, then dry them for winter storage, just as she did in the Urals." She loves the area: "The air, the weather, the quietness, . . . I think I'm there at home."[67]

There has always been a smattering of non-Jewish bungalow colonies in the Borscht Belt, mostly owned by Italians. Some, such as Borellos in Hasbrouck, rented to a largely Jewish population. Others cater to a Christian clientele. An altogether new non-Jewish group has appeared lately, the Koreans. Sullivan County reminds them of the countryside near Seoul. (Who says Sullivan

County lacks universal appeal?) A Korean businessman, Soung Kiy Min, even owns Grossinger's, the hotel of legend, and there is at least one Korean colony owned by Ye Shik Choi, a Presbyterian elder from Queens. One problem for both of these resort owners is that Koreans have not yet become used to the concept of vacations.[68]

The most exotic change to the Sullivan County landscape has been the number of hotels that have become "New Age Havens." The most successful of these is the sprawling Shree Muktanada Ashram, a Hindu meditation center with a strong, formerly Jewish following. This center has swallowed up three former kosher hotels and several bungalow colonies in South Fallsburg. The complex, which can accommodate three thousand guests seeking enlightenment, is even more self-contained than the Hasidic world. They have armed guards to keep the outside world away. Like many Hasidic colonies turned into religious camps, it is tax exempt and, therefore, disliked by the locals.[69]

Sullivan County is not the Jewish Alps of yesterday. It is more diverse, and perhaps more bizarre, than the county of my youth. Even if increasing numbers of secular Jews "rediscover" it, it will never again be the Borscht Belt of legend.

Bertha's friend Fran poses at the entrance to bungalow 24 at the Sunshine Colony in Greenfield Park in 1993. She and her husband, Sid, outlived the colony, which never opened for the 1994 season. They lost their substantial deposit at what had been a premium quality bungalow colony.

The Nob Hill Country Club in Kiamesha was making the sometimes rocky transformation from bungalow colony to "Resort Co-Operative" in 1993. Note that they have units both for sale and rent.

In 1993, Green Acres, near Liberty, was a very well-kept colony turned co-op. This building houses three units. Notice the wonderful, idiosyncratic garden design. A bungalow is visible at right.

Lansman's Play House (casino) in Woodbourne in 1993. A professional staff maintains the co-op grounds.

A vendor selling novelty merchandise at Lansman's in 1993. Peddlers of all kinds visit the colonies regularly. It is only at the co-ops and colonies that rent to recent Russian immigrants that you would see secular young Jews today.

One of Richman's bungalows repositioned on the grounds of The Aladdin in Woodbourne, N.Y., in 1993. The windows in the gables over the porch are the give-away. the disparity of style of the bungalows at this assembled colony is overwhelming. A heat-and-air-conditioning unit is in the window on the right.

This 1993 sign on a Kiamesha bungalow colony says it all regarding the change taking place at bungalow colonies throughout the Catskills as the orthodox and the Hasidim replace secular Jews. Bertha Richman's wonderful, live-wire cousins Adele and Harry Goldenberg used to go to this once very secular colony in the 1950s.

In the summer of 1993, Sullivan County storefronts are plastered with notices of Yiddish and Hebrew entertainment being offered at hotels, camps, bungalow colonies, and second-home communities.

(lower right) New Orthodox and Hasidic women often wear clothing that is as fashionable as it can be within their constraints. Upscale ladies even wear Armani, "hemmed discreetly . . . below the knee." Merchants with stores in the city, catering to the religious market, will often bring clothing up to the Catskills to sell to their co-religionists. Consider this 1993 sign to be an invitation to a *fromme* (religious) "trunk show." Holiday Park Bungalow Colony is in Woodbourne. Ultraorthodox, it is one of the few colonies that has kept the name given to it by its former owner—the very secular Woodbourne pharmacy owner, Abe Godlin.

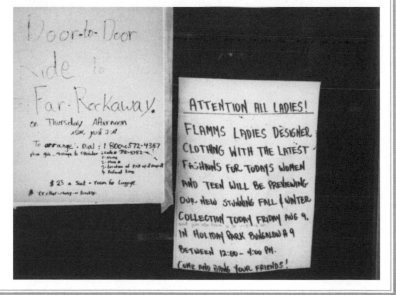

The "line" at an Hasidic colony, 1993. Most Hasidic colonies are surrounded by chain-link fences, and some have become very security conscious after the Papier murders. Air conditioning is a blessing to people who wear heavy clothing, even in the summer. The units are in the rear windows, out of range of this photograph. Typical of the casual attitude Hasidim often have toward their external surroundings, tricycles litter the lawn and a washing machine needs a home. One unit has a screen that conceals the wooden piers supporting the bungalow.

The *mechitza* around the swimming pool in 1993 delineates this orthodox colony near Loch Sheldrake, which closed in 1996. Plastic panels are attached to the chain-link fence surrounding the pool, providing the required privacy for separate-sex swimming.

Mountaindale's *mikva,* or ritual bath, had a very informal sign in 1993 that is typical of the slapdash attention given to exterior appearances among many ultraorthodox. The *mikva* itself follows rigid rules of construction and upkeep. By the 1990s, every Sullivan County town in the bungalow belt has at least one ritual bath to serve their orthodox summer crowd.

Be both orthodox and modern. Prepared foods free the modern matron from the rigors even of cooking for the Sabbath. This sign of the times was posted in a Woodbourne shop window in 1993. In 1997 the Shabbos special at the nearby Chinese restaurant features won ton soup and egg rolls.

A "knishmobile" parked in Loch Sheldrake in 1993. *Glatt* kosher food vendors all display proof of being under the supervision of a particular rabbi or rabbinical council. "Izzy's Knish Nosh is the only one to carry Mom's Knishes. Recipe was *not* sold to Dagan's Pizza in Woodbourne or anybody." The sign refers to a local knish war. Mom's is the lineal descendant of Ruby, the knish man who delivered to Kassack's Bungalow Colony when Irwin worked at their day camp.

Orthodox women shopping on an August day in 1993. The sign Woodbourne Cholov Yisroel Pizza and Falafel is testimony to the area's very special nature. In summertime, Woodbourne is often so busy that several police officers are needed to control traffic. Trying to reconcile the needs of pedestrians, drivers, and parkers, additional local police were hard at work just outside the picture frame when Irwin shot this photo.

On a Saturday afternoon in August 1993, Hasidic boys from a nearby camp walk across the new bridge in Woodbourne. Ordinary daily life is suspended and Woodbourne becomes very quiet on the Sabbath. Most businesses are closed, and parking space is available everywhere.

The Centre Theater in 1993. Once a center of Woodbourne's summer life, it was finally sold in 1996, and it will be converted into a legitimate theater. Next door is Congregation B'nai Isreal where Grandpa Richman was so active.

The end of a dream, Woodbourne, 1996. The fate of many a small or medium-size bungalow colony was a fire (either accidental or planned) or a date with a bulldozer.

A ruined casino in 1996 defaced with graffiti, "Led Zeppelin," is very visible. Located along Route 52 in Dairyland, this sad relic was once the hub of the Joyland Bungalow Colony. The owners were Grandpa Richman's clients. Their name was Halbreich. Grandpa used to joke that they were "half rich," which is the English translation of their name.

The year is 1996. Bertha Richman (second from the left) is the only secular Jew in the Woodbourne bakery. The woman third from the right is obviously wearing a wig under her hat. The lady at the extreme right wears a snood over her close-cropped hair.

15

Ghosts along the Road

As I drive along the roads in Sullivan County, especially those that lead into Woodbourne, I see ghosts. I see hotels that have been converted into schools, drug rehabilitation centers, or bungalow colonies, or that have completely disappeared. I go by bungalow colonies that are now orthodox, and I go by colonies that have vanished. My mind's eye remembers a Sullivan County of vital towns, undrained by the shopping centers that have sprung up outside of Liberty and Monticello drawing year-round business, and the day-to-day business of many summer visitors as well. Even if they don't buy all their food at those malls, the Hasidim and New Orthodox are very evident today, buying milk, orange juice, canned goods, and Pampers. All of these are much cheaper here than in the small town stores or in the on-site grocery stores that still exist—and which continue to exist because they can sell *glatt* kosher products in a *glatt* kosher environment.

Route 42, as it leaves South Fallsburg, is a typical road running through Sullivan County's resort belt. South Fallsburg, itself, is an important Sullivan County community, once a railroad town whose station is now the Town of Fallsburg Municipal Offices. It was a boomtown in the 1920s. Weiner's Resort Furniture is gone, Paul Freed's Hong Kong Shop of "South Fallsburg and Miami Beach" is gone. During the day, Main Street is filled with New Orthodox and Hasidim buying at a *glatt* kosher fish store and at *glatt* kosher butchers. And there's a Jewish bookshop—a branch of Woodbourne's bookshop. The Rivoli theater is an active second-run movie operation, owned by the Rosenshein family. At night, South Fallsburg changes complexion. Apart from the movie and a Chinese restaurant, the only action is at several Black bars, which cater to people who came, and continue coming, to the county to work in the hotels or at the colonies. Many have become year-round residents; many are chronically underemployed.

On the road, my memories pass by. The Irvington Hotel is now an orthodox colony. You pass the new sewage plant. Across the road is a large colony, now orthodox. You pass another colony, with a high fiberglass fence around a swimming pool. There are very few cars in the lot, at midweek. This place must be Hasidic. The New Orthodox women drive—and many have cars. For me, the most poignant stretch of road passes the site of the Senate Hotel, which has vanished. The Flagler Hotel's golf course, where I worked as a caddy at fifteen (albeit briefly), is a sand quarry, and the once elegant Flagler Hotel, the mountain's first grand hotel, is now the Crystal Run School—a facility for retarded adults. Its mission-style main building was torn down. Nestling the hotel is Barron's Bungalow Colony, once one of the most expensive in the mountains—next to The Flagler, no less! In 1991, Barron's advertised in *Der Yid: Voice of American Jewry:* "One and two bedrooms for rent, day camp, lifeguard, groceries on premises, close to camps." No mention of being next to Crystal Run.[1] In 1995, Barron's is the "Summer Garden Cottages"—a *shtetl* renewed. Catskills Playland, a religiously oriented amusement park (it is kosher and it observes the Sabbath), opened a few years ago on the site of the Ambassador Hotel, which had the mountain's first nightclub.

The crossroads town of Fallsburg is next. The Crossways, where we waited in line for pizza, is closed and for sale. (Years earlier it had been the Wunderbar, one of the Catskills' hot late-night clubs, which attracted the fast crowd from the hotels and the bungalows. It was notorious for its drag shows in the late 1940s and early 1950s.) Yit's Garage is still there. A new Stewart's convenience store just opened on the site of a nice old house. The town church went from Methodist church to Porno Shop to Afro-Methodist church to vacant lot. Abe Godlin's branch drugstore is gone. The post office remains.

I pass the former Hotel Furst and the old Murray Hill Hotel. Both were places Grandma Schwebel sometimes summered; both now treat recovering drug addicts. As I approach Woodbourne, I pass the site of Keystecher's Cottages—"Old Man Keystecher" was Grandpa's buddy. Then past the site of the Woodcrest Villa—a rooming house and bungalow colony. The five-mile drive is over. On the right, past the traffic light, is the synagogue, B'nai Israel, and then the Centre Theater.

"One weekend at the Woodbourne theatre patrons were offered a first-run Hollywood feature on Saturday evening followed by a midnight show of Jewish singers," Steven Kanfer reported. "On Sunday, the center held a rally for Schmuel Pressburger, rival of Teddy Kollek for the mayoralty of Jerusalem."[2] The theater never reopened for the 1989 season, but it was rented for a few grossly overcrowded Hasidic events and thoroughly trashed. It was boarded up in the summer of 1991: A bright spot for the future, it is now being developed into a legitimate theater.

I drive through Woodbourne on the new bridge that crosses the Neversink and turn left with Route 42. On the left is the new post office on the site of a Victorian-era hotel and beer parlor. Across the street is the Georgian-Revival lawyer's office, which was the town's most elegant residence. I drive past private homes of many styles. There are arts-and-crafts bungalows, 1920s colonial revivals, and 1960s ranch houses. They are lived in by year-round people, many of whom are prison guards, teachers, and hotel workers.

I pass the River Haven Colony, now a co-op, and George Vantran's farm, now owned by a heavy-equipment firm that uses the barn for storage. I pass John's Garage, which belonged to his father, Art, and I turn right into Richman's. The patio is there, as are the pump house, the garage, and the house—no bungalows, no tenants. I know that I will try to keep this place after my mother passes away. I am ambivalent about Woodbourne, but it is a central aspect of my family's American Dream. Fortunately we were not destroyed by it, as many owners of small colonies were. When the time came, the family could support the colony as we now support the house. While they have spent many summer holidays there, the old house is not as central a part of my children's lives as it is of mine. They have fond memories. But they are very different memories, mixed as they are with remembrances of our Lancaster County summers and trips to Europe.

I think about the colonies I worked at, about the teams we played. What was "Kassack's" is now ultraorthodox. When the Kassacks sold it, it underwent a name change to Robbi Lane Cottages. I had so little interest in it afterwards, I didn't even know it had a newer name along with an orthodox clientele. For this book I learned it is "Golden Gardens." Our athletic archrival, Lansman's, has become a semideluxe secular co-op with eighty-five families in houses made by combining units. There are living rooms, video games, and kids, tennis courts, gas-fired grills, and kids. "Martin Friedman, president of the co-op's board of directors, advised a visitor to disregard the incorporated title. 'We're Lansman's . . . [but] we don't consider ourselves a bungalow colony anymore. We call ourselves a summer resort.'"[3] Kare Free, Woodland, and Jacoby's, like Kassack's, are all orthodox or Hasidic. Meyer Furman's has disappeared. First his "Downtown" became a one-family home, then his "Uptown" became a one-family home, as all the bungalows were sold or demolished. His casino burned down, and twenty-five years after he built it, his beautiful pool was dismantled for the steel plates.

The landscape elsewhere is marred with rotting and decayed resorts waiting to be cleared. An article in a local paper blares, "Filthy, Condemned Bungalows Razed. Welfare tenants cheer as bulldozer levels five dwellings." Like many owners of slum property in New York State, a Greenwood Lake colony owner had been renting her rotting summer cottages to welfare recipients for $650 to $700 per month.[4] Society's ills are Sullivan County's ills. The only constant about the Catskill resorts is change that—since the late nineteenth century—has reflected, in slightly distorted form, the Jewish community of New York and of America.

What will the future hold for the region's bungalows? The answer probably rests with demographics. Every year more old-line bungalow people die. Fewer snowbirds return to bungalow nests. Co-ops, some attracting an artsy non-Jewish crowd, will continue—they provide relatively inexpensive summer homes that can be used for weekends now, for summer-long stays after retirement. Gentrification has not yet become significant in Sullivan County. And while the infusion of new blood, the Russian Jews, is encouraging, the long-term implications are unclear. The future most likely belongs to the New Orthodox and the Hasidim, who are among the fastest growing groups in America.

One letter to the editor of the *New York Times* is a vision of this future. Fifty-year-old Naomi Goldberg writes that at a young age she chose orthodoxy: "Thirty years later, I am the mother of fourteen. I am the grandmother (so far) of seventeen grandchildren." She continues, "calculating conservatively I may have one hundred grandchildren, [and] become great-grandmother to a thousand." Proudly she notes, "In my community, I am not an exception but the norm." Naomi Goldberg had written in response to an op-ed piece in which Jeanne Safer defends her choice not to have children: "Ms. Safer says that she and the women like her are 'models' for the next generation! What generation? They did not have children."[5]

Many of Mrs. Goldberg's fourteen children, one hundred expected grand-children, and one thousand expected great-grandchildren will need some place to go in the summer. Bound by self-imposed restrictions, they will not be able to go to trendy spots. If they remain true to the faith—and most "FFB" do—they will come to completely dominate the bungalow colonies of Sullivan County, and also those of the nearby counties of Orange, Ulster, and Delaware. David Weiss is a Satmar Hasid from Williamsburg who manages a colony in Swan Lake with a wonderful tax-exempt sounding name: "Nel Education Center." The rental in 1993 is a very modest $1,200 a summer. "The women cluster in lawn chairs encircled by baby carriages and small children . . . and play board games like Otello." Their husbands come up for the weekends "and spend much of their days inside a study hall." Manager Weiss observes that "studying is one thing you never take a vacation from." When asked about the impact on the Catskills made by the newer arrivals—the Koreans and the Russians—he is unimpressed. He expects that within a generation or two they will become upwardly mobile and move elsewhere. "They won't last," he said. "The Hasidim have no choice. You can't take ten children and go off to Europe."[6] Tomorrow belongs to the New Orthodox and the Hasidim, as yesterday belonged to my grandparents and my parents. I am the observer, the historian, and, perhaps, the seer.

Notes

I Introduction

1. The spellings of both of these were taken from record labels, the first from *The Barry Sisters: Their Greatest Yiddish Hits,* Tradition Records 2215; and the second from *Connie Francis Sings Jewish Favorites,* MCM Records E3869. Variations often appear in the transliteration of Yiddish and Hebrew words.
2. Arthur Koestler, *The Sleepwalkers* (New York: Viking Penguin, 1969), 416.
3. Leonard Dinnerstein, *Anti-Semitism in America* (New York: Oxford University Press, 1994), 39–40.
4. Alf Evers, *The Catskills: From Wilderness to Woodstock* (Garden City, N.Y.: Doubleday and Co., 1972), 545, 697.
5. Abraham D. Lavender and Clarence B. Steinberg, *Jewish Farmers of the Catskills: A Century of Survival* (Gainesville: University Press of Florida, 1995), 3.
6. Shalom Goldman, *The Jewish Experience in the Catskills* (Burroughs's essays were discussed in this lecture recorded at Sullivan County Community College, Loch Sheldrake, N.Y. [West Hurley, N.Y.: Creative Seminars, 1995]).
7. Lavender and Steinberg, *Jewish Farmers,* 31.
8. Esterita Blumberg, *Remember the Catskills: Tales by a Recovering Hotelkeeper* (Fleishmanns, N.Y.: Purple Mountain Press, 1996), 28.
9. Lavender and Steinberg, *Jewish Farmers,* 30–31. In the period 1940–1960, the Shawanga Lodge was known for its lively young crowd. Bungalow people laughingly referred to it as *"Schvenga* Lodge." *"Schvenga"* is a play on the Yiddish word for 'pregnant.' The hotel had a fast reputation and a young crowd.
10. There is some disagreement about the use of the word *"kuchalein."* My grandfather and his cronies used the term generally. Many others equate *kuchaleins* with rooming houses. They consider bungalows to be of a higher and separate order.

11. Stefan Kanfer, *A Summer World* (New York: Farrar Straus Giroux, 1989), 71–72, 126, 153, 234, 257, 279–83.

12. Harold Jaediker Taub, *Waldorf-in-the-Catskills: The Grossinger Legend* (New York: Sterling Publishing, 1952), fly leaf. The author's copy of this fawning book was autographed by Jennie Grossinger for then Sullivan County Historian Manville B. Wakefield.

13. Oscar Israelowitz, *Catskills Guide* (Brooklyn, N.Y.: Israelowitz Publishing, 1992).

14. From an advertisement flier kept in the Richman archives, *"The History of the Borscht Belt": Part 1* (21 August 1995), 1. This flier was printed by an *ad hoc* group of "writers, artists, musicians, and scholars," who would later form the basis for the Catskill Institute, now housed at Brown University.

15. Donna Gaines, "The Lost Daughters of Zion Return to the Catskills," *Village Voice,* 5 October 1993, 33.

16. Ibid., 36.

17. Barbara Shea, "At Resorts in Catskills, Everyone Is Family," *Lancaster (Penn.) Sunday News,* 10 November 1996, 6.

18. Kendall Hamilton and T. Trent Gegax, "Young Fogies," *Newsweek,* 28 October 1996, 65.

19. Arthur Kober, *Thunder over the Bronx* (New York: Simon and Schuster, 1935), 193–97.

20. Clay Lancaster, *The American Bungalow* (New York: Abbeville Press, 1985), 19.

21. Ibid., 77–78.

22. Ibid., 16.

23. Ibid., 182.

24. Manville B. Wakefield, *To the Mountains by Rail* (Grahamsville, N.Y.: Wakefair Press, 1970), 121.

25. "The Hollywood Country Club," *The Brooklyn Bridge,* writ. Peter Schneider, prod. Gary David Goldberg, CBS Network (30 July 1993), television series.

26. Is the town South Fallsburg or South Fallsburgh? The U.S. Postal Service says Fallsburg. No "h." After World War II, the Postal Service began a conscious effort to remove the "h" from town and city names in the United States. Only communities with clout retained their "h." Pittsburgh, Pennsylvania, is an example of a city that fought for its "h."

27. Sybil Adelman Sage, "Hollywood by Hearse: A Zany Undertaking," *New York Times,* 6 January 1991, N.E., sec. xx, p. 15.

28. Norman Ober, *Bungalow Nine* (New York: Walker and Company, 1962).

29. Cupping was the popular immigration-era medical practice of bringing blood to the skin's surface via the vacuum created by applying bell-shaped cupping glasses to the skin. "Dry cupping" only raised welts. If the skin was scarified before the application of the cups, "wet cupping" resulted as blood was drawn. A scene in the film *Zorba the Greek* (1964) illustrates dry cupping.

30. Miriam Damico, personal interview with the author (Loch Sheldrake, New York), 12 August 1993.

31. Joey Adams, with Henry Tobias, *The Borscht Belt* (New York: Bobbs-Merrill, 1966), 29.

32. Michael Straus, "A Bungalow in the Hills," *New York Times,* 10 June 1956, sec. xx, p. 9.

33. Joseph Berger, "New Accents for Old Ritual: Vacationing in the Catskills," *New York Times,* 12 July 1993, late city edition, B5.

34. Adams, *The Borscht Belt,* 16–34.

35. Henry Tobias, *Music in My Heart and Borscht in My Blood* (New York: Hippocrene Books, 1987), 71–80.

36. Ober, *Bungalow Nine.*

37. Edwin L. Dale Jr., "Floods Batter the Northeast," *New York Times,* 20 August 1955, late city edition, A1.

38. Sidney Offit, *He Had It Made* (New York: Crown Publishers, 1959), 185.

39. Reuben Wallenrod, *Dusk in the Catskills* (New York: Reconstructionist Press, 1957).

40. Harvey Jacobs, *Summer on a Mountain of Spices* (New York: Harper and Row, 1975), 19.

41. Kober, *Thunder*, 92–93.

42. Ibid., 96.

43. Martin Boris, *Woodridge 1946* (New York: Crown Publishers, 1980), 2–3.

44. Ibid., 3.

45. Ibid.

46. Ibid., 22.

47. Ibid.

48. Wallenrod, *Dusk*, 6.

49. *The Rise and Fall of the Borscht Belt,* dir. Peter Davis, 90 min., Villon Films, 1988, video-cassette; distributed by Arthur Cantor, Inc.

2 A. Richman, Woodbourne, New York

1. Russian Jews of Grandpa's time who lived in small towns looked very much like Tevye's family in the movie *Fiddler on the Roof,* dir. Norman Jewison, United Artists, 1971.

2. Materials on the Wilner Benevolent Association are in the Richman archives, as are Abraham Richman's membership ring, dated 1906, and presidential gold watch, dated 1916. "Wilna" is the common spelling, but the organization used "Wilner" because a Wilner is one who comes from Wilna. The story of the Wilna ghetto is shown in the documentary *The Partisans of Vilna,* dir. of photography Danny Shneuer, Euro-American Home Vidco, 1987.

3. Leo Rosten, *The Joys of Yinglish* (New York: McGraw-Hill, 1989).

4. Joey Adams, with Henry Tobias, *The Borscht Belt* (New York: Bobbs-Merrill, 1966), 28.

5. Isaac Landman, "Catskills: Playground of the Masses," *The American Hebrew,* 31 August 1928, 460–63.

6. Ibid.

7. Ibid., 463.

8. Ibid., 460.

9. Ibid.

10. Ibid.

11. Ibid.

12. Myrna Katz Frommer and Harvey Frommer, *It Happened in the Catskills* (New York: Harcourt Brace Jovanovich, 1991), 13.

13. Abraham D. Lavender and Clarence B. Steinberg, *Jewish Farmers of the Catskills: A Century of Survival* (Gainesville: University Press of Florida, 1995), 160–61.

14. Ibid., 161.

15. Dave Barry, "Party Host Turns Batty Landlord," *Harrisburg (Penn.) Sunday Patriot News,* 26 January 1992, G3.

16. Irving Howe and Kenneth Libo, *How We Lived* (New York: Richard Marek, 1979), 42–46.

17. Neil M. Cowan and Ruth Schwartz Cowan, *Our Parents' Lives* (New York: Basic Books, 1989), 44–52.

18. The story of the railroad and its often unpleasant trips is told in Manville B. Wakefield, *To the Mountains by Rail* (Grahamsville, N.Y.: Wakefair Press, 1970).

19. His drugstore at 1631 Eastern Parkway in Brooklyn was used as a location for scenes in

a major motion picture, but they ended up on the cutting-room floor (*Last Angry Man,* dir. Daniel Mann, Columbia Pictures, 1959).

20. Quoted in Frommer and Frommer, *It Happened,* 13.
21. Adams, *Borscht Belt,* 24.
22. Ibid.
23. Quoted in Frommer and Frommer, *It Happened,* 13.
24. David Gold, personal interview with the author, 1 September 1996.

3 Farmer's Life

1. Reuben Wallenrod, *Dusk in the Catskills* (New York: Reconstructionist Press, 1957), 64.
2. Ibid., 80–81.
3. Ibid., 86.
4. Oleg Volkov, *"Leningrad Reve de Saint-Petersbourg,"* Le Figaro (Paris), 8 June 1991, Magazine sec., 95.
5. Brian Lazarus, "This Is Your Life," *Meyer Furman's Camp Neversink Weekly Camper,* 6 August 1954, 1.
6. *Hemerocallis fulva* rather than true lilies.
7. *Hydrangeae paniculata,* "grandiflora."
8. At this time, many are persons of color.
9. *Sweet Lorraine,* dir. Steve Gomer, Autumn Pictures/Angelika Co., 1987, film.
10. Joey Adams, with Henry Tobias, *The Borscht Belt* (New York: Bobbs-Merrill, 1966), 28.
11. Stefan Kanfer, *A Summer World* (New York: Farrar Straus Giroux, 1989), 126.
12. Miriam Damico, personal interview with the author (Loch Sheldrake, New York), 12 August 1993.
13. Michael Straus, "A Bungalow in the Hills," *New York Times,* 10 June 1956, late edition, sec. xx, p. 9.
14. Sonia Pressman Fuentes, "A Woodridge Kuchalyn," audiotape recorded at the "Borscht Belt Weekend" in 1996 in Woodridge, N.Y. (West Hurley, N.Y.: Creative Seminars, 1996).
15. *The Rise and Fall of the Borscht Belt,* dir. Peter Davis, 90 min., Villon Films, 1988, videocassette; distributed by Arthur Cantor, Inc.
16. Myrna Katz Frommer and Harvey Frommer, *It Happened in the Catskills* (New York: Harcourt Brace Jovanovich, 1991), 8.
17. Henry Tobias, *Music in My Heart and Borscht in My Blood* (New York: Hippocrene Books, 1987), 36.
18. Ibid.
19. Ibid.
20. Ibid.
21. The Joyland Colony was in Dairyland on Route 52. Before it fell into ruin several years back, it served as a training site for the militant Jewish Defense League, followers of Rabbi Meir Kahane.
22. Frommer and Frommer, *It Happened,* 62.
23. Martin Boris, personal interview with the author (Woodridge, New York), 31 August 1996.
24. This name has been changed because I do not want to embarrass the "Krinsky" children.
25. In *Music in My Heart,* Tobias recalls "convenient" fires at many resorts. One of his stock jokes was: "We had a little fire in the Social Hall. The fire was supposed to be after the summer, but something went wrong," p. 36.
26. Names have been changed.

27. Bernard Kalb, "Catskill Birthday," *New York Times,* 10 May 1953, late edition, sec. xx, p. 13.
28. Abraham D. Lavender and Clarence B. Steinberg, *Jewish Farmers of the Catskills: A Century of Survival* (Gainesville: University Press of Florida, 1995), 163–64.
29. Adams, *Borscht Belt,* 22–23.
30. Ibid.
31. Advertisements in *Der Yid: Voice of American Orthodox Jewry,* 1 March 1991, 63.
32. Adams, *Borscht Belt,* 22–23.

4 *Unzereh Menschen* (Our People)

1. *The Rise and Fall of the Borscht Belt,* dir. Peter Davis, 90 min., Villon Films, 1988, video-cassette; distributed by Arthur Cantor, Inc.
2. Joey Adams, with Henry Tobias, *The Borscht Belt* (New York: Bobbs-Merrill, 1966), 27. Adams actually never believed that anyone would prefer a *kuchalein* or a bungalow to a hotel: "Nobody actually preferred a *kuchalane* unless he couldn't afford better," p. 28.
3. Ibid., 30.
4. Bern Sharfman, personal interview with the author (Harrisburg, Penn.), 22 July 1996.
5. Myrna Katz Frommer and Harvey Frommer, *It Happened in the Catskills* (New York: Harcourt Brace Jovanovich, 1991), 117.
6. Ibid., 7.
7. Ibid., 63–64.
8. *The New Grove Dictionary of American Music,* s.v. "Cahn (Cohen, Kahn), Sammy (Samuel)." For a rendition of *"Bei Mir Bist du Schön,"* listen to *The Best of the Andrews Sisters,* MCA Records MCA 2–4024.
9. Norman Ober, *Bungalow Nine* (New York: Walker and Company, 1962), 147.

5 River and the Woods

1. Tony Gould, "Part I: The Rise and Fall of Epidemic Poliomyelitis," *A Summer Plague: Polio and Its Survivors* (New Haven and London: Yale University Press, 1995), 1–226. This gives an excellent overview of a changing world.
2. *Sweet Lorraine,* dir. Steve Gomer, Autumn Pictures/Angelika Co., 1987, film.
3. "The Hollywood Country Club," *The Brooklyn Bridge,* writ. Peter Schneider, prod. Gary David Goldberg, CBS Network (30 July 1993), television series.
4. *Radio Days,* dir. Woody Allen, Orion Pictures, 1989, film.
5. Myrna Katz Frommer and Harvey Frommer, *It Happened in the Catskills* (New York: Harcourt Brace Jovanovich, 1991), 15–16.
6. The story of the region's Jewish farmers is interesting and complex. It is explored in its many facets in Abraham D. Lavender and Clarence B. Steinberg, *Jewish Farmers of the Catskills: A Century of Survival* (Gainesville: University Press of Florida, 1995).

6 Noodling Around: Kids at Large

1. Unfortunately, several reels were damaged because of a water leak in the Woodbourne house; however, the surviving reels are a rich resource of life at the bungalow colony in the 1950–1970 period.

2. Little Joey and his friends often watch the skies for enemy aircraft in *Radio Days*, dir. Woody Allen, Orion Pictures, 1989, film.
3. Harvey Jacobs, *Summer on a Mountain of Spices* (New York: Harper and Row, 1975), 108–9, and passim.
4. Mell Lazarus, "Angry Fathers," *New York Times Magazine*, 28 May 1995, 20.

7 To Town: The Escape

1. Sidney Offit, *He Had It Made* (New York: Crown Publishers, 1959), 233.
2. See the photograph of Congregation B'nai Israel illustrated in Abraham D. Lavender and Clarence B. Steinberg, *Jewish Farmers of the Catskills: A Century of Survival* (Gainesville: University Press of Florida, 1995), 72.
3. *The Rise and Fall of the Borscht Belt*, dir. Peter Davis, 90 min., Villon Films, 1988, video-cassette; distributed by Arthur Cantor, Inc.
4. "Village Bypass Slated," *New York Times*, late edition, 6 August 1954, A14.
5. Ibid.
6. Harvey Jacobs, *Summer on a Mountain of Spices* (New York: Harper and Row, 1975), 16–17.
7. "Eleven Stores Hit by Woodbourne Fire," *Monticello (N.Y.) Republican Watchman*, 6 February 1964, 1.
8. *Sweet Lorraine*, dir. Steve Gomer, Autumn Pictures/Angelika Co., 1987, film.
9. Martin Boris, *Woodridge 1946* (New York: Crown Publishers, 1980), 4–6.
10. Joey Adams, with Henry Tobias, *The Borscht Belt* (New York: Bobbs-Merrill, 1966), 30.
11. T. F. Kane, "Performing Arts Moves to Theater," *Middletown (N.Y.) Times Herald Record*, 4 September 1996, 5.
12. Barbara Gref, "The Story of Sam, Rose, and the Rivoli," *Middletown (N.Y.) Sunday Record*, 16 July 1995, Magazine sec., 3–5. The Rivoli closed 31 August 1997. It lasted seventy-five seasons.

8 Daily Life: Mostly Adults

1. Joey Adams, with Henry Tobias, *The Borscht Belt* (New York: Bobbs-Merrill, 1966), 23–24.
2. Ibid., 25.
3. Ibid., 25–26.
4. Ibid., 25. While its official name was Orseck's 999, everyone called it "Orseck's," or "the Orseck boys," or just "999." *Quo Vadis* (1951) is an epic movie known for its lavish use of extras.
5. Ibid., 26.
6. Myrna Katz Frommer and Harvey Frommer, *It Happened in the Catskills* (New York: Harcourt Brace Jovanovich, 1991), 98.
7. Ibid., 96.
8. Adams, *Borscht Belt*, 26–27.
9. Ibid., 27.
10. Norman Ober, *Bungalow Nine* (New York: Walker and Company, 1962), 1.
11. Stefan Kanfer, *A Summer World* (New York: Farrar Straus Giroux, 1989), photographs between pp. 46 and 47.
12. Adams, *Borscht Belt*, 30.

13. For a description of a bungalow colony clinic and its milieu, see Robert Eisenberg, *Boychiks in the Hood* (San Francisco: Harper, 1995), 197–201.
14. Frommer and Frommer, *It Happened,* 128.
15. "It's Time to Order Your 1997 Mah-Jongg Card," Lancaster (Penn.) Jewish Community Center's *The Center News,* November 1996, 3.
16. Ober, *Bungalow Nine,* 141.
17. Miriam Damico, personal interview with the author (Loch Sheldrake, New York), 12 August 1993.
18. Harvey Jacobs, *Summer on a Mountain of Spices* (New York: Harper and Row, 1975), 13. "Taft" was a Bronx high school. Thomas Jefferson High School is in Brooklyn.
19. Adams, *Borscht Belt,* 30.
20. Robert K. Plumb, "Upstate Hydroelectric Plant Will Tap City's Water System," *New York Times,* 3 March 1954, late city edition, A20.
21. *Sweet Lorraine,* dir. Steve Gomer, Autumn Pictures/Angelika Co., 1987.
22. Robert L. Schain, "A Study of the Historical Development of the Resort Industry of the Catskills" (Ph.D. diss., New York University, 1969), 368.
23. Ibid.
24. *The Rise and Fall of the Borscht Belt,* dir. Peter Davis, 90 min., Villon Films, 1988, videocassette; distributed by Arthur Cantor, Inc.
25. Ober, *Bungalow Nine,* 70.
26. Ibid., 71.
27. Ibid. A "fungo" is a bat with a ball attached to it by an elastic cord. You can hit at the ball endlessly.
28. Mimi Sheraton, *From My Mother's Kitchen* (New York: Harper and Row, 1979), 243.
29. Ibid.
30. *Mr. Saturday Night,* dir. Billy Crystal, Castle Rock Entertainment, 1992, film. For recipes, see Raymond Socolow, *The Jewish-American Kitchen* (New York: Stewart, Tabori, and Chang, 1989). There are many Jewish cookbooks in print, but this one is the most authentic for eastern European-based cookery.

9 The Quest for Entertainment

1. *Goodbye Columbus,* dir. Larry Peerce, Willow Tree/Paramount, 1969, film.
2. Norman Ober, *Bungalow Nine* (New York: Walker and Company, 1962), 68.
3. Ibid., 251–52. *Roggalach* or, more commonly, *rugelach* are crescent-shaped, cinnamon-flavored, sweet pastries stuffed with nuts and raisins. Dairy *rugelach* often incorporate sour cream in the dough. Pareve ones are made with vegetable oil. (Now, I wonder where they got cider in summer!)
4. Ibid., 253.
5. Miriam Damico, personal interview with the author (Loch Sheldrake, New York), 12 August 1993.
6. *The Rise and Fall of the Borscht Belt,* dir. Peter Davis, 90 min., Villon Films, 1988, videocassette; distributed by Arthur Cantor, Inc.
7. Irving Howe and Kenneth Libo, *How We Lived* (New York: Richard Marek, 1979), 44.
8. *Rise and Fall of the Borscht Belt.*
9. Harvey Jacobs, *Summer on a Mountain of Spices* (New York: Harper and Row, 1975), 240–41.
10. *Rise and Fall of the Borscht Belt.*

11. *Webster's New Twentieth-Century Dictionary of the English Language,* 2d ed., s.v. "casino."

12. John Zukowsky and Robbe Pierce Stimson, *Hudson River Villas* (New York: Rizzoli, 1985), 178–79.

13. Ober, *Bungalow Nine,* 7.

14. *Rise and Fall of the Borscht Belt.*

15. Ober, *Bungalow Nine,* 49.

16. Bernard Kalb, "Catskill Birthday," *New York Times,* 10 May 1953, late edition, sec. xx, p. 13.

17. For the sounds of Catskill entertainment, 1920–1960, many good recordings are available. Dave Tarras, *Dave Tarras Plays Again* (Standard-Colonial Records 718), and Sholom Secunda, *A Yiddish Sing-Along with Sholom Secunda* (Liberty Records 7254), are outstanding. The sounds of other early entertainers are also available on record. Never to leave a dry eye in the house, Jennie Goldstein is heard in *Jennie Goldstein Sings Fourteen of Her Most Famous Yiddish Theatre Hits* (Greater Recording Company GRC90). Husband and wife team Miriam Kressyn and Seymour Rexsite were long popular with songs drawn from the Yiddish tradition; listen to *Miriam Kressyn and Seymour Rexsite Sing the Yiddish Hit Parade* (Greater Recording Company GRC212). Called the "Maurice Chevalier" of Jewish entertainers, Aaron Lebedeff can be heard in *The Best of Aaron Lebedeff* (Greater Recording Company GRC182). For the sound of comedy, laugh while listening to the Barton Brothers, *Jewish Comedy Songs* (Apollo Records 475), and Mickey Katz, *The Very Best of Mickey Katz* (Capital Records T298). These performers are the inspiration for Allan Sherman, whose record *My Son, the Folk Singer* (Warner Brothers Records 1475) was enormously popular. Most people didn't realize they were laughing at Catskill material. I saw and heard all of these and others perform. For a remarkable example of a Yiddish performance that would have been at home on any Catskill stage, see Feyvush Finkel's turn in *Itzhak Perlman: In the Fiddler's House,* dirs. Don Lenzer and Glenn DuBose, special television broadcast, 1996.

18. The Senate, The Levitt, The Pollack, The Irvington, and The Ambassador.

19. Joey Adams, with Henry Tobias, *The Borscht Belt* (New York: Bobbs-Merrill, 1966), 33.

20. Abraham D. Lavender and Clarence B. Steinberg, *Jewish Farmers of the Catskills: A Century of Survival* (Gainesville: University Press of Florida, 1995), 179–80.

21. *Radio Days,* dir. Woody Allen, Orion Pictures, 1989, film.

22. *Rise and the Fall of the Borscht Belt.*

23. Adams, *Borscht Belt,* 30–31.

24. Henry Tobias, *Music in My Heart and Borscht in My Blood* (New York: Hippocrene Books, 1987), 72.

25. Myrna Katz Frommer and Harvey Frommer, *It Happened in the Catskills* (New York: Harcourt Brace Jovanovich, 1991), 93.

26. Ibid., 72. Note the spelling variant; "Feyvush" is more correctly Yiddish than "Feibish," which is possibly more Anglicized.

27. *Broadway Danny Rose,* dir. Woody Allen, Orion Pictures, 1984.

28. "The Hollywood Country Club," *The Brooklyn Bridge,* writ. Peter Schneider, prod. Gary David Goldberg, CBS Network (30 July 1993), television series.

29. Frommer and Frommer, *It Happened,* 117.

30. *Goodbye Columbus.*

31. Dave Tarras, *Yiddish-American Klezmer Music, 1925–1956,* compact disk (Yazoo Records 7001). *"Klezmer,"* in Hebrew, means "instrument of song," according to Itzhak Perlman in *In the Fiddler's House.* Klezmer is traditionally the music of itinerant

Central European musicians, as seen in the classic film *Yidn Mitn Fidl* (dir. Joseph Green, 1936). In America, the term relates to the 'soul music' of American Yiddish speakers. Comedian Red Buttons recalls, "When I started playing the Catskills in 1935, there was dance music and there was klezmer music. . . . The klezmer music was to get your heart started" *(In the Fiddler's House)*. After going out of fashion, klezmer is now enjoying a revival. Biographer Henry Sapoznic wrote that "Dave Tarras was not a little amused by the reinvention of the word *klezmer* itself." For Tarras, "a klezmer was a guy that couldn't play—he could only scratch out a tune for the cheap goyim" (annotated on the Dave Tarrus album cover, *Yiddish-American Klezmer Music*.)

32. Jeannie Reynolds, *Jeannie Reynolds Remembers* (LM Records, no recording number). LM Records was Jeannie's own label. L and M are the initials of her and Hal's children, Lanny and Mindy.

33. Lavender and Steinberg, *Jewish Farmers*, 187. (The Resnicks owned Channel Master, Inc., a pioneer manufacturer of TV antennas. The Slutskys own the Nevele and Fallsview Hotels; one is *tref* and one is kosher.)

34. Ibid.

35. Robert L. Schain, "A Study of the Historical Development of the Resort Industry of the Catskills" (Ph.D. diss., New York University, 1969), 402–3.

36. Dora Huss, "My View: Indian Gambling Is Sullivan's Only Answer," *Middletown (N.Y.) Times Herald Record*, 6 July 1996, 35; and T. R. Pavis-Weil, "Gambling on the Future," *Middletown (N.Y.) Sunday Record*, 7 July 1996, 7.

10 Religion

1. Joey Adams, with Henry Tobias, *The Borscht Belt* (New York: Bobbs-Merrill, 1966), 23.

2. David Boroff, "Don't Call It 'The Borscht Belt,'" *New York Times Magazine*, 9 May 1965, 58.

3. Oscar Israelowitz, *Catskills Guide* (Brooklyn, N.Y.: Israelowitz Publishing, 1992), 38–62.

4. *The Rise and Fall of the Borscht Belt*, dir. Peter Davis, 90 min., Villon Films, 1988, videocassette; distributed by Arthur Cantor, Inc.

11 Summer Emergencies and Other Unforgettable Events

1. Stefan Kanfer, *A Summer World* (New York: Farrar Straus Giroux, 1989), 288.

2. Ibid.

3. Abraham D. Lavender and Clarence B. Steinberg, *Jewish Farmers of the Catskills: A Century of Survival* (Gainesville: University Press of Florida, 1995), 188.

4. "Upstate Resorts Isolated: Helicopters Save Scores," *New York Times*, 20 August 1955, late edition, A1.

5. Ibid., 10.

6. Ibid.

7. Ibid., 1.

8. Norman Ober, *Bungalow Nine* (New York: Walker and Company, 1962).

9. Harvey Jacobs, *Summer on a Mountain of Spices* (New York: Harper and Row, 1975), 121.

10. Ibid., 123.

11. Ibid., 121.

12. "Sullivan County, New York: Number One in the Nation for a Zestful, Restful Vacation," advertisement distributed by the Sullivan County Board of Supervisors, n.d.
13. Recipes and descriptions of all these dishes can be found in Raymond Socolow, *The Jewish-American Kitchen* (New York: Stewart, Tabori, and Chang, 1989).
14. "Eleven Stores Hit by Woodbourne Fire," *Monticello (N.Y.) Republican Watchman*, 6 February 1964, 1.
15. Ibid.
16. "Woodbourne to Rebuild Modern Shopping Center," *Monticello (N.Y.) Republican Watchman*, 13 February 1964, 1.
17. Pamela Moore, "Some Personal Glimpses at the Woodbourne Fire," *Monticello (N.Y.) Republican Watchman*, 6 February 1964, 1.

12 The Day Camp

1. Robert L. Schain, "A Study of the Historical Development of the Resort Industry of the Catskills" (Ph.D. diss., New York University, 1969), 362–63.
2. In 1956, a day camp "costs an average of $50 a season a child" (Michael Straus, "A Bungalow in the Hills," *New York Times*, 10 June 1956, late edition, sec. xx, p. 9). A recent camp flier advertised the 1996 cost per child at $550, with lunch and transportation extra.
3. Norman Ober, *Bungalow Nine* (New York: Walker and Company, 1962), 41–42.
4. *Meyer Furman's Camp Neversink Weekly Camper*. Articles from this newspaper were mostly written by counselors and campers. Three of the more prolific authors were Arlene Mittleman, Carole Berman, and Linda Rademan—all Rancherettes, or senior girls. This particular article was written by a counselor named Rachel Rotenkowsky who was a tenant at Richman's. She was a displaced person who stayed with her aunt.
5. Ibid.
6. Ibid.
7. Ibid.
8. Ibid.
9. Ibid.
10. I've changed his name to protect his identity.
11. Names are altered.
12. "Jay" could drive at eighteen because he claimed that his summer address was his legal one. Various counties in New York had differing ages for driving.
13. Name is altered.
14. *Meyer Furman's Camp Neversink Weekly*.
15. Ober, *Bungalow Nine*, 136.
16. *Meyer Furman's Camp Neversink Weekly*.
17. Ibid.
18. Ober, *Bungalow Nine*, 247.
19. "Lansman's Day Camp," advertisement, *Middletown (N.Y.) Record*, 6 May 1996, 42.

13 Crime and Punishment

1. "Work Begins on New Prison," *New York Times*, 26 May 1934, city edition, A32.
2. The growth of Florida's popularity, especially condominium growth there, would have a great effect on the year-round population of Sullivan County. For more insight into

this phenomenon, see Richard Nagler, *My Love Affair with Miami Beach* (New York: Simon and Schuster, 1991); and Deborah Dash Moore, *To the Golden Cities* (New York: Free Press, 1994).

3. *Goodfellas,* dir. Martin Scorsese, Warner Brothers, 1990, film. The Brownsville section of Brooklyn was the home of many working-class Jews and Italians and also the base of operation of many mobsters. Neighborhood kids knew the mob-related places.

4. I have changed her name to protect her identity.

5. Stefan Kanfer, *A Summer World* (New York: Farrar Straus Giroux, 1989), 119. Listen to Miriam Kressyn and Seymour Rexsite, *Miriam Kressyn and Seymour Rexsite Sing the Yiddish Hit Parade,* Greater Recording Company GRC212.

6. Harvey Jacobs, *Summer on a Mountain of Spices* (New York: Harper and Row, 1975), 16.

7. Craig Wolff, "Summer Calm in Catskills Shattered by Slayings," *New York Times,* 14 July 1991, Metropolitan sec., 23.

8. Ibid.

9 Ibid.

10. Ibid.

11. Josh Kurtz, "Hotel Worker Held in Catskills Killings," *New York Times,* 18 August 1991, 24.

12. Ibid.

13. Ibid.

14. "Man Sentenced to Seventy-Five Years in Slayings of Elderly Couple," *New York Times,* 22 November 1992, A55.

15. Ibid.

14 An Age of Change

1. Margaret Washington, town clerk of Thompson, N.Y., telephone interview with my research assistant Matt Singer, 16 July 1991; Charlotte Feigenbaum Spector, personal interview with the author (Middletown, Penn.), 8 November 1995; and Harvey Jacobs, *Summer on a Mountain of Spices* (New York: Harper and Row, 1975), 16.

2. "Regency Country Club," advertisement, *Catskill Summer Calendar and Directory: A Comprehensive Guide,* 7th ed. (South Fallsburg, N.Y.: Yeshiva Gedolah-Zichron Moshe, 1991), 43. Note that the use of glamorous allusion is still alive and well.

3. Abraham D. Lavender and Clarence B. Steinberg, *Jewish Farmers of the Catskills: A Century of Survival* (Gainesville: University Press of Florida, 1995), 164.

4. *Rear Window,* dir. Alfred Hitchcock, Patron, 1954, film.

5. For an interesting view of one family whose odyssey leads them from the Catskills, see Donald Katz, *Home Fires: An Intimate Portrait of One Middle-Class Family in Postwar America* (New York: Harper Collins, Aaron Asher Books, 1992).

6. David Tashman, "Singing the Blues for the Catskills Bungalow Belt," *New York Daily News,* 5 July 1971, 7C.

7. Joseph Berger, "New Accents for Old Ritual: Vacationing in the Catskills," *New York Times,* 12 July 1993, late edition, A1.

8. Stephen Isreal, "A Kaddish to Catskill Kitsch," *Middletown (N.Y.) Sunday Record,* 29 August 1993, Magazine sec., 4.

9. "The paid nonstop social director, entertainer, and 'fun maker' in those Catskill resorts that constitute the 'Borsht [*sic*] Belt!'" Leo Rosten, *The Joys of Yinglish* (New York: McGraw-Hill, 1989), 532.

10. Isreal, "A Kaddish," 4.

11. Ibid.

12. Ibid., 5. The "Copa" was a famous New York City nightclub, "The Copacabana."

13. Ibid.

14. Stefan Kanfer, *A Summer World* (New York: Farrar Straus Giroux, 1989), 279.

15. Ibid., 280. Also quoted in Constance L. Hays, "Catskill Bungalows: Rustic Goes Co-op," *New York Times,* 24 August 1987, late edition, B1, B2.

16. Ibid.

17. Ibid.

18. David Gold, personal interview with the author, 1 September 1996.

19. Alan Wechsler, "They Tell so All Will Know: Holocaust Survivors Summon Painful Stories for Video," *Middletown (N.Y.) Sunday Record,* 18 August 1996, 4.

20. Roslyn Bernstein, "Colonizing the Catskills," *New York Magazine,* 17 August 1981, 48–49.

21. Ibid.

22. The *pishke* is "a little can or container kept in the home, often in the kitchen, in which money to be donated to charity is accumulated." Various charities provided their own *pishke* to donators. Among the labels found on these boxes are: "For Farm Equipment to Be Sent to Jewish Farmers in Kansas," "For the Hebrew Home for the Aged," and "To Send a Rabbi-Saint to the Holy Land before He Dies." From Rosten, *Joys of Yinglish,* 424.

23. Joel R. Burcat, personal interview with the author, 3 March 1996.

24. George Kranzler, *Hasidic Williamsburg* (Northvale, N.J.: Jason Aronson, 1995), 50.

25. Burcat, interview.

26. "The Catskills on Self Destruct," *TV VUES* (Catskill Edition), 10–16 August 1991, 19. Printed in extremely small type, this essay packs a lot of vitriol in a small space.

27. Ibid.

28. Robert Eisenberg, *Boychiks in the Hood* (San Francisco: Harper, 1995), 197.

29. Ibid., 196–97.

30. *"Glatt* literally means smooth, beyond any question. It is usually [although not exclusively] used in connection with kosher meat. A term introduced by Hungarian *Hasidim* to indicate their more stringent requirement for kosher food. Connotation of higher standards of dietary laws." Definition from Kranzler, *Hasidic Williamsburg,* 299.

31. It is commonly believed by many non-Jews and many nonobservant Jews that "kosher" pertains only to food. It can also pertain to all aspects of a pious life. One Talmudic prohibition holds that mixing natural fibers, especially wool and linen, is an affront. Hence kosher socks have the proper fiber content.

32. Kranzler, *Hasidic Williamsburg,* 50.

33. Kanfer, *Summer World,* 182.

34. "A divider, a wall or curtain that separates the sections reserved for men and women in the synagogues and at social affairs" (Kranzler, *Hasidic Williamsburg,* 302).

35. Kanfer, *Summer World,* 281–82.

36. Ibid., 282.

37. Kranzler, *Hasidic Williamsburg,* 181.

38. Kanfer, *Summer World,* 282.

39. Oscar Israelowitz, *Catskills Guide* (Brooklyn, N.Y.: Israelowitz Publishing, 1992), 19. *Tzitzit* are "ritual fringes attached to the four corners of a garment . . . in accordance with *Numeri* 16, 38" (Kranzler, *Hasidic Williamsburg,* 306).

40. *The Chosen,* dir. Jeremy Paul Kagan, Contemporary Films, 1981. This event is also described in Chaim Potak's novel *The Chosen* (Greenwich, Conn.: Fawcett Publications, 1967), upon which the film is based.

41. "Orthodox Jews Play Ball in the Catskills," narr. John Kalish, *All Things Considered*, National Public Radio (WITF, Harrisburg, Penn.), 24 August 1993.

42. Ibid.

43. "International Campaign to Bring Moshiach," advertisement, *New York Times*, 31 January 1996, late edition, A11; and William Berezansky, "Signs of the Times," *Middletown (N.Y.) Times Herald Record*, 12 August 1991, sec. 1, p. 12.

44. Ari L. Goldman, "Thruway Rest Stop Provides Place for Jews to Pray," *New York Times*, Sunday, 25 July 1993, Metro sec., 34.

45. Ibid.

46. Ibid.

47. The *sheitel*—a wig worn to cover the hair of married women—once looked like a hat and was very obvious. Traditionally worn by women from Eastern Europe, its purpose was to make Jewish women less attractive to would-be assailants. However, modern orthodox women often wear very fashionable, attractive *sheitelen*. Modern wigs can be very expensive. Top-of-the-line wigs like Olgas—made by "Olga Berman, a Hungarian wig maker in Besonhurst"—cost around $2,000. Specialty wigs by other makers go up to $3,500. Always made of human hair and often imported from Eastern Europe, the wigs are also expensive to maintain and restyle. Clients of Mark Garrison, a Madison Avenue wig stylist, "pay at least $600 to have their wigs transformed." (Elizabeth Hayt, "For Stylish Orthodox Women, Wigs that Aren't Wiggy," *New York Times*, 27 April 1997, Styles sec., 48.)

48. Advertisements found in the *Catskill Summer Calendar and Directory*, 37, 105.

49. Ibid., 53, 67, 109. *Heimish*, which translates as "homey," is a very popular word in use by both normative and orthodox Jews. It denotes a friendly, traditional atmosphere.

50. Advertisement in *TV VUES* (Catskill Edition), 10–16 August 1991, cover.

51. Advertisement for the *mikvah* at Camp Shearith, in *Catskill Summer Calendar*, 49.

52. Kanfer, *Summer World*, 281.

53. Advertisement in *Catskill Summer Calendar*, 105.

54. Jennifer Brylinski, Sullivan County Department of Planning, telephone interview with my research assistant Matt Singer, 16 July 1991.

55. The *payess*, or *peyot*, are derived from the Hebrew *pe'ot*, which translates as "earlocks" or "curls." The custom among orthodox Jews for wearing *payess* and letting their beards grow full comes from Leviticus 19:27—"Ye shall not round the corners of your head, neither shalt thou mar the corners of thy beard." Rosten, *Joys of Yinglish*, 404–5.

56. *Streimlen* are round fur hats worn by Hasidic men, especially on the Sabbath and on many holidays.

57. Advertisement in *TV VUES*, cover.

58. Advertisement in *Catskill Summer Calendar*, 35.

59. Kanfer, *Summer World*, 283.

60. For a view of life in a suburbanizing former bungalow colony and an Hasidic girl's coming of age, see the novel by Pearl Abraham, *The Romance Reader* (New York: Putnam Group, 1995).

61. Alan Wechsler, "Summer Folk Find Trouble: Bias Crime Alleged as Fight Draws Crowd," *Middletown (N.Y.) Times Herald Record*, 8 July 1996, 5.

62. Alan Wechsler, "Woodbourne Gets Religion," *Middletown (N.Y.) Times Herald Record*, 15 July 1996, 3, 11.

63. Nancy Greene, "Woodbourne Doesn't Close Up," *Middletown (N.Y.) Times Herald Record*, 9 August 1996, 39.

64. For another view of the orthodox scene in Woodbourne, see Eisenberg, *Boychiks*, 191–95.

65. Lavender and Steinberg, *Jewish Farmers,* 161.
66. Berger, "New Accents," B5.
67. Ibid.
68. Ibid., A1, B5.
69. Shirley Chaiet, "SYDA Puts Its Interests First, Town's Second" *Middletown (N.Y.) Times Herald Record,* 10 August 1991, 47; and Ari L. Goldman, "'New Age' Enlivens Catskills: New Life for the Old Hotels, though Not for Tax Rolls," *New York Times,* 14 August 1992, late edition, Metro sec., B1, B6.

15 Ghosts along the Road

1. Advertisement in *Der Yid: Voice of American Orthodox Jewry,* 1 March 1991, 63.
2. Stefan Kanfer, *A Summer World* (New York: Farrar Straus Giroux, 1989), 281.
3. Constance L. Hays, "Catskill Bungalows," *New York Times,* 24 August 1987, late edition, B2.
4. Laura A. Fahrenthold, "Filthy, Condemned Bungalows Razed," *Middletown (N.Y.) Times Herald Record,* 14 August 1996, 4, 11.
5. Naomi Goldberg, "What Childless Women Are Missing," letter to the editor, *New York Times,* Sunday, 28 January 1996, E12.
6. Joseph Berger, "New Accents for Old Ritual: Vacationing in the Catskills," *New York Times,* 12 July 1993, late edition, B5.

Bibliography

A book like this has many sources that are impossible to document in the traditional fashion, as they are drawn from my memories and from many years of conversation and observation that were not strictly "field work." Research in the traditional sense did not provide me with surprises or extraordinary insights, but rather told me, and I hope the reader as well, that my bungalow colony experiences and those of my family were not unique but part of a continuing tradition.

Abelow, Sam P. *History of Brooklyn Jewery.* New York: Sheba Publishing, 1937.

Abraham, Pearl. *The Romance Reader.* New York: Putnam Group, 1995.

Abramowicz, Dina. YIVO (Institute for Yiddish Culture). Letter to Matt Singer, 10 July 1991. Richman Archives.

Adams, Arthur G. *The Catskills: An Illustrated Historical Guide with Gazetteer.* New York: Fordham University Press, 1990.

Adams, Joey, with Henry Tobias. *The Borscht Belt.* New York: Bobbs-Merrill, 1966.

Adler, Cyrus, ed. *The American Jewish Year Book.* Philadelphia: Jewish Publication Society of America, 1990.

Almonds and Raisins: A History of the Yiddish Cinema. Directed by Russ Karel; narrated by Orson Wells. Ergo Media, 1983. Videocassette.

Andrews Sisters. *The Best of the Andrews Sisters.* MCA Records MCA 2–4024.

"Anti-Hebrew Crusade: Not so Extensive in the Catskills as Reported." *New York Times,* 7 May 1889, late edition, 1.

Associated Co-Operative Fire Insurance Company. *50 Years of Working Together.* Woodridge, N.Y.: Associated Co-Operative Fire Insurance Company of Sullivan and Adjoining Counties, 1963.

Avalon. Directed by Barry Levinson. Baltimore Pictures, 1990. Film.

Barry, Dave. "Party Host Turns Batty Landlord." *Harrisburg (Penn.) Sunday Patriot News,* 26 January 1992, G3.

Barry Sisters. *The Barry Sisters Sing.* Cadence CH30012.

———. *Their Greatest Yiddish Hits.* Tradition Records 2213.

Barton Brothers. *Jewish Comedy Songs.* Apollo 475.

Beers, F. W. *County Atlas of Sullivan, New York.* New York: Walker and Jewett, 1875.

Berezansky, William. "Signs of the Times: Sect Proclaims, 'Messiah on Way.'" *Middletown (N.Y.) Times Herald Record,* 12 August 1991.

Berger, Joseph. "New Accents for Old Ritual: Vacationing in the Catskills." *New York Times,* 12 July 1993, late edition, A1.

Bernheimer, Charles, ed. *The Russian Jew in the United States.* Philadelphia: John C. Winston, 1905.

Bernstein, Roslyn. "Colonizing the Catskills." *New York Magazine,* 17 August 1981, 48–49.

Birmingham, Stephen. *The Rest of Us.* New York: Harper and Row, 1984.

Black, Kathryn. *In the Shadow of Polio: A Personal and Social History.* Reading, Mass.: Addison-Wesley, 1996.

Blackman, Betsy. *Resorts of the Catskills.* New York: St. Martin's Press, 1979.

Blumberg, Esterita. *Remember the Catskills: Tales by a Recovering Hotelkeeper.* Fleischmanns, N.Y.: Purple Mountain Press, 1996.

———, ed. *Fifty Years of Working Together.* South Fallsburg, N.Y.: Fallsburg Printing, 1963.

Boris, Martin. *Woodridge 1946.* New York: Crown Publishers, 1980.

———. Personal interview with the author. Woodridge, N.Y., 31 August 1996.

Boroff, David. "Don't Call It the Borscht Belt." *New York Times Magazine,* 9 May 1965.

Broadway Danny Rose. Directed by Woody Allen. Orion Pictures, 1984. Film.

Brown, Phil. "Catskill Culture: The Rise and Fall of a Jewish Resort Area Seen through Personal Narrative and Ethnography." *Journal of Contemporary Ethnography* 25 (1996): 83–119.

Bruce, Ira. "Samuel Badisch Ornitz, 1891–1957." *Jewish Writers of North America.* Detroit, Mich.: Gale Research, 1981.

Brylinski, Jennifer. Sullivan County Department of Planning, Monticello, N.Y. Telephone interview with research assistant Matt Singer. 16 July 1991.

Burcat, Joel R. Personal interview with the author. Harrisburg, Penn., 3 March 1996.

"Bypass Is Opened: Lieut. Gov. Wilson Predicts Many New Road Projects." *New York Times,* 9 August 1959, late edition.

Cahan, Abraham. *The Rise of David Levinsky.* New York: Harper and Brothers, 1917.

———. "The Russian Jew in America." *Atlantic Monthly,* July 1898, 128–39.

Catskill Guide. Millbrook, N.Y.: Taconic Press, Summer/Fall 1991.

Catskill Summer Calendar and Directory: A Comprehensive Guide, 7th ed. South Fallsburg, N.Y.: Yeshiva Gedolah-Zichron Moshe, 1991.

Catskills on Broadway. Produced by Kenneth Greenblatt and Stephen D. Fish; performance by Freddie Roman, et al. 44 Productions, n.d. Videocassette.

Chaiet, Shirley. "SYDA Puts Its Interests First, Town's Second." *Middletown (N.Y.) Times Herald Record,* 10 August 1991, 47.

Chernow, Jay, and his Hi-Hats Ensemble. *Let's Be Frielach.* Aleph ALP1001

Chosen, The. Directed by Jeremy Paul Kagan. Contemporary Films, 1981.

Cohen, Stanley. *The Game They Played.* New York: Farrar Straus Giroux, 1977.

Cohn, Sarah B., ed., *From Hester Street to Hollywood.* Bloomington: University of Indiana Press, 1983.

Cowan, Neil M., and Ruth Schwartz Cowan. *Our Parents' Lives: The Americanization of Eastern European Jews.* New York: Basic Books, 1989.

Curley, Edward F. *Old Monticello*. Monticello, N.Y.: *Republican Watchman,* 1930.

Dale, Edwin L., Jr. "Floods Batter the Northeast: Seventy-Three Killed, Damage in Billions; Four States Declare Emergencies." *New York Times,* 20 August 1955, late edition, A1.

Damico, Miriam. Personal interview with the author. Loch Sheldrake, N.Y., 12 August 1993.

Danziger, Herbert. *Returning to Tradition: The Contemporary Revival of Orthodox Judaism.* New Haven, Conn.: Yale University Press, 1989.

Davidson, Gabriel. "A Glimpse at Jewish Life in the Mountains." *Mountain Hotelman,* April 1933.

———. *Our Jewish Farmers and the Story of the Jewish Agricultural Society.* New York: L. B. Fischer, 1943.

Davis, William A. "Changing Times Come to the Catskill Resorts." *Miami Herald,* 2 October 1988, late edition, 3F.

DeLisser, R. Lionel. *Summer Resorts Directory.* Brooklyn, N.Y.: *Brooklyn Daily Eagle,* 1903.

Deutsch, Phyllis. "Theatre of Mating: Jewish Summer Camps and Cultural Transformations." *American Jewish History* 75 (1986): 307–21.

Dinnerstein, Leonard. *Anti-Semitism in America.* New York: Oxford University Press, 1994.

Dunphy, Robert J. "What's Doing in Sullivan County." *New York Times,* Sunday, 10 June 1979, sec. x, p. 15.

Eisenberg, Robert. *Boychiks in the Hood.* San Francisco: Harper, 1995.

"Eleven Stores Hit by Woodbourne Fire." *Monticello (N.Y.) Republican Watchman,* 6 February 1964, 1.

Ellenville Hebrew Aid Society. *Fifty Golden Years.* Ellenville, N.Y.: Ellenville Hebrew Aid Society, 1959.

Elliot Erna. *Centreville to Woodridge: The Story of a Small Community.* Woodridge, N.Y.: privately printed, 1976.

Evers, Alf. *The Catskills: From Wilderness to Woodstock.* Garden City, N.Y.: Doubleday, 1972.

Evers, Alf, et al., eds. *Resorts of the Catskills.* New York: St. Martin's Press, 1979.

Fahrenthold, Laura A. "Filthy, Condemned Bungalows Razed." *Middletown (N.Y.) Times Herald Record,* 14 August 1996.

"Farmer and Hotelman." *Mountain Hotelman,* 9 May 1930, 12.

Feder Sisters. *Yiddish Maestro Please.* United Artists Records UAL3227.

Feinsilver, Lillian M. *The Taste of Yiddish.* New York: Thomas Yoseloff, 1970.

Fiddler on the Roof. Directed by Norman Jewison. United Artists, 1971. Film.

Fine, Morris, ed. *The American Jewish Year Book.* New York: American Jewish Committee, 1950.

Fine, Morris, and Milton Himmelfarb, eds. *The American Jewish Year Book.* New York: American Jewish Committee, 1961.

———, eds., *The American Jewish Year Book.* New York: American Jewish Committee, 1970.

Fishman, Priscilla, ed. *The Jews of the United States.* New York: Quadrangle, 1973.

Foster, Lee. "The Magic Words in the Catskills: 'More, More, More.'" *New York Times,* Sunday, 5 March 1972, sec. xx.

Francis, Connie. *Connie Francis Sings Jewish Favorites.* MGM Records E3869.

Friedenwald, Herbert, ed. *The American Jewish Year Book.* Philadelphia: Jewish Publication Society, 1910.

Friedman, Lester D. *Hollywood's Image of the Jew.* New York: Ungar, 1982.

Frommer, Myrna Katz, and Harvey Frommer. *It Happened in the Catskills: An Oral History in the Words of Busboys, Bellhops, Guests, Proprietors, Comedians, Agents, and Others Who Loved It.* New York: Harcourt Brace Jovanovich, 1991.

Fuchs, Daniel. *A Summer in Williamsburg.* New York: Vanguard Press, 1934.

Fuentes, Sonia Pressman. *A Woodridge Kuchalyn.* ("Recorded Borscht Belt Weekend, Woodridge, N.Y.") West Hurley, N.Y.: Creative Seminars, 1996. Audiotape.

Gaines, Donna. "The Lost Daughters of Zion Return to the Catskills: A Journey to the Source of Jewish Identity, Featuring Gefilte Fish, Matzoh Ball Soup, Borscht Chicken, Pot Roast, Corned Beef, Potato Kugel, and Memories." *Village Voice,* 5 October 1993, 33.

Glazer, Nathan. *American Judaism.* Chicago: University of Chicago Press, 1972.

Glazer, Nathan, and Daniel P. Moynihan. *Beyond the Melting Pot.* Cambridge, Mass.: M.I.T. Press, 1970.

Gold, David. *The River and the Mountains: Readings in Sullivan County History.* South Fallsburg, N.Y.: Marielle Press, 1994.

———. Personal interview with the author. Woodridge, N.Y., 1 September 1996.

Goldberg, Naomi. "What Childless Women Are Missing." Letter to the editor. *New York Times,* Sunday, 28 January 1996, E12.

Golden Age of Second Avenue, The. Directed by Morton Silverstein. Arthur Cantor Films, n.d. Film.

Goldman, Ari L. "Brooklyn Project Shatters Hispanics, Hasidim Peace." *New York Times,* 1 October 1990, late edition, B1.

———. New Age' Enlivens Catskills: New Life for the Old Hotels, Though Not for Tax Rolls." *New York Times,* 14 August 1992, late edition, Metro sec., B1.

———. "Thruway Rest Stop Provides Place for Jews to Pray." *New York Times,* Sunday, 25 July 1993, Metro sec., 34.

Goldman, Shalom. "The Jewish Experience in the Catskills." Lecture recorded at the Sullivan County Community College, Loch Sheldrake, N.Y. West Hurley, N.Y.: Creative Seminars, 1995. Audiocassette.

Goldscheider, Calvin. *The American Jewish Community.* Providence, R.I.: Brown University Studies, 1986.

Goldsheider, Calvin, and Alan S. Zuckerman. *Jewish Community and Changes.* Bloomington: University of Indiana Press, 1986.

Goldstein, Jennie. *Jennie Goldstein Sings Fourteen of Her Most Famous Yiddish Theatre Hits.* The Greater Recording Company GRC90.

Goodbye Columbus. Directed by Larry Peerce. Willow Tree/Paramount, 1969. Film.

Goodfellas. Directed by Martin Scorcese. Warner Brothers, 1990. Film.

Goodman, Philip, and Hannah Goodman. *The History of Jewish Marriage.* Philadelphia: Jewish Publication Society of America, 1965.

Gould, Tony. *A Summer Plague: Polio and Its Survivors.* New Haven and London: Yale University Press, 1995.

Greenburg, Dan. *How to be a Jewish Mother.* Performed by Gertrude Berg. Amy Records. AMY8007.

Greene, Nancy. "Woodbourne Doesn't Close Up." *Middletown (N.Y.) Times Herald Record,* 9 August 1996, 39.

Gref, Barbara. "The Story of Rose, Sam, and the Rivoli." *Middletown (N.Y.) Sunday Record Magazine,* 16 July 1995, 3–5.

Gross, Theodore, ed. *The Literature of American Jews.* New York: Free Press, 1975.

Grossinger, Tania. *Growing Up at Grossinger's.* New York: McKay, 1975.

Hamilton, Kendall, and T. Trent Gegax. "Young Fogies." *Newsweek,* 28 October 1996, 64–67.

Hart, Moss. *Act One.* New York: Random House, 1959.

Hays, Constance L. "Catskill Bungalows: Rustic Goes Co-op." *New York Times,* 24 August 1987, late edition, B1.

Hayt, Elizabeth. "For Stylish Orthodox Women, Wigs that Aren't Wiggy." *New York Times,* 27 April 1997, N.E., 48.

Heilman, Samuel. *Defenders of the Faith: Inside Ultra-Orthodox Jewry.* New York: Schocken Books, 1992.

Helmer, William F. *O and W: The Long Life and Slow Death of the New York, Ontario, and Western Railway.* Berkeley, Cal.: Howell North, 1970.

Hester Street. Directed by Joan Michlin Silver. Midwest Films, 1974. Film.

History of the Borscht Belt, The: Part 1. Descriptive advertisement brochure. Privately printed, 21 August 1995. Maintained in Richman Archives.

"Hollywood Country Club, The." *The Brooklyn Bridge.* Written by Peter Schneider; produced by Gary David Goldberg. CBS Network, 30 July 1993. Television series.

Howe, Irving, with Kenneth Libo. *World of Our Fathers.* New York: Harcourt Brace Jovanovich, 1976.

Howe, Irving, and Kenneth Libo. *How We Lived: A Documentary History of Immigrant Jews in America, 1880–1930.* New York: Richard Marek, 1979.

Huss, Dora. "My View: Indian Gambling Is Sullivan's Only Answer." *Middletown (N.Y.) Times Herald Record,* 6 July 1996, 35.

Image before My Eyes. Directed by Josh Waletzky. Axon Video, 1988. Film.

"International Campaign to Bring Moshiach," advertisement. *New York Times,* 31 January 1996, A11.

Isreal, Stephen. "A Kaddish to Catskill Kitsch." *Middletown (N.Y.) Sunday Record Magazine,* 29 August 1993.

Isrealowitz, Oscar. *Catskills Guide.* Brooklyn, N.Y.: Isrealowitz Publishing, 1992.

"It's Time to Order Your 1997 Mah-Jongg Card," advertisement. *The Center News.* Lancaster, Penn.: Jewish Community Center, November 1996, 3.

Itzhak Perlman: In the Fiddler's House. Directed by Don Lenzer and Glenn DuBose; performance by Red Buttons and Feyvush Finkel. 1996. Special television broadcast (Harrisburg, Penn.: WITF-TV, 7 March 1996).

Jacobs, Glenn, ed. *The Participant Observer.* New York: George Braziller, 1970.

Jacobs, Harvey. *Summer on a Mountain of Spices.* New York: Harper and Row, 1975.

Jewish Luck. Directed by Alecsander Granowskij. Yiddish Film Collection, 1925. Film.

John, William. "Bridgeville Bottleneck." *New York Times,* Sunday, 14 June 1953, Travel sec., 7.

Joselit, Jenna Weissman. *The Wonders of America: Reinventing Jewish Culture, 1880–1950.* New York: Hill and Wang, 1994.

Kalb, Bernard. "Catskill Birthday: Fifty Years Ago Sullivan County Had Its First Visitor—And Look at it Now." *New York Times,* 10 May 1953, late edition, sec. xx, p. 13.

―――. "Where Hotelmen Improve on Nature: Sullivan County Literally Converts Its Mountains into Pleasure Palaces." *New York Times,* 14 June 1953, late edition, sec. xx, p. 6.

Kane, T. F. "Performing Arts Moves to Theater." *Middletown (N.Y.) Times Herald Record,* 4 September 1996, 5.

Kanfer, Stefan. *A Summer World: The Attempt to Build a Jewish Eden in the Catskills—From the Days of the Ghetto to the Rise and Decline of the Borscht Belt.* New York: Farrar Straus Giroux, 1989.

Katz, Donald. *Home Fires: An Intimate Portrait of One Middle-Class Family in Postwar America.* New York: Harper Collins, Aaron Asher Books, 1992.

Katz, Mickey. *The Very Best of Mickey Katz.* Capitol Records T298.

King, Anthony D. *The Bungalow: The Production of a Global Culture.* London: Routledge and Kegan Paul, 1984.

Klezmer Conservatory Band. *Yiddishe Renaissance.* Vanguard VSD79450.

Kober, Arthur. *Having a Wonderful Time.* New York: Dramatists Play Service, 1948.

229

———. *Thunder over the Bronx.* New York: Simon and Schuster, 1935.

Koestler, Arthur. *The Sleepwalkers.* New York: Arcana Books, Viking Penguin, 1969.

Kranzler, George. *Hasidic Williamsburg: A Contemporary American Hasidic Community.* Northvale, N.J.: Jason Aronson, 1995.

———. *Williamsburg: A Jewish Community in Transition.* New York: Feldheim Books, 1961.

Kressyn, Miriam, and Seymour Rexsite. *Miriam Kressyn and Seymour Rexsite Sing the Yiddish Hit Parade.* Greater Recording Company GRC212.

Kurtz, Josh. "Hotel Worker Held in Catskill Killings." *New York Times,* Sunday, 18 August 1991, Metropolitan sec., 24.

Kurzweil, Arthur. *From Generation to Generation: How to Trace Your Jewish Geneology and Family History,* rev. ed. New York: Harper Collins, 1994.

Lancaster, Clay. *The American Bungalow.* New York: Abbeville Press, 1985.

Landman, Isaac. "Catskill, Playground of Jewish Masses: A Tour of the Mountains, Where 3,000 Farmers Provide Summer Vacation Places for a Multitude of New Yorkers." *The American Hebrew,* 31 August 1928, 460–63.

Landon, Ron. *The Book of Jewish Lists.* New York: Stein and Day, 1982.

Last Angry Man. Directed by Daniel Mann. Columbia Pictures, 1959. Film.

Lavender, Abraham D., and Clarence B. Steinberg. *Jewish Farmers of the Catskills: A Century of Survival.* Gainesville: University Press of Florida, 1995.

Lazarus, Mell. "Angry Fathers." *New York Times Magazine,* 28 May 1995, 20.

Lebedeff, Aaron. *The Best of Aaron Lebedeff.* Greater Recording Company GRC182.

Levenson, Gabe. "Catskill Resorts Still the Place to Relax." *Miami Jewish Tribune,* 26 April–2 May 1991, late edition, 10B.

Levenson, Sam. *Meet the Folks.* New York: Citadel Press, 1949.

Lifson, David S. *The Yiddish Theatre in America.* New York: Thomas Yoseloff, 1965.

Lipzin, Sol. *The Flowering of Yiddish Theatre.* New York: Thomas Yoseloff, 1963.

Lyons, Richard D. "Catskills Reawakening after a Long Sleep." *New York Times,* 25 July 1981, late edition, A25.

"Man Sentenced to 75 Years in Slaying of Elderly Couple." *New York Times,* Sunday, 22 November 1992, A55.

Metzker, Isaac. *A Bintel Brief.* Garden City, N.Y.: Doubleday and Company, 1971.

Meyer Furman's Camp Neversink Weekly Camper, 6 August 1954. Maintained in Richman Archives.

Michaels, Joanne, and Mary Barile. *The Hudson Valley and Catskill Mountains.* New York: Crown Publishers, 1988.

"Milk and Honey" (The Original Broadway Cast Recording). RCA Victor LOC-1065.

Moore, Deborah Dash. *To the Golden Cities: Pursuing the American Jewish Dream in Miami and L.A.* New York: Free Press, 1994.

Moore, Pamela. "Some Personal Glimpses at the Woodbourne Fire." *Monticello (N.Y.) Republican Watchman,* 6 February 1964, 1.

"Mosiach," advertisement. *New York Times,* 31 January 1996, A11.

Mr. Saturday Night. Directed by Billy Crystal. Castle Rock Entertainment, 1992. Film.

Nagler, Richard, *My Love Affair with Miami Beach.* New York: Simon and Schuster, 1991.

Newman, Cathy. "The Love of the Catskills." *National Geographic,* November 1992, 108–30.

"New Route 17 Bypass Opened in Ceremony." *New York Times,* 24 October 1958, late city edition, 29.

Ober, Norman. *Bungalow Nine.* New York: Walker and Company, 1962.

Offit, Sidney. *He Had It Made.* New York: Crown Publishers, 1959.

Oliver, Donald, ed. *The Greatest Review Sketches.* New York: Avon, 1902.

"Orthodox Jews Play Ball in the Catskills." Narrated by John Kalish. *All Things Considered*. Natl. Public Radio, 24 August 1993.

Oysher, Moishe, with Fraydele Oysher and Marilyn Michaels. *An Oysher Album*. Michaels Records MIC102.

Partisans of Vilna, The. Director of photography, Danny Shneuer. 90 min. Euro-American Home Video, 1987. Videocassette.

Pavis-Weil, T. R. "Gambling on the Future." *Middletown (N.Y.) Sunday Record*, 7 July 1996, mid-Hudson edition, 7.

———. "Mohawks Offering State 10.5 Percent Cut: Casino Revenue-Sharing Not Yet Accepted." *Middletown (N.Y.) Times Herald Record*, 27 June 1996, mid-Hudson edition.

Performance '94': The Catskill's Ethnic Entertainment Showcase. Brochure, 1994.

Plesur, Milton. *Jewish Life in Twentieth Century America*. Chicago: Nelson-Hall, 1982.

Plumb, Robert K. "Upstate Hydroelectric Plant Will Tap City's Water System." *New York Times*, 3 March 1954, late edition, A20.

Pomerantz, Joel. *Jennie and the Story of Grossinger's*. New York: Grosset and Dunlap, 1968.

Pontier, Glenn. "A Personal Perspective." *Monticello (N.Y.) Independent Weekly Review*, 6 June 1996, 2.

Potok, Chiam. *The Chosen*. Greenwich, Conn.: Fawcett Crest, 1967.

Quinlan, James E. *History of Sullivan County*. 1873. Reprint, South Fallsburg, N.Y.: Sullivan County Historical Society, 1965.

Radio Days. Directed by Woody Allen. Orion Pictures, 1989. Film.

Rear Window. Directed by Alfred Hitchcock. Patron, 1954. Film.

Reynolds, Jeannie. *Jeannie Reynolds Remembers*. LM Records. No recording number.

Richman, Jacob. *Laughs from Jewish Lore*. New York: Funk and Wagnalls, 1926.

Richman Family Archives, Woodbourne, N.Y., is located in Bainbridge, Penn.

Rischin, Moses. *The Promised City*. Cambridge: Harvard University Press, 1962.

———, ed. *Grandma Never Lived in America: The New Journalism of Abraham Cahan*. Bloomington: Indiana University Press, 1985.

Rise and Fall of the Borscht Belt, The. Directed by Peter Davis. Villon Films (New York), 1988. Distributed by Arthur Cantor, Inc. Videocassette.

"Roads Bond Issue Pushed Upstate." *New York Times*, 30 October 1955.

Rosten, Leo. *The Joys of Yinglish*. New York: McGraw-Hill, 1989.

Rubin, Lucille Dee. "First Aid for Sick Route 17." *New York Times*, Sunday, 8 June 1952, Resorts sec., 12.

Sacher, Abraham L. *A History of the Jews*. New York: Alfred A. Knopf, 1967.

Sage, Sybil Adelman. "Hollywood by Hearse: A Zany Undertaking." *New York Times*, Sunday, 6 January 1991, sec. xx, p. 15.

Schain, Robert L. "A Study of the Historical Development of the Resort Industry of the Catskills of New York State in Order to Determine the Changing Patterns of Leisure Pursuits of the Guests." Ph.D. diss., New York University, 1969.

Schneiderman, Harry, ed. *The American Jewish Year Book*. Philadelphia: Jewish Publication Society of America, 1924.

———. *The American Jewish Year Book*. Philadelphia: Jewish Publication Society of America, 1932.

Schneiderman, Harry, and Morris Fine, eds. *The American Jewish Year Book*. Philadelphia: Jewish Publication Society of America, 1949.

Schwartz, Marvin. "Music, Scenery, and Fishing in the Catskills." *New York Times*, Sunday, 10 June 1956, sec. xx, p. 7.

Secunda, Sholom. *A Yiddish Sing-Along with Sholom Secunda*. Liberty Records LST-7254.

Sharfman, Bern. Personal interview with the author. Harrisburg, Penn., 22 July 1996.

Shea, Barbara. "At Resorts in Catskills, Everyone Is Family." *Lancaster (Penn.) Sunday News,* 10 November 1996, P6.

Sheraton, Mimi. *From My Mother's Kitchen: Recipes and Reminiscences.* New York: Harper and Row, 1979.

Sherman, Allan. *My Son, the Folk Singer.* Warner Brothers Records 1475.

Silberman, Charles E. *A Certain People: American Jews and Their Lives Today.* New York: Summit Books, 1985.

Simons, Howard. *Jewish Times.* New York: Houghton Mifflin, 1988.

Sing-Along in Yiddish with Marv Kurz. Golden Crest. No recording number.

Singer, David, and Ruth Seldin, eds. *The American Jewish Yearbook.* New York: American Jewish Committee, 1991.

Socolow, Raymond. *The Jewish-American Kitchen.* New York: Stewart, Tabori, and Chang, 1989.

Spalding, Henry D. *Encyclopedia of Jewish Humor.* Middle Village, N.Y.: Jonathan David Publishers, 1969.

Spector, Charlotte Feigenbaum. Personal interview with the author. Middletown, Penn., 8 November 1995.

"State Drafts Plan to Better Route 17: Connection with New Thruway, Dubbed 'Quickway' by Some, Follows Southern Tier." *New York Times,* 4 November 1951, late edition, 46.

Stember, Charles H., et al. *Jews in the Mind of Americans.* New York: Basic Books, 1966.

Stranger among Us, A. Directed by Sidney Lumet. Hollywood Pictures, 1992. Film.

Straus, Michael. "A Bungalow in the Hills." *New York Times,* Sunday, 10 June 1956, sec. xx, p. 9.

———. "Busy Catskills Take Spring in Their Stride." *New York Times,* Sunday, 3 April 1966, sec. xx, p. 11.

———. "The Catskill Revolution." *New York Times,* Sunday, 7 June 1959, sec. xx, p. 5.

———. "Catskills Turn to Tennis." *New York Times,* Sunday, 12 June 1966, sec. xx, p. 3.

———. "A Day and a Night at the Races." *New York Times,* 5 June 1960, late edition, sec. xx, p. 3.

———. "Monticello Raceway Marking a Milestone." *New York Times,* Sunday, 7 May 1967, sec. xx, p. 3.

Sullivan County Board of Supervisors. *"Sullivan County, New York:* Number One in the Nation for a Zestful, Restful Vacation." Advertisement distributed by the Sullivan County Board of Supervisors, n.d.

Sweet Lorraine. Directed by Steve Gomer. Autumn Pictures/Angelika Co., 1987. Film.

Tarras, Dave. *Dave Tarras Plays Again.* Standard-Colonial Records ST-LP-718.

———. *Yiddish-American Klezmer Music, 1925–1956.* Yazoo Records 7001.

Taub, Harold Jaediker. *Waldorf-in-the-Catskills: The Grossinger Legend.* New York: Sterling Publishing, 1952.

Thruway public information officer (Albany, N.Y.). Telephone interview with research assistant Matt Singer, 16 July 1991.

Tishman, David. "Singing the Blues for Catskill Bungalow Belt." *New York Daily News,* 5 July 1971, city edition, C7.

Tobias, Henry. *Music in My Heart and Borscht in My Blood: An Autobiography.* New York: Hippocrene Books, 1987.

Turkus, Burton, and Sid Feder. *Murder, Inc.* New York: Farrar Straus and Young, 1951.

TV VUES, Catskill edition, 10–16 August 1991.

"Upstate Resorts Isolated: Helicopters Save Scores." *New York Times,* 20 August 1955, late edition, A1.

"Village Bypass Slated: Dewey Orders Project in Area Where Truck Killed Three." *New York Times,* 6 August 1954, late edition, A14.

Volkov, Oleg. *"Leningrad Reve de Saint-Petersbourg."* *Le Figaro* (Paris), 8 June 1991, Magazine sec., 88–98.

Wakefield, Manville B. *To the Mountains by Rail: People, Events, and Tragedies . . . the New York, Ontario, and Western Railway and the Famous Sullivan County Resorts.* Grahamsville, N.Y.: Wakefair Press, 1970.

Wallenrod, Reuben, *Dusk in the Catskills.* New York: Reconstructionist Press, 1957.

Washington, Margaret. Town Clerk of Thompson. Telephone interview conducted by research assistant Matt Singer. 16 July 1991.

Waxman, Chiam I. *America's Jews in Transition.* Philadelphia: Temple University Press, 1983.

Wechsler, Alan. "Borscht Belt Heyday Relived." *Middletown (N.Y.) Sunday Record,* 3 September 1995, Magazine sec., 4.

———. "Summer Folk Find Trouble: Bias Crime Alleged as Fight Draws Crowd." *Middletown (N.Y.) Times Herald Record,* 8 July 1996, 5.

———. "They Tell so All Will Know: Holocaust Survivors Summon Painful Stories for Video." *Middletown (N.Y.) Sunday Record,* 16 August 1996, Region sec., 4.

———. "Woodbourne Gets Religion." *Middletown (N.Y.) Times Herald Record,* 15 July 1996, 3.

Weissman, Jenna J., ed., with Karen S. Mittleman. *A Worthy Use of Summer: Jewish Summer Camping in America.* Philadelphia: National Museum of Jewish History, 1993.

"Widening to Ease Tie-Ups in Route 17: State to Improve Resort Road in Three Areas without Interfering with Travels." *New York Times,* 18 August 1951, A12.

Williams, Alexander H. "Uneasy Return to the Catskills: Family, Friends of Murdered Pair Are Still Healing." *Middletown (N.Y.) Times Herald Record,* 7 July 1992, 3.

Wolff, Craig. "Summer Calm in Catskills Shattered by Slayings." *New York Times,* 14 July 1991, late city edition, A23.

"Woodbourne to Rebuild Modern Shopping Center." *Monticello (N.Y.) Republican Watchman,* 13 February 1964, 1.

"Work Begins on New Prison." *New York Times,* 26 May 1934, late edition, 32.

Wouk, Herman. *Marjorie Morningstar.* New York: Pocket Books, 1955.

Yaffe, Ephraim. *A Good Life.* Ellenville, N.Y.: privately printed, 1974.

Yiddish American Sing-A-Long. Solomon Schwartz and his orchestra and the Emanuel Fisher Singers. London Records SW99428.

Yiddish Dream, The. Sung by Hershel Bernadi, et al. Vanguard USD 715/16

Yidl Mitn Fidl (Little Jew with a Fiddle). Directed by Joseph Green (1936). Ergo Media, 1988. Videocassette.

Zborowski, Mark, and Elizabeth Herzog. *Life Is with People: The Culture of the* Shetetl. New York: Schocken Books, 1952.

Zukowsky, John, and Robbe Pierce Stimson. *Hudson River Villas.* New York: Rizzoli, 1985.

Index

236

bungalow colonies, 1, 4, 5, 6–7, 8, 12, 14, 24, 25, 29, 51, 52, 71, 80, 104, 131; activities for adults, 101–14; advertising of, 59–60; with casinos, 128–29; changes in clientele, 181–204; crime, 175–80; daily life at, 68–70; emergencies and disasters, 149–56; foods, 115–19, 155; future of, 208–9; handymen, 40–41, 104; influence of Hasidic and New Orthodox Jews, 193–204, 205–6, 208–9; in literature, 12–17, 35–36; owners, 38, 51, 53–54, 58; parties, 120–29; recreation at, 71–84, 87–93; professional entertainment at, 132–33, 137–42; and religion, 143–48; renting, 41–42, 59–62; telephones, 129–31; television, 132–33; tenants, 41–42, 56–58, 63–68. *See also* bungalows, day camps, *and names of specific bungalow colonies*

bungalows, 7, 8–9, 9–10, 24, 25, 64; floor plans, 30, 33; furnishings, 11–12, 29–32; in literature, 12–17. *See also* bungalow colonies

Burcat, Dave, 110–11, 164–65
Burcat, Jessie, 110–11
Burroughs, John, 3
Burton, Anthony Valentino, 179–80

Cahill, Michael F., 179
Cahn, Sammy, 66
Camp Neversink, 36
Camp Shearith, 197
Camp Tiferes, 193
Cantor, Eddie, 64–65
Capone, Alfonse, 178, 181
casinos, 128–29, 135, 136, 138
Catskill Funland, 201
Catskill Game Farm, 168
Catskill, N.Y., 168
Catskills, The, 27, 39, 69, 99, 102, 127, 131, 147, 201; and bungalow colonies, 1, 4, 9, 12, 23, 24, 29, 41, 45, 64, 182, 186, 191, 192, 194, 195, 196, 198, 208; and crime, 179, 180; and day camps, 157; and food, 115, 118, 119; and hotels, 1, 64, 134, 157, 182, 184; and Jews, 2, 3, 4, 20, 21, 22, 182, 208; and *kuchaleins*, 1, 4; literature about, 5, 6, 12, 16, 17, 64, 106; and New Orthodox

and Hasidic Jews, 202; and professional entertainment, 139, 140, 141, 142
Catskills Guide (Israelowitz), 147
"Catskills on Self Destruct, The," 188–91
Catskills Playland, 206
Centerville, N.Y. *See* Woodridge, N.Y.
Centre Theater, 95, 99, 132, 207
Chaplin, Saul, 66
Chertkoff, Eddie, 156
Chertkoff, Jeffrey, 156
Chester's, 133, 134–35
Chosen, The, 194
Cino, Anthony, 174
Clearview Country Club, 194
Cohen, Mary, 139
Cohn, Leah, 180
Concord, The, 5, 64, 65, 134, 179
Coney Island, 2
Conway, John (*Gangsters of the Catskills*), 178
Corbin, Austen, 2
Country Kosher Bakery, 118
Cowans, Neil and Ruth (*Our Parents' Lives*), 26
Crabbe, Buster, 65
Crossways, The, 206
Cutler's Cottages, 8, 29, 53, 104, 186

Daily News, 69
Dairyman's League, 22
Damico, Miriam, 10, 31, 42, 110, 125
Damoshack's Woodland Colony, 159, 165
Dan family, 3
Daniels, B., 168
Dareff, H., 166
Dareff, S., 168
Davis, Monroe, 53
day camps, 56, 76, 110, 140, 156, 157–74. *See also names of specific day camps*
Day, The, 69
Delmont, The, 64
Diamond, Jack "Leggs," 178
Dickin's, 94
Dill, Harry, 32
Dill's, 94
Dominion family, 55
Duberstein, Elyse, 163
Dubofsky family, 26, 144–45, 155
Dubofsky, Jerry, 80